The British New Wave

A certain tendency?

B. F. TAYLOR

Manchester University Press

MANCHESTER AND NEW YORK

distributed exclusively in the USA by Palgrave

Published by Manchester University Press
Oxford Road, Manchester M13 9NR, UK
and Room 400, 175 Fifth Avenue, New York, NY 10010, USA
www.manchesteruniversitypress.co.uk

Distributed exclusively in the USA by
Palgrave, 175 Fifth Avenue, New York,
NY 10010, USA

Distributed exclusively in Canada by
UBC Press, University of British Columbia, 2029 West Mall,
Vancouver, BC, Canada V6T 1Z2

British Library Cataloguing-in-Publication Data
A catalogue record for this book is available from the British Library

Library of Congress Cataloging-in-Publication Data applied for

ISBN 0 7190 6908 4   *hardback*
EAN 978 0 7190 6908 6

First published 2006

15 14 13 12 11 10 09 08 07 06   10 9 8 7 6 5 4 3 2 1

Typeset in Apollo with Rotis
by Graphicraft Limited, Hong Kong
Printed in Great Britain
by Biddles, King's Lynn

Shall we for ever make new books, as apothecaries make new mixtures, by pouring only out of one vessel into another? Are we for ever to be twisting, and untwisting the same rope?

(Laurence Sterne, *The Life and Opinions of Tristram Shandy*)

Contents

Plates

Acknowledgements

To my father, Peter. I am eternally grateful for your unfailing support. Without you, the serious study of film would have passed me by completely.

Catherine Grant deserves a special mention. You rescued me when my research was floundering, gave me purpose, encouragement and restored my confidence. It has been a pleasure to work with you.

Various other colleagues and friends at the University of Kent need to be acknowledged. Many thanks to Michael Grant for inspiring me as an undergraduate. Thank you to Andrew Klevan for not only inspiring me in a similar way but also giving me the idea for this project in the first place. Thank you also to Murray Smith, Elizabeth Cowie and Sarah Cardwell for their ongoing demonstration of the importance of studying the cinema. Thank you also to William Collier. Your support has meant more than you will ever know. I also want to mention the members of Lunch Club – Nigel, Gary, Dave, Alex, Steve, Dan and Thalia.

Thank you to new colleagues at Trinity College Dublin, especially Brian Singleton, Dennis Kennedy, Kevin Rockett and Paula Quigley. Additionally, Matthew Frost at Manchester University Press for all his patience and Peter Hutchings for kindness, insight and observation.

Hugo, for faith, understanding and the relentless insults that one brother would expect from another. Thanks also to dear friends Mark and Matt, Paul and the other founding members of the Hastings and Bexhill Amateur Wrestling Ring. My mother Lois, Helen and Michael.

Finally, thanks to Paula for everything.

Dublin 2005

1 The British New Wave: a certain tendency?

The terrible thing about the cinema is the way it uses up everything. It exhausts ideas, stories, brands of stories, and suddenly finds itself faced with a kind of gulf, a ditch across which it must leap to capture some new and absolutely unforeseen territory. We're not talking, obviously, about eternal masterpieces: clearly Shakespeare always had something to say, and he didn't have to jump any ditch. But it's a situation ordinary film production is likely to run into every five years or so. In France the New Wave has been lucky enough to jump the ditch. In England the same thing could happen. (Jean Renoir)[1]

'Queen' magazine recently ran a 'Space-age guide for Social Astronauts' which replaced the expressions like 'In' and 'Out' with 'Go,' 'Rogue' and 'Abort.' 'The cinema is generally "Go,"' twittered this glossy publication, 'but films in foreign languages are "Rogue" (released on the right course, but now in the wrong orbit); English films are usually "Abort."' (Mark Shivas)[2]

There is, in any art, a tendency to turn one's preferences into a monomaniac theory; in film criticism, the more . . . single-minded and dedicated . . . the theorist is, the more likely he is to be regarded as serious and important and 'deep' – in contrast to relaxed men of good sense whose pluralistic approaches can be disregarded as not fundamental enough. (Pauline Kael)[3]

The British New Wave: definitions and directions

The British New Wave is the name conventionally given to a series of films released between 1959 and 1963. Here is the series in full: *Room at the Top* (Jack Clayton, 1959); *Look Back in Anger* (Tony Richardson, 1959); *The Entertainer* (Tony Richardson, 1960); *Saturday Night and Sunday Morning* (Karel Reisz, 1960); *A Taste of Honey* (Tony Richardson, 1961); *A Kind of Loving* (John Schlesinger, 1962); *The Loneliness of the Long Distance Runner* (Tony Richardson, 1962); *This Sporting Life* (Lindsay Anderson, 1963); *Billy Liar* (John Schlesinger, 1963).

Conventional approaches to these films place their greatest emphasis upon viewing them as a series, stressing their similarities, and use these similarities to include the films in broader debates about class, gender and/or ideology. The time is now right to take an alternative approach and consider each of the films individually. This is not to deny that the similarities between these films do exist. Nevertheless, for the sake of revivifying the study of British cinema, there is little methodological sense in merely reproducing existing critical discussions. Instead, I will define my own critical position in relation to the British New Wave and demonstrate that we can fruitfully consider the detail of these films individually without continually re-emphasising their similarities. The spirit of this approach has been shaped by Peter Hutchings's recent discussion of the British New Wave. The innovation of this approach is also complemented by the position its subjects occupy within the history of British cinema. As their collective title suggests, the arrival of these films was marked by a similar sense of innovation. This is because, as Peter Hutchings observes:

> Often shot on location in cities in the Midlands or the north of England and featuring relatively unknown actors and relatively untried directors, these films were generally seen by critics of the time as a step forward for British cinema, a move towards a mature, intelligent engagement with contemporary British social life and a welcome breath of fresh air after the conformist entertainment provided by studio-bound British film-makers in the first part of the 1950s.[4]

Hutchings continues by outlining three key points which will guide this book. He reminds us that these films, though constantly thought of and defined as a series, are, in certain respects, different from each other. Hutchings also argues that all of the New Wave films are 'fictions that seek, often in very seductive ways, to involve us in their narratives in a manner that still has the potential to neutralise any critical distance, in effect to make us sympathetic participants in their world'. Finally, and crucially, whilst not denying the central position that the concept of cinematic realism holds in the British cinema, Hutchings suggests that the concern 'to deconstruct realism and the aesthetic practices associated with it impacted especially severely' on the British New Wave.[5] Let's begin by considering Hutchings's final suggestion.

The innovation of a film like *Room at the Top* was its engagement with a contemporary British social life, and the emphasis in these new films was on the relationship between a character's leisure time and their working life. This was accompanied by an increased willingness to deal openly with the representation of sexual behaviour, especially of the extra-marital kind. The result of this was that the films displayed 'a deeper attention to the articulation of character and individuality', achieved by their narratives being 'resolutely organised around a single central protagonist, a single psychology and subjectivity'.[6] Furthermore, it was this willingness to depict sexual relationships more explicitly, combined with a use of vernacular language and the breaking of conventional shooting techniques that led to an idea of social realism being attributed to the British New Wave. For Julia Hallam and Margaret Marshment:

> The roots of the social realist aesthetics of these 'kitchen sink' dramas are found in the British documentary movement of the 1930s (particularly the poetic realism of Humphrey Jennings), the Free Cinema movement of the 1950s and a new class consciousness in British theatre and literature centred on the experiences of aggressive and rebellious working-class males – the so-called 'angry young men' epitomised in successful plays such as John Osborne's *Look Back in Anger* and novels such as Alan Sillitoe's *Saturday Night and Sunday Morning*.[7]

The idea of social realism, however, has always been a contentious issue, especially as the term itself – like the phrase 'kitchen sink' – has become something of a convenient, and uncritical, way to describe the contents of these films as 'gritty', 'raw' and offering a 'slice of life'. Worse still is the fact that the term itself is difficult to define owing to its being so politically and historically contingent. As Samantha Lay writes:

> Specific stylistic concerns are utilised at different times, in different ways by film-makers. Their use of certain styles in camera work, iconography, editing and soundtrack stand in a relationship of contrast not just between the mainstream products of the day but also to the stylistic preferences of the social realist film-makers who preceded them.[8]

A further problem stems from the suggestion that 'the new "realism" of these films was no more "realistic" than previous modes of representation had been. What was new was the drawing of a different boundary between the realms of "fiction" and "life." '[9] Finally, since the 1970s, realism in the cinema has been treated with suspicious and considered ideologically suspect.[10]

The relationship between social realism and the British New Wave is a troubled one and I am reluctant to engage with broader debates of realism and the cinema. My concern is that the question of realism in the cinema has always carried strong overtones in film aesthetics and has meant that successive critics have had to come to terms with some variation on the theme. The end result of this is usually the adding of another interpretation on to what Andrew Tudor has called 'the already creaking cart'.[11]

Lay usefully defines several pertinent features of the form of social realism associated with these films, and prominent among these is the way 'character and place are linked in order to explore some aspect of contemporary life'. The term can generally imply an independent production, the use of real locations and the employment of non-professional or little-known actors. Lay outlines three overlapping aspects: practice and politics, style and form, and content. Practice has already been defined above. If politics is defined as intentions then we can see that the New

Wave directors 'were interested in extending the range of cinematic representation to include the working class beyond London to the industrial towns and cities of the north of England'. The style and form of these films reflected this new range of cinematic representation but quickly became labelled as drab and gritty, with depressing portrayals of settings and characters. As Lay concludes:

> 'Style' refers to the aesthetic devices employed by film-makers and the artistic choices they make. These aspects of social realism refer to the specific formal and stylistic techniques employed by social realist film-makers to capture, comment on, and critique the workings of society. Form and style refer to elements within the text, though it is important to note that they may be informed by practice, politics and content.[12]

With the emphasis on the idea of difference, I will begin by outlining an approach to film criticism that places the greatest value on considering a film in its own right. An approach of this kind allows the individual details of one film to be brought to our attention in such a way as to negate the need always to compare one film with another. This will be followed by considering the idea of a 'critical distance'. The focus will be on the critical reception that these films received at the time and will consider some of the ways in which this reception has coloured subsequent examinations of the New Wave. I will conclude by continuing to investigate the relationship between British New Wave 'style' and social realism. Bearing in mind that the question of realism in the cinema is an enormous one, my discussion will be restricted to the impact that the desire to deconstruct these issues of realism has had upon the films. I will also propose a way in which the severity of this impact might be lessened.

Roman candles and rockets

Neil Sinyard hints at some of the reasons why the British New Wave films may have always suffered in terms of the critical response to them. The arrival of *Room at the Top* and the films that followed it coincided with a seismic shift in the British critical culture. For this period was the heyday of auteurism and 'by the side of the big names of Europe and Hollywood, it was felt that British film had little to offer'. Though the arrival of Clayton's film was greeted with considerable optimism, changes in the critical climate meant that some commentators were less sympathetic. This was particularly evident in the first edition of *Movie*, the British film journal which 'set the intellectual tone of the debate about British film for the rest of the decade'. Published in 1962, just as the British New Wave was in its prime, *Movie* contained a broad survey of the then contemporary state of British cinema, Victor Perkins's 'The British Cinema'.

British cinema has since undergone an extensive critical re-evaluation yet the shockwaves from Perkins's damning indictment still ensure that the discussion of New Wave 'style' is still what Sinyard calls a tentative affair.[13]

Discussions of these films began in 1959 with *Room at the Top* and have continued ever since. In fact, as Anthony Aldgate and Jeffrey Richards write in their recent re-evaluation of *The Loneliness of the Long Distance Runner*:

> Just as the notion of fifties cinema as necessarily a 'doldrums era' is now undergoing a well merited albeit tardy revision so, too, that aspect of late 1950s and early 1960s British cinema which has hitherto attracted most attention when discussing the advances evidently made during the period – in debates, principally, surrounding the 'new wave' films – is once more, and for its own part, receiving renewed and closer scrutiny.[14]

Yet, the critical attention that these films have received, and are now receiving once again, is less to do with discussing the details of individual films and more concerned with still viewing them as a series. This is because, as Richards argues elsewhere, the study of film can be divided into two approaches: film studies and cinema history. Whereas the former concerns itself with 'minute visual and structural analysis of individual films' the latter places 'its highest priority on context, on the locating of films securely in the setting of their makers' attitudes, constraints and preoccupations, on audience reaction and contemporary understandings'. Both are valuable yet, as Richards continues, there still remains a 'hostility' between some adherents of the two approaches.[15] Nowhere is this hostility more apparent than in the case of the British New Wave. Admittedly, this division is a highly artificial one. Nevertheless, the implications of this division are directly relevant to the debates that surround the British New Wave. This is because films such as *Room at the Top* or *Billy Liar* lend themselves almost too easily to broader accounts of their context and construction. This is evident in famous discussions such as John Hill's 1986 book *Sex, Class and Realism: British Cinema 1956–1963*, or Andrew Higson's investigation into the realist tendencies inherent in their use of locations,[16] to name but two of the most famous accounts. The problem is that the balance between the two approaches has become weighted too far in favour of cinema history. This imbalance is due to an extremely persuasive historical reason why the 'minute visual and structural analysis of individual films' has not been applied to the New Wave.

In 1958 Penelope Houston, the then editor of *Sight and Sound*, invited a selection of eminent British film critics and film makers to contribute to a round-table discussion about the state of British film criticism.[17] Paul Rotha and Lindsay Anderson felt *Sight and Sound*, in a sentiment later echoed by the writers of *Movie*, to be 'an organ of the enemy'. Anderson, summing up his view of *Sight and Sound*'s position, expressed a certain disappointment:

> But what it [*Sight and Sound*] lacks, I feel, is a certain vitality – *creative* feeling for the cinema. There's too much of the charmed circle about it. What we need is something at once more edgy and more personal . . . The criticism we desperately need should be enthusiastic, violent and responsible, all at the same time.

Basil Wright was also keen for film criticism to become much more radical. As he declared: 'What we seem to need at this stage is an anarchic paper, run by a group of probably rather scruffy young men between 17 and 22, who will let off squibs and roman candles and rockets in all directions and generally stir up the whole thing.'[18]

Whilst Wright's desire for scruffy anarchists was never realised, the critical pyrotechnics he called for soon arrived, first in the form of *Oxford Opinion* then, in June 1962, with the first edition of *Movie*.[19] It was here that Anderson's desire for enthusiasm, violence and responsibility found its expression in the writings of Ian Cameron, Mark Shivas and Victor Perkins, amongst others.

Exactly a year after its first issue, *Movie* published a round-table discussion designed to demonstrate the critical differences between its regular contributors, and Victor Perkins outlined his ambitions for both *Movie* and the future of British film criticism. He began by suggesting that any criticism is valuable, as long as it is related to the film itself and, more importantly, opens up 'avenues for discussion rather than closing them down'. 'I think we all attempt', he continued, 'to write criticism which is useful, whether or not it meets with agreement, criticism which suggests more questions than it answers.' All of which led him to conclude that he would rather be an orator than an oracle. Or, 'To put it another way, this magazine won't really be a success until it's regarded as a witness stand rather than a judgement seat.'[20]

Movie's primary aim was to advocate a more specific style-based approach to British film criticism. David Bordwell traces the development of this form of criticism from the postwar writings on film found in *Cahiers du Cinéma* and developed by the journal's American champion, Andrew Sarris. *Movie*, following the American tradition, was primarily concerned with merging 'the analysis of technique with the delineation of themes'. This was because the 1960s boom in explicatory interpretation was undergirded by the presumption that a film was actually 'a composite of implicit meanings given material embodiment in formal patterns and technical devices'. This trend incorporated two distinct approaches. On the one hand, the critic 'might choose to emphasize the meanings, as did Sarris and most *Cahiers* writers in their attempt to distinguish each director's underlying vision or metaphysic'. Or, 'the critic could take the themes as given and go on to study how form and style make them concrete and vivid'. This second method was an important feature of most *Movie* critics' approach to narrative and technique.[21]

The implications of the kind of exploration of visual style offered by *Movie*, their valuing the detail of a film's style, might be 'most markedly shown in relation to Hollywood films'. However, 'the debate about Hollywood demonstrates what is at stake in mise-en-scène particularly clearly, these ideas are just as relevant to other forms of cinema.' As John Gibbs continues:

> Ultimately, the concept of mise-en-scène may be more important than the arguments about authorship which it supported. It enabled critics to understand film as a visual and sensory experience rather than just a literary one, to engage with film as a medium in its own right, and to consider the determining influence of style upon meaning. *And, in the case of Movie particularly, it formed the basis of a detailed criticism, which strove to understand the relationship between a film's meanings and the evidence on the screen. Mise-en-scène criticism made possible a more profound sense of how films work.* [italics mine][22]

Valuing the influence of style upon meaning will be central to my examination of the British New Wave. There are significant differences among these films, and it is through an examination of the style and meaning of each film that these differences will be most clearly demonstrated. In this way, the balance between film studies and cinema history will be restored. However, despite their talk of being a witness stand rather than a judgement seat, the form of mise-en-scène criticism advocated by *Movie* was never applied to films such as *Room at the Top* or *The Entertainer*. This suggests that mise-en-scène criticism only made possible a more profound sense of how *certain* films work. The pressing question here is: why was *Movie* not prepared to apply its critical methods to these films? In order to answer this question we need to consider the process of film criticism in more detail.

An artistic conscience?

The practical activity of film criticism is beset by two specific problems. With the critic having to construct a sufficiently compelling argument for the chosen film to be considered worthy of critical interpretation, the first problem is one of *appropriateness*. The films of British New Wave were not deemed to be an appropriate subject for sustained critical interpretation and received little in the way of positive critical attention from *Movie*. This means that the avenues for positive critical discussion remained limited and, were it not for the fact that the next problem facing the film critic is one of *novelty*, there is little point in trying to apply a style-based critical model to the British New Wave. Bordwell defines novelty in the following way:

> the interpreter is expected either to (a) initiate a new critical theory or method; (b) revise or refine an existing theory or method; (c) 'apply' an existing theory or method to a fresh instance; or (d) if the film is familiar, point out significant aspects which previous commentators have ignored or minimized.[23]

Applying an approach to film criticism that originated in the 1950s hardly qualifies as the initiation of a new critical method. Nevertheless, these observations are crucial because the reasons for examining the New Wave films in this way still fulfil the remaining criteria. An existing method of criticism will be refined and will also be applied to a fresh instance. With films as familiar as *Room at the Top* or *A Taste of Honey*, part of the task will also involve pointing out significant aspects that have been both minimised and ignored. The question at this point is, of course: why didn't the writers of *Movie* apply the form of film criticism they helped to pioneer to their national cinema in the first place? The answer to this will become clearer when the idea of a critical distance is considered. Before this, however, more needs to be said about this kind of critical approach.

Having decided to examine a film, there are two ways for the critic to proceed. One way is to note the 'compatibilities that the film affords with respect to concepts currently in circulation in criticism'. The other is based on the idea of 'anomalies'. As Bordwell continues:

> Within the film, perhaps a scene or a bit of behaviour does not initially seem to fit with the others; or perhaps previous critical interpretations have ignored or overlooked something I can pick out; or perhaps the film as a whole does not square with some current conception of genre or style or mode. I can then hypothesize that the film will somehow justify its difference by virtue of certain other properties that are institutionally acceptable (for example, internal plot logic, thematic coherence or ideological aspects).[24]

Bordwell's observations depend upon the idea of our examination of a particular film being sufficiently different from previous examinations. But, if we are to successfully justify the appropriateness of the British New Wave films as the basis for the kind of critical discussion that *Movie* reserved for other films, then these ideas of novelty and difference must be extended further. Deborah Thomas is helpful here when she discusses what she feels it might mean to 'read' a film. For her, the aim of the process:

> is to engage with [the film] in all of its detail as a starting point for talking about things that matter and, in the process, to discover the common ground between the film and us, in some cases in spite of a considerable passage of time between the film's initial appearance and our subsequent reading.[25]

It is not necessary for these readings to match up with the intentions of the film makers who produced the films in the first place. Rather furthering Bordwell's ideas of compatibilities and anomalies, Thomas offers the following advice:

> [The readings] can most usefully be understood as sustained meditations grounded in the detailed specifics of their texts. At their best, such accounts invite those to whom they are offered to revisit the films and see for themselves, enriching their own experiences with new depth and bringing significant details to their attention in fresh and productive ways, while ultimately encouraging such viewers to make up their own minds as to how true to their own experiences of the film the readings may be, and how illuminating and important the issues that they raise.[26]

Thomas's offer to revisit a particular film and produce a sustained meditation sits comfortably with Bordwell's desire for novelty. Both suggest a way in which overlooked or (critically) 'unworthy' films might benefit from re-evaluation. Also, both commentators emphasise the attention that must be paid to the specific detail of an individual film.

Stanley Cavell continues this idea of the details specific to a single film when he famously asks 'What Becomes of Things on Film?' The process of reading a film, of interpretation, must 'account for the frames of the film being what they are, in the order they are in, e.g., to say what motivates the camera to look and to move as and where it looks and moves'. As Cavell concludes:

> the question of what becomes of objects when they are filmed and screened – like the question what becomes of particular people, and specific locales, and subjects and motifs when they are filmed by individual makers of film – has only one source of data for its answer, namely the appearance and significance of those objects and people that are in fact to be found in the succession of films, or passages of films, that matter to us. To express their appearances, and define those significances, and articulate the nature of this mattering, are acts that help to constitute what we might call film criticism.[27]

Cavell, then, continues this idea of film interpretation being a sustained meditation upon the film in question. With words such as expression, definition and articulation, the interpretative process is a highly personal one. For example, as Cavell considers elsewhere:

> How could we show that it [the film] is equally, or anyway, sufficiently, *worth* studying? Now we are at the heart of the aesthetic matter. Nothing can show this value to you unless it is discovered in your own experience, in the persistent exercise of your own taste, and hence the willingness to challenge your taste as it stands, to form your own artistic conscience, hence nowhere but in the details of your encounter with specific works.[28]

Cavell proposes an approach to film criticism that not only emphasises, once again, the importance of considering the specific details of a
specific film but also suggests that the problem of appropriateness noted
by Bordwell might be best overcome by adopting a purely personal
response to the film in question. However, questions of experience, taste
and a personal response to an individual film need careful handling. This
was why *Movie* rejected films such as *Room at the Top* in the first place.
Therefore, applying this idea of developing a critical conscience whilst
discussing *A Kind of Loving*, say, is a process that needs further definition, and a better understanding can be developed by considering Robin
Wood's response when challenged to formulate his critical position.

The disciplines of film criticism and theory share a contradictory
relationship. Though they may partly overlap and though they might be
capable of supporting one another, they ultimately lack compatibility.
A theorist erects systems whilst a critic explores works. To the theorist
a 'personal response to a given work will be an irrelevance, even an
obstruction'. For the critic 'while he will be aware that it must be continually probed, questioned, tested – personal response is central to his
activity'. There is the possibility that such an 'ideal' will never be fully
attainable. Nevertheless, 'the function of an ideal is to provide a means
of measuring degrees of success and failure'. One reason for the unat-
tainability of this ideal takes us to the heart of what Wood calls the critical
dilemma: 'the intense personal involvement in the work which is inseparable from any genuine response will inevitably make our "reading" to some
degree biased and partial'. Despite this, Wood concludes with a call for
critical integrity:

> I see no way of eliminating this problem from criticism, though the chief
> function for the critic of the tools provided by the theorists is to discipline
> and counterbalance this personal/subjective element: any theory of art, any
> scholarship, any historical or cultural research, any analytical procedure, that
> can help us see the work as it is and ensure that we are responding to
> something that is there and not something we have invented, is obviously to
> be welcomed.[29]

Following Bordwell, Thomas, Cavell and Wood, I will develop my
own artistic conscience by examining the specific details of films such
as *Saturday Night and Sunday Morning* or *A Taste of Honey*. The examination of each film will take the form of a sustained personal reading,
bringing the significant details of each film to the forefront in a fresh and
productive way. The reader will be offered the opportunity to revisit the
films of the British New Wave for themselves and allow my discussions
to enrich their own experiences of these films. Finally, as well as being
continually probed, questioned and tested, my personal response to each
of these films will also be underpinned by the three conclusions Wood

reaches in his discussion. Firstly, 'Valid criticism must never lose touch with the critic's whole response, in which instinctual and emotional elements play at least as important a role as intellectual.' Secondly, the suppression of a personal element in critical discourse is neither 'possible nor desirable'. Its 'apparent absence should always be regarded with distrust'. Thirdly, 'the true end of criticism is evaluation, the evaluation of the total experience of the work is felt by the critic to offer; experience derived, that is, from what the work *is* rather than from what it *says*, structure, style, method all playing their roles'.[30]

We now need to turn to the question of why it is that this form of critical approach has never been applied to these films. Considering the fact that all of these films have been re-released and are now available on DVD, there is every reason to suspect that critical interest will once again turn to *This Sporting Life* or *A Kind of Loving*. Yet, the writers of *Movie* made it clear from the outset that they didn't feel the mise-en-scène of these films to be worthy of such sustained attention. Quite simply, *Movie*'s stance in relation to these films is responsible for the existence of a specific critical distance.

Movie and the British film

Penelope Houston believed that the weakness of 'the *Cahiers du cinéma* school' – as she called *Movie* (and its precursor, *Oxford Opinion*) – lay in the fact that they paid scant attention to 'experience which does not take place in the cinema'. Self-limiting in its enthusiasm, criticism of this sort was, for Houston, 'shop talk for the initiated'. As she continues:

> it turns inward upon itself, so that a film's validity is assessed not in relation to the society from which it draws its material but in relation to other cinematic experiences. It is all a bit hermetic, as though its practitioners had chosen to live in the dark, emerging to blink, mole-like, at the cruel light, to sniff the chilly air, before ducking back into the darkness of another cinema.[31]

Ian Cameron countered by pointing out that the journal was motivated more through a perceived absence of ideas in Britain than from an abundance of ideas from the continent. Cameron was happy to acknowledge that the obvious influence of *Cahiers* could be found in the confidence with which *Movie* developed its own cinematic tastes. Nevertheless, this confidence was tempered with a practicality. As Cameron explained:

> In comparison with the flamboyant intellectualism of *Cahiers*, *Oxford Opinion* [*Movie*'s predecessor] was almost doggedly practical, keeping very close to its subjects, usually keeping within them rather than referring out . . . The closeness to the films and the desire to investigate the way they *worked* continued into *Movie*; the best antidote to the prevalent wooliness about the cinema seemed to us to lie in detailed, descriptive criticism.[32]

Movie was not trying to be fashionable but was attempting 'to establish a solid critical tradition in an art form that has been so badly served by its critics'. Cameron felt that *Movie*'s contribution was to initiate discussion of the 'extraordinary richness of expression that the medium has inspired'.[33]

The journal saw itself as a response to the failure of British film criticism, a failure it saw characterised by *Sight and Sound*'s reverence for declining European art cinema as well as 'a set of liberal and aesthetic platitudes which stood in for a deeper and more analytical response' which 'meant that the critical approach to all films was equally impoverished'.[34]

Movie was motivated by a conscious effort to stand apart from the existing British critical community and move closer to the style-based criticism more commonly practised in France and America. Taking their lead from abroad, the journal's first edition contained its own ranking of directors in order of their perceived critical worthiness. Charles Barr has described this as an elaborate chart set out on two halves of the same page. The editors' judgement of the talents of all practising Hollywood and British directors led to them being graded in a series of six categories and 'almost all the British were huddled in the two lowest ones'.[35] Such a practice contained 'inevitable extravagances'[36] with only Hawks and Hitchcock designated as 'Great' directors and more than the vast majority of British directors being ranked as 'Competent or ambitious' at best or, alternatively, just dismissed as 'The Rest'. The result of this chart was 'a spectacular, eloquent and polemically very effective asymmetry'. From *Movie*'s point of view, this 'asymmetry' was a clear indication of where its collective sympathies lay.[37] The moment that this chart was published, the style and construction of the British New Wave films was critically doomed. For it was alongside this chart that Victor Perkins, writing on behalf of the journal's editorial board, outlined his famous assault on 'The British Cinema'.

The Woodfall answer?

'The British Cinema' opens with a wry acknowledgement of the changing face of the industry. As Perkins begins:

> Five years ago the ineptitude of British films was generally acknowledged. The stiff upper lip movie was a standard target for critical scorn. But now the British cinema has come to grips with Reality. We have had a breakthrough, a renaissance, a New Wave. More than that, we are now on the crest of a Second Wave: 'In the new spirit of freedom the British cinema moves on to explore worlds outside the conventional middle-class drama.'[38]

This breakthrough was nothing more than a change of outlook and still did nothing to hide the fact the British cinema was as lifeless as before. If British films had improved then this was only in terms of their intentions for Perkins was 'still unable to find evidence of artistic sensibilities in working order' and this lead him to famously conclude that there 'is as much genuine personality in "Room at the Top", method in "A Kind of Loving" and style in "A Taste of Honey" as there is wit in "An Alligator named Daisy", intelligence in "Above us the Waves" and ambition in "Ramsbottom Rides Again".' Though Perkins is quick to point out that his opening remarks might sound 'peevish', this does not stop him from continuing his claims for the lack of 'artistic sensibilities' evident in the British cinema by comparing British films with the best movies from Europe, Japan and the United States. *Movie*'s stance on British cinema is first revealed by Perkins asking 'where are the British films that we can compare with, say, *Lola*, *The Keeper*, *Rebel Without a Cause*, or *Man of the West*?' As he continues:

> The cinema of Fritz Lang, Raoul Walsh or Jacques Tourneur is different from, not superior to, the cinema of Godard, Nicholas Ray, Franju, Losey, Bergman, or George Cukor. The request is not for a 'correct' approach to the necessary subjects. It is for a cinema which has style, imagination, personality and, because of these, meaning.[39]

But why might Perkins have felt this way? To begin with, he places the blame on the industry itself for a lack of artistic sensibility. Producers and backers lacked ambition and adventure and were paralysed by the fear of commercial failure. This led to an over-reliance upon the formulae set by previous commercial successes.[40] These problems are not dissimilar from the problems faced by the film industries of other countries. Nevertheless, the problems peculiar to Britain are compounded by the concept of what Perkins terms 'The Good Film'. As he complains:

> The traditional British 'quality' picture follows a recipe for which the ingredients are: an important and if possible controversial subject . . . ; a popular story; a fair representation of all points of view; a resolution which makes the audience 'think'; a 'cinematic' treatment; lastly, but importantly, a few 'personal' idiosyncrasies (in the hope that mouthpieces will thus resemble people).[41]

This list of ingredients created a cinema of such 'awfulness' that a new and more responsible approach was needed, one that was prepared to deal seriously with human relationships and social problems. This was precisely what the 'new wave' of films, either produced or influenced by the Woodfall company, had to offer. Despite their 'difference' from the 'quality' picture, however, Perkins was still not convinced. Whereas the failure of the 'quality' picture could be attributed to its use of stereotypes, its spurious excitement and its attempts at intellectualising its subjects, the newer forms of British cinema failed stylistically. Despite gaining praise for their attempts to break away from formulaic constraints of the 'quality' picture, Perkins felt that these films were unable to connect their characters effectively with their environments. As he famously notes:

> Richardson, Reisz, Schlesinger and Clayton are weakest exactly where their ambitions most demand strength: in the integration of character with background. Because of this weakness they are constantly obliged to 'establish' place with inserted shots which serve only to strengthen our conviction that the setting, though 'real', has no organic connection with the characters.

As a result, for Perkins and, by extension, *Movie*, the 'new wave' was as clumsy as it was ambitious.[42]

These objections were founded upon the belief that the first task facing a film critic was to look for 'a harmony between action and presentation', a task further guided by the need for a correspondence between the event and its presentation. As he concludes elsewhere: 'There's a huge range of filming any piece of action but I would insist that the chosen method maintain the integrity of the event.'[43] This was where the British New Wave directors were alleged to have failed. Perkins's objections were founded on the belief that directors such as Schlesinger, Clayton and Reisz sacrificed 'the integral relationship between décor and action' in order to 'make a directorial point'.[44]

One way that we might understand these objections to the British New Wave is to see them in terms of an aesthetic standard. Perkins's objections become the criteria by which these new British films were deemed to have fallen below this standard. When compared to the finest films that Hollywood and Europe had to offer, the British New Wave, was, for *Movie*, devoid of personality and reduced to making clumsy points. These films also lacked style, imagination and, ultimately, as a result of all of these deficits, meaning. Further compounding their failure was the lack of a suitable correspondence between the form of a particular film and its content. This created a gap between the event and its presentation. For Perkins, and by association, for *Movie*, the new British films were not worthy of positive critical comment.[45] As Charles Barr concludes elsewhere:

> Such British films as did get occasionally get praised were presented as being marginal and atypical, exceptions which, in the true sense of the term, proved the rule – they tested and bore out, by their demonstrable difference, and by the fact that they seemed to lead nowhere, caught in a cinematic cul-de-sac, the 'rule' that certain notions and practices of cinema were somehow embedded in Britain which were inimical to the kind of high achievement of skill and moral seriousness valued by *Movie*.[46]

Why did the style and construction of these new British films cause Perkins so much consternation?

Between form and content

The problem with the British New Wave was a simple one. Allegedly, these new British films were unable successfully to contain their use of locations within their narratives. We need to understand that the position that Perkins adopted in relation to these films finds its origins in discussions of the cinema's essentially bastard nature. Believing the medium to be an intrinsically hybrid form of expression, Perkins felt that there was too much variety and conflict between its facilities and components for the cinema to be considered otherwise. Yet, crucially, he also suggested that the exclusive opportunities offered by the medium were the essential factors in the questions of choice and style. Allied to this was the belief that these specific opportunities were better served when considered in terms of their inter-relatedness. On a broader scale this is because:

> The fictional film exploits, where purer forms attempt to negate, the conflict between reality and illusion. Instead of trying exclusively either to create or record, the story film attempts a synthesis: it both records what has been created and creates by the manner of its recording.[47]

Admittedly, these last ideas are taken from Perkins's *Film as Film*, a book written some ten years after the publication of 'The British Cinema' and it is highly likely that critical positions and perspectives will change over time. This is all part of what Cavell calls 'the persistent exercise of your own taste'.[48] With its concern for coherence and synthetic relationships, *Film as Film* is a broader development of some of the concerns expressed in 'The British Cinema' and, as such, bears a direct relevance to this discussion. Nevertheless, despite the time that has elapsed between the publication of 'The British Cinema' and the present day, there has been no evidence of Perkins reconsidering or recanting the views on the British New Wave he expressed in 1962. At this point it is also worth pointing out that I do not intend to extend this discussion into a broader debate about the medium's essence. Instead, I will concentrate on the relationship between this idea of synthesis and the objections Perkins raised about the British New Wave. Indeed, it is Perkins himself who usefully suggests the limits of this debate when he argues that the essence of the medium itself is not a sufficiently compelling subject when it comes to the business of film criticism. This is because, as he continues:

> We do not deduce the standards relevant to Rembrandt from the essence of paint; nor does the nature of words impose a method of judging ballads and

novels. Standards of judgement cannot be appropriate to a medium as such but only to particular ways of exploiting its opportunities.[49]

This is crucial because Perkins's original objections were wholly based upon the ways in which the New Wave directors exploited the opportunities offered by the medium. We have come to understand the scorn with which Perkins viewed these films, and it was his standards of judgement that led him to condemn these films as failures. Putting aside the more personal claim that these films lacked style and meaning, we have also seen that the bulk of Perkins's objections were based upon the failed integration of a character with its background, the constant 'obligation' to 'establish place with inserted shots', and the setting lacking an organic connection with the characters – with each objection being an example of the ways in which these films failed to make the most of their opportunities. This was where the films failed. As John Hill later explains:

> The ideas and attitudes expressed by . . . the films of the British 'new wave' do not derive simply from the focus on the subject-matter but also from their deployment of certain types of conventions (in accordance with what a audience 'accustomed to the cinema' expects) which, then, inevitably structure and constrain the way in which that subject matter can be presented in the first place.[50]

Perkins's idea of opportunities presented by the medium becomes redefined as the deployment of conventions, and this is crucial because, as Hill continues, it is the 'conventionality' of realism which makes its usage so vulnerable to change. As the conventions change (either in reaction to previously established conventions or in accordance with new perceptions of what constitutes reality) so too does our sense of what then constitutes reality.[51] Perkins acknowledged that there was a need for British films to avoid what he called the cinema of awfulness, with its stereotypes and spurious excitement, and adopt a more responsible approach to dealing with human relationships and social problems. However, these new Woodfall-influenced films were also damned by their efforts to be more responsible. For Hill, it is through these efforts that the vulnerability of the British New Wave was most clearly demonstrated. This is because the narrative elements of a particular film are not only the actions and events themselves but also the way in which these actions and events are presented. These specific conventions will be motivated in terms of the presentation of actions and events. However as Hill continues, the inclusion of certain scenes can be considered to be redundant, unwarranted and, ultimately, 'surplus'. Despite similarities with other films, this inclusion gives the British New Wave a degree of 'noticeability'.[52]

Andrew Higson continues this idea of noticeability when he describes this inclusion of scenes or actions in terms of the tension that they create within the narrative. Seen in this way, these stylistic procedures

> at one level construct a *narrative space* in which the protagonists of the drama can perform the various actions of the plot. Narratives require space in which they can unfold. But because British New Wave films are promoted as realist, landscape and townscape shots must always be much more than neutral narrative spaces. Each of these location shots demands also to be read as a real historical place which can authenticate the fiction.

At the same time, however, the demands of the New Wave narratives require these spaces to be active rather than passive. This is because they must also authenticate the fiction by being easily read as real historical places and here the two demands create a tension, 'with the narrative compulsion of the film working continually to transform place once more back into space'. There are two ways in which this tension might be resolved. One is when the characteristic shots of these films become incorporated into the movement of the narrative. 'In these cases', Higson notes, 'place becomes a signifier for character, a metaphor for the state of mind of the protagonists.' The second way is to understand them to be cutting against the narrative flow, allowing these shots to be read a spectacle, 'as a visually pleasurable lure to the spectator's eye'.[53]

For Perkins, these shots achieved neither of these things. It is true that he felt these shots to be cutting against the narrative flow but the tension they created within the workings of the film served only to enhance his idea of landscape-mongering. It is this degree of noticeability that leaves these films at their most vulnerable to adverse criticism. This is because any innovation in cinematic realism is best understood in terms of a rejection of those conventions that preceded it. In this way, 'location shooting and the employment of unknown regional actors' were a means by which 'new wave' realism might place a distance between itself and 'the "phoney" conventions of character and place characteristic of British studio procedure'. This was exactly what Perkins called for in his article. However, it was the replacement of these 'phoney' conventions with location shooting that then led Perkins to complain that these films constantly had to re-establish their setting. It was the deployment of ostensibly non-functional actions and locations which became a characteristic of the British New Wave. In contrast to a high degree of ordering allegedly apparent in 'conventional narrative films', this deployment only loosely fitted into the logic of narrative development. As Hill suggests: 'Place as place is less important than its function in the narrative as a site for action.' One explanation for this approach to space and place can be found in the films' concern for realism. With its 'apparent "mismatch" between place and action', a distance is (arguably) placed between these films and the 'more ordered and less 'wasteful' fictions of Hollywood where, also, 'place' is not 'accredited an autonomy and "integrity" outside the demands of the narrative'. This is the conclusion that Perkins reached. As Hill concludes:

> It was because of such stylistic 'manipulation' that a number of critics (including those attached to *Movie* such as V.F. Perkins) had objected to the British 'new wave' films. For them the virtue of mise-en-scène in traditional American cinema was precisely its relative unobtrusiveness: style and technique amplified the themes of a film without distracting from the film's forward movement. By contrast, the style and iconography employed by the British 'new wave' is obtrusive.[54]

Perkins also demanded a correspondence between the form of a film and its actual content, so that the distance between a cinematic event and its presentation might be reduced and/or removed. Higson is useful here when he defines the obtrusiveness of this these films as an example of 'surface realism' – 'an iconography which authentically reproduces the visual and aural surfaces of the 'British way of life'. The problem with this definition is that such a surface realism prevents the total incorporation of these iconographical details into their respective narratives. Rather than a complete sense of mise-en-scène we are presented with 'the spectacle of the real, as distinct from its narrativization'.[55]

The views of Hill and Higson are vital for two reasons. They make clear the relationship between Perkins's objections and the artistic choices made by the New Wave directors. Equally importantly, both Hill and Higson demonstrate a willingness to place as much emphasis upon the collective failings of these films as Perkins originally did. Their observations are indicative of the same tendency towards overemphasising the similarities between these films that Perkins's article initiated. We can see that one aspect of the historical legacy left by 'The British Cinema' has been the tendency to view these films collectively. For a final example of this tendency we need to move forward ten years from 'The British Cinema'.

Corruption and repetition

Thomas Elsaesser outlined two things that particularly troubled him about the British New Wave. He felt that directors such as Schlesinger, Anderson and Richardson demonstrated 'an excessive modesty'. Echoing the comparative theme evident in Perkins's earlier discussions, Elsaesser felt that these directors just didn't measure up to the new wave of French directors such as Rohmer, Rivette and Godard. Specifically, this meant that the British directors lacked 'a cinematic eye' and by this Elsaesser meant an approach to the material he [the director] is dealing with, which is shaped by the requirements and possibilities of the cinema, and that there is consequently no director who has an awareness of style and form sufficiently sensitive that each movement of the camera counts, each angle and composition of the frame is there to advance the thematic movement, embody a point of view or clarify the action.[56]

This 'modesty' allowed Elsaesser to bemoan the fact that this lack of a cinematic eye resulted in 'loose-jointed narratives, careless handling of camera movements' and, echoing Perkins's earlier indictment, a 'misplaced visual emphasis'. The alleged problems of style and construction in the films of Schlesinger *et al*. were further compounded by questions about the representation of location and atmosphere. As Elsaesser continues:

> The fact is that by seeking 'realism' primarily on the level of location and atmosphere, the British cinema, especially during its 'renaissance' has remained almost as naïve as ten years earlier: it confined itself to a sometimes astute but more often mechanical combination of an industrial (northern) working-class setting with readily identifiable characters and class stereotypes.[57]

It was this mechanical combination which caused the initially fresh images of the New Wave, the shots of urban industrial skylines and rolling moors, for example, to eventually become formulaic and demonstrate their 'vulnerability'. This resulted in two additional problems. Firstly, there was an obvious effect on the way the films were constructed. Elsaesser also felt that the films' dramatic conflicts were either 'pushed into melodrama or they dissipated themselves in squalid little compromises'. These two problems came to demonstrate what he saw as one of the fundamental problems with realism in the cinema; namely, its corruption through repetition. As if this wasn't enough, these films also lacked a sufficiently well-established psychological or moral conflict and a theme or argument that allowed the setting of the film to be absorbed into 'the metaphoric language of emotions and actions'. This meant that the British New Wave was unable to avoid the exploitation of its social milieu.[58]

Like Perkins previously, Elsaesser's objections focus on the films' systematic use of landscape and location. Perkins's disdain for the apparent lack of effective connection between character and landscape has become, for Elsaesser, a problem with 'misplaced visual emphasis'. In both cases, it is the link between the style of the British New Wave and their use of realistic locations that leads to these films being seen as having failed. By making this link, Elsaesser was able to suggest famously that realism in these films meant nothing more than living in a terraced house and riding a bicycle to work. A further result of this repetition was the spawning of cliché after cliché, 'until the scene of a couple overlooking belching gas-works and a row of sooty houses from the surrounding hills became as meaningful as a shot of the Eiffel tower in a picture about Paris'.[59]

Appropriate criteria?

If standards of judgement can only be appropriate to ways in which a particular film takes advantage of the opportunities offered by the medium then this also must mean that the criteria applied by the critic must be based upon what he or she can sustain and not on the demands that he or she might make. This is crucial because, as Perkins concludes:

> The clarification of standards should help to develop the disciplines of criticism without seeking to lay obligations on the film-maker. Criticism and its theory are concerned with the interplay of available resources and desirable functions. They attempt to establish what the medium is good for. They cannot determine what is good for the medium, because the question is useless. The search for appropriate criteria leads us to observe limitations; it does not allow us to prescribe them. Anything possible is also permissible, but we still have to establish its value. We cannot assess worth without indicating function.[60]

It is the interplay of resources and functions that is crucial here. The resources available to these films would be the locations where they were filmed and their functions, desirable or otherwise, would be to establish the spaces and places where the New Wave narratives unfold. However, Perkins felt that there was a problem with the interplay between them. This meant an alleged discrepancy between action and its presentation. This discrepancy allowed him to decide upon the relatively low critical value of these films. Having decided that the function of the locations prevented them from being fully integrated into the narrative Perkins felt able not only to list the criteria appropriate to their failure but also to dismiss these films arbitrarily.

The concern here is that, despite claims to the contrary, Perkins's claims for the failings of the British New Wave appear to do more than merely observe their limitations. In the case of these British films, this 'lack' of correspondence meant, for Perkins, that they appeared imbalanced. As he writes:

> This balance, the delicate relationship between what is shown and the way of showing, justifies and exalts the movie's mongrel confusion of reportage with narrative and visual art. A single image is made to act both as a recording, to show us what happens, and as an expressive device to heighten the effect and significance of what we see.[61]

However, this balance can be appreciated only if we respond to movies as a synthetic form and understand that the parts of a film are of interest only in relationship not in isolation. With its characteristic use of apparently isolated establishing shots, the British New Wave apparently lacked the capacity to be considered in this way. 'The British Cinema', then, marked the point at which British style-based criticism and the New Wave films diverged. Also, as is evident in the responses of Elsaesser, Higson and Hill, Perkins's original objections were wholly responsible for the creation of a certain tendency to treat these films collectively. Yet, the case for refusing to examine the style and meaning of these films individually is not as watertight as impressions might suggest. Perkins's accusations of 'landscape-mongering' sit at odds with his call for an interest in relationships and not isolation and, as we are about to see, the relationship between *Movie* and the British New Wave becomes an increasingly complicated one.

One true church?

The practical critical approach advocated by *Movie* was the specific way in which the journal would set itself apart from the existing critical community in Britain. In particular, they were keen to stand in opposition to the British Film Institute journal *Sight and Sound*. As Perkins explained in 1961:

> Our reaction was provoked by *Sight and Sound*'s influence over 'serious' film criticism in Britain. During the past five years, the magazine has retreated further and further from the difficult business of coming to grips with the most complex of art forms, and has hidden behind a screen of well-meaning 'liberal' clichés. Its reviews became increasingly dull and unhelpful.[62]

Elsewhere, Ian Cameron was even more brutal: 'The ultimate reason for bad criticism in Britain is intellectual laziness which shows itself as a reluctance to make the effort to understand more than the superficial meaning of a film.'[63] However, *Movie*'s antagonism towards *Sight and Sound* was also responsible for a contradiction that lies at the very heart of their objections to the British cinema.

As Thomas Elsaesser argues, Perkins's repudiation of British cinema, especially its 'new wave', was simply an attempt to dispel the belief that directors such as Richardson, Schlesinger, Clayton and Anderson had 'somehow given the British cinema an artistic form and a sense of style'.[64] Critically, for Perkins and the others at *Movie*, there was just no comparison between a Nicholas Ray film, say, and one from Tony Richardson. As Geoffrey Nowell-Smith continues, the belief in a new British cinematic 'style' was sacrilegious. As he writes:

if they [*Movie*] are interested at all to elucidate what Preminger has to say about Israel, or what Rossellini has to say about freedom in *Vanina Vanini*, it is because Preminger (or, as the case may be, Rossellini) is saying it, and Preminger and Rossellini are members of the True Church, like Donen, Minnelli, Hawks.

'There is,' as Nowell-Smith concludes, 'be it noted, only One True Church, even if it has many prophets, and there is one cult – the almost mystical and certainly hermetic movie experience.'[65]

For *Movie*, the suggestion that the style and construction of a film such as *Room at the Top* was worthy of positive critical discussion was tantamount to heresy. This heretical belief in the development of a British 'style' could be blamed on the infidels writing for *Sight and Sound*.

Sight and Sound hoped that this mode of British film making might bring about what they saw as a specifically British 'sense of style'. Though Houston felt that there was nothing great about the film she did declare it to have the 'impact of a genuine innovation'. Also, with a new subject, a new setting and new talent, Houston concluded that 'half a loaf, in this context, looks very much better than the usual bread substitute'. Additionally, there was also a real cause for optimism that the newer independent companies such as Remus (which produced *Room at the Top*), Woodfall and Associated British would be able to demonstrate innovation. However, as she warned: 'What happens next will depend on the talent and persuasiveness of half a dozen writers and directors, on the imponderables of public response, and on whatever weight the critics are prepared to throw into the scale.' This meant that it was now up to the critics 'to play their own part in trying to keep the road signposted and the traffic moving'.[66] David Robinson felt *Look Back in Anger* to be a 'breakthrough'.[67] Penelope Houston echoed Robinson's optimism in her cinematic summary of 1959. As she declared:

> However and wherever we are going to do our film-making, one encouraging certainty remains. 1959 has been a year of intense vitality, an amazingly confident contrast to the uneasy 'fifties. The cinema has been killed off in the headlines several times during the past few years. The corpse has never looked healthier.[68]

With its 'attempt to interpret the spirit behind a large part of British life today', *Saturday Night and Sunday Morning* was, for Peter John Dyer, the next step forward for this new wave of British films. Mindful of the tendency always to compare a British film with a more 'acceptable' film from elsewhere – a tendency that epitomised *Movie*'s position – Dyer's review is an attempt to make a claim for the critical acceptance of the British New Wave.

Whilst prepared to acknowledge that the film might lack the 'sublimity and universality' of *Pather Panchali* and *Tokyo Story*, Dyer doubts whether such a comparison is really necessary. This kind of comparative argument – as revealed by the stance taken by Perkins in 'The British Cinema' – demonstrated 'something notoriously inbred and exclusive about the British which tugs against the broader, deeper expressions of feeling – against, if you like, universality'. As he argues:

> Why, in any case, should not the Nottingham wilderness of trade-marked houses and digital smokestacks be as likely a setting for important truths as Tokyo or Taormina? It would be a great pity if our sensibilities, our stand-ards of what is major and minor art, should continue to be directed, despite the example of *Saturday Night and Sunday Morning*, by sophisticates and romantics, sceptics and theorists, of every shade and hue.

Dyer concludes with a critical challenge which demonstrates a more reasonable approach to the New Wave: 'Grant us more such "minor" films and directors. Then, and – in the context of contemporary British cinema – only then, can we start asking for something "major." '[69]

For *Sight and Sound*, *A Kind of Loving* appeared to keep the momentum going. Eric Rhode begins by connecting the film's 'documentary' style with the inner conflicts of the characters. In this way, the style of Schlesinger's film 'establishes the bewilderment of his lovers through the ambiguity of their motives'. Of course, as Rhode continues:

> this documentary style is as awkward as gunpowder: the mildest implausibil-ity is liable to blow the film sky-high. Yet June Ritchie and Alan Bates, who play the lovers, carry this dangerous burden with an almost breathtaking nonchalance, and perform with a range of gesture, genuine and unexpected, which is not usually found outside the documentary.

The result of this, for Rhode, is a 'curious objectivity'. The camera 'holds us back from the characters so that people are almost seen as things – leaden, weighted with texture. Rather than let us identify ourselves with these characters . . . it restrains us, makes us think again.' As Rhode concludes: 'Somehow, we are forced to fuse these two points of view: and this, in effect, is the achievement of *A Kind of Loving*. It presents us with a complex situation and then compels us to face it squarely.'[70]

Like Dyer's previously, the tone of Rhode's review demonstrates a more even-handed approach. Rather than just praising the film for its own sake or dismissing it out of hand, Rhode makes a significant claim for the achievements of Schlesinger's film. However, if Rhode gave the impression that the style of these new films was capable, after all, of bearing a serious critical weight then this optimism was short-lived, as Peter Harcourt's discussion of *The Loneliness of the Long Distance Runner* demonstrates. Once again, this review will be considered in greater detail later. Harcourt's review has a decidedly disappointed tone to it, and the implication is that *Sight and Sound*, despite its initial optimism, soon came to share the same disillusionment with these films as *Movie*.

Hollow promises?

In each of these examples a sense of the relationship between style and theme was clearly evident for *Sight and Sound*. However, the initial optimism soon faded and for the journal, as for *Movie*, the supposed breakthrough in British cinema appeared to be only a hollow promise. As Penelope Houston writes:

> Three years or so ago, films like *Room at the Top* and *Look Back in Anger* had critics talking about a breakthrough in British cinema. A breakthrough to what? Other than a responsible look at a new kind of subject, it was never all that clear; but we could feel that the British cinema was poised on the edge of something. In 1962, it is still hovering on the edge.[71]

However, just like Perkins, a disappointed Houston was unable to resist the urge to look elsewhere for inspiration. As she laments:

> But perhaps we know now, as we didn't then, what a breakthrough might mean: we've had films as varied as *La Notte* and *Il Posto*, *Lola* and *A Bout de Souffle* to teach us. There is not a glimmer of a chance, on the existing evidence, that any of these films could have come out of Britain, either from our studios or from the young film-makers working independently.

Finally, echoing Perkins's thoughts on the stylistic failures of the new British films, Houston concludes by suggesting that 'a film like *Lola* or *Il Posto* seems entirely at home in the place where it's made; a British film, when it gets outside the studio, becomes location-conscious'.[72]

Houston's despair at the lack of progress made by these films meant that the distance between her and Perkins was smaller than either would care to admit. In fact, as her review of Seth Holt's *Nowhere to Go* (1958), demonstrates, Houston was expressing a real concern about those aspects of a film's construction that later troubled Perkins. As she writes, describing the film's ending:

> It is the film's final shot which comes closest to giving the game away. This is a really striking atmospheric landscape, a view of the Welsh countryside with the chimneys of an industrial town smoking in the distance. We don't often see this sort of view in a British film, and the shot is held for emphasis, designed clearly to make a point. But what point? . . . a shot which would make a fine conclusion to a bigger film merely imposes a pretentious final comment on a film not large enough to contain it.

As Houston concludes, 'Here, fully exposed, is one of the traps that catch the contemporary serious film-maker: the temptation to impose "significance", as it were, from outside.'[73]

Ultimately, Houston, like Perkins, bemoaned the lack of a break-through. *Sight and Sound*, like *Movie*, felt that the overall failings of the British New Wave were symptomatic of an industry that was itself a failure. Another conclusion that both journals arrived at was that Britain's home-grown product just could not compare with its European and Hollywood counterparts. As Houston writes: 'Accepting that Britain cannot, except in co-productions, expect to challenge the American cinema in terms of spectacle . . . then there is the challenge of French and Italian "quality" product to be met.'[74] However, as she eventually admits elsewhere: 'Comparisons between the young cinemas of Britain and France are becoming monotonous. We have made them ourselves in *Sight and Sound*.' Whereas 'across the channel the *Cahiers du cinéma* writers . . . have made it woundingly apparent that as far as they are concerned Britain's cinema is not yet ready to join Europe'. The result of this, for Houston, was that compared to a cinema 'headed by Truffaut, Godard, Resnais, Demy, Rivette etc., we are fielding a second eleven and', as she concedes, 'that is all there is to it'.[75] Despite the many protestations made by *Movie* to emphasise the difference of their critical position, Perkins reaches the same conclusion at the end of 'The British Cinema'. As he complains: 'We know that we can't have a *L'Avventura* or an *À Bout de Souffle* under the present system. We are much more disturbed by the fact that we are not getting equivalents for *Psycho*, *Elmer Gantry* and *Written on the Wind*.'[76]

The relationship between the form of expressive criticism advocated by *Movie* and the films of the British New Wave is a complicated one. Despite the claims that Perkins made for the study of cinema to be based upon ideas of difference not superiority, it is clear that British cinema in general, and the New Wave in particular, was not considered worthy of the kind of individual attention that *Movie* devoted to other films. Despite its initial euphoria, *Sight and Sound* succumbed to the same disappointments and reached the same conclusions. The historical reason why making a positive style-based case for the British New Wave has always been a problematic one is more complicated than originally imagined. If *Movie*'s objections to these films were solely dependent upon a considered examination of their style and construction then this would be enough to suggest that a new style-based interpretative approach to these films might well be a waste of time. Certainly, according to the aesthetic standards set by Perkins in his article, this would appear to be the case. Also, it is clear that, for Perkins the differences between the films of the British New Wave and those films from Hollywood and France could be found primarily at the level of their respective mise-en-scène. However, *Movie*'s objections to the stylistic flaws of these films were fatally influenced by its dislike of *Sight and Sound*'s desire to champion them. With a contradiction underpinning *Movie*'s stance it is sensible to suggest that the relationship between style-based criticism and the New Wave needs to be reconsidered. The existence of this contradiction offers sufficient opportunity for an examination of the style and meaning of *A Kind of Loving*, say, to begin in earnest and not just be dismissed as unnecessary. Indeed, as Perkins claims elsewhere, adding a further complication:

> So long as we see the definition of criteria as a means of validating enthusiasm rather than contempt, our standards of judgement will be useful for what they include but will have limited reference. The limits are not destructive but necessary. A positive claim, provided that it is rationally sustained, should be given greater weight than a denial of value. If we fail to perceive functions and qualities it may well be because we are looking for them in inappropriate ways.[77]

Here, though, Perkins's call for a positive claim sits at odds with his views on the films themselves. Consider, also, another statement that he makes on the same subject:

> The corollary is that values which *are* claimed should be argued in the clearest and most positive terms. A failure to discern quality is not a demonstration of its absence, but equally its presence cannot be indicated by the kinds of negative statements which movie reviewers have frequently invoked in the past decade to solicit approval for films which 'escape the confines of narrative' and so forth.[78]

A continued emphasis upon the issues and conventions of social realism that inevitably accompany these films will always result in the kind of negative statements that have always prevented any discernment of quality. Though Perkins avoids the term 'social realism' it is obvious that his concerns over the mismatch between locations and characters amount to a dissatisfaction with the same thing. Thus, a continued emphasis upon the collective failings of the films appears to be incompatible with the desire to make an evaluative assessment of the style and meaning of each individual film. This is especially true when we relate this desire to Perkins's involvement in the promulgation of style-based evaluative film criticism in Britain. The real problem here is that to understand the use of location only in terms of the deployment of a specific convention places a dubious double weight upon the question of the use of location. Over time the idea of a convention becomes tainted by accusations of repetition and corruption. This has meant that these accusations then become the reason why expressive discussions of New Wave style and meaning have never been started. This double weight has always placed an unnecessary limit upon the discussion of these films.

Despite the apparent contradictions and asymmetrical tendencies that we have uncovered, a style-based approach of the kind advocated by Perkins is still the best way in which our subsequent discussions of these films can avoid the overworked emphasis upon the realist issues that inevitably accompany them. There are two reasons for this. Firstly, an evaluative approach to film criticism has little choice but to rely upon a personal response to the film(s) in question. That there is little choice here is because, as Perkins suggests, the alternative to a personal response is to restrict criticism to a descriptive role and this would be highly unsatisfactory. Also, as he continues: 'A descriptive analysis will need at the least to make claims about the distribution of the film's emphasis; and emphasis is as subjectively perceived, relies as much on a personal response, as judgement.'[79]

Perkins's words here unwittingly become the moment at which British style-based criticism and the New Wave can begin to converge once again. If claims about the distribution of a film's emphasis are reliant upon a personal response then this explains Perkins's original stance concerning these films. However, I certainly have no intention of reducing my examination of the New Wave to mere description. My interest is in making claims for the differences that distinguish one film from another – relying on description alone would serve only to highlight similarities.

My personal response will inevitably involve my own claims about the distribution of emphasis in each film. The traditional tendency has been to place the greatest emphasis on the use and abuse of social realist conventions, but the weight of this emphasis has always restricted discussions of the films. In order for the redistribution of this emphasis to begin we need to return to the questions of conventions.

Plausibility and common sense

For Andrew Tudor, it is the idea of 'plausibility' that is more interesting than 'what can be claimed as realistic representation'. We all have conventional ideas of what is appropriate to the context of the film we are watching. If a film is set in a northern industrial town and the protagonist works on a lathe in a factory then it surely stands to reason that he is more likely to live in a terraced house and go to work on a bicycle than wake up in a penthouse apartment before setting off in a Cadillac. As Tudor concludes:

> All the discussions of realism in film aesthetics, all the claims of film-makers to be making realist films, all these have contributed to forming our notions of the 'real' in films. Sometimes directly, sometimes indirectly. But we shall never understand the working of the conventional image of 'realism' as long as we go on looking for some absolute aesthetic standard.[80]

It is also interesting to consider what Robin Wood has to say on the same subject. He begins by suggesting that discussions of realism demonstrate formidable theoretical elaboration but lack common sense. This is followed by a list of what he believes to be the fundamental features of realism: the tendency to become interested in characters as if they were real people; the tendency to care about the characters and what happens to them; the tendency to become emotionally involved, 'to participate, to identify'.[81] As Wood explains:

> The reason why representational or narrative art has been dominant in all ages is simple: it makes possible a human richness – an appeal from human beings, to human beings, about human beings – that abstract art or art that denies us emotional involvement and satisfaction cannot (for all their potential interest) possibly encompass.[82]

As Wood is led to conclude: 'The narrative film – owing as much to the development of the novel as to the invention of the camera – provides, then, a remarkable synthesis of the manifold strivings towards Realism in the arts.' However, the problem here is that, owing to 'its complicated mechanics' film, 'the most realistic of art forms', becomes the easiest 'to deconstruct'. As each of its technical innovations moves the camera closer to perfecting 'the illusion of reality' it also 'offers further possibilities for deliberately artificial (hence anti-Realist) effects'.[83] Yet 'Realism is a concept generally taken for granted' and is in fact 'very difficult to define satisfactorily. For Wood, as for Tudor, the commonest notion of it would probably be 'the plausible reproduction of reality as we know it.' However, as he finally warns:

> The criterion by which Realism is assessed is our own experience of life, beside which we place the work in a straight 'one to one' relationship; its value is determined by how recognizable we find its characters or by how we would like those characters if we had to live with them.[84]

The problem here is twofold. Firstly, 'our experience of life may be limited'. Secondly, a film defines its own reality through its 'method, presentation, style, structure'. Therefore, '"Realism" is relative, not absolute, and can only be judged by reference to the work's internal relationships'. This means that a better notion of Realism might be 'a particular artistic method or strategy'. Crucially, the relativity of realism becomes clears through the question of the emphasis placed upon it. By questioning this emphasis and refusing to accept an absolute standard of judgement, one that can then be applied to define a series of films collectively, the precise nature of our involvement will 'differ appreciably' from film to film, with 'each writer or director determining our relationship to his characters through method and style'.[85]

The chapters that follow will become the demonstration of a personal response to the films of the British New Wave. This demonstration will take the form of a series of sustained meditations upon the films in question. Also, following Wood, the precise nature of my involvement with each film will differ appreciably. In each case, I will show that a redistribution of critical emphasis not only allows discussions of the British New Wave to be based around questions of their style and meaning but will also allow the problematic relationship between these films and the questions of realism to be reconsidered. There is an important distinction to make here. I am not suggesting that social realist conventions were not utilised by the films but it should also be clear by now that a repeated emphasis upon the use of these conventions leading to a flawed series of films has become little more than an effective means of closing down discussion. Surely there is something else that we might start to say about these films? To this end, my discussion of the British New Wave will be based upon the idea of difference. Though there might be inevitable or unavoidable similarities between *Room at the Top* and *A Kind of Loving*, the main focus of my examination of these films will be upon the differences that can be found at the level of their respective style and meaning. Some of the chapters will be concerned primarily with producing sustained readings of individual films. Whilst continuing the interpretative trend that underpins this book, other chapters will also address other notable discussions that have accompanied these films. Finally, other chapters will also aim to demonstrate the ways in which detailed film analysis will allow the critic to move beyond generalised discussions of history and context and really gets to grips with the mise-en-scène of an individual film. It will also become immediately apparent that, with the exception of the Richardson films, the chapters are not arranged chronologically in relation to the films' release. This is a deliberate attempt to demonstrate that the films might be better understood in their own right and not as part of a series.

Chapter 2 will begin by considering Tony Richardson's contribution to the British New Wave. Beginning with 1959's *Look Back in Anger* and ending with 1962's *The Loneliness of the Long Distance Runner*, this chapter will comprise a series of shorter interrelated test-cases designed to demonstrate how an analysis of style and meaning might be undertaken. By including his two other films, 1959's *The Entertainer* and 1961's *A Taste of Honey*, in this demonstration I will also consider in greater detail the concerns over realist conventions raised by commentators such as Hill and Higson. This chapter will also evaluate the development of Richardson's approach to film making and reveal that the critical trajectory that his films initiated can be seen as symptomatic of the broader critical trajectory that accompanied the series as a whole. Ultimately, as this chapter will demonstrate, Richardson's four films from this period need to be seen as indicative of a talent being developed rather than the achievements of a director at the height of his creative ability.

Chapter 3 will examine Jack Clayton's 1959 *Room at the Top* and will concentrate on the film's opening sequences in order to achieve two related objectives. I will explore in detail the ideas of arrivals and new beginnings that these sequences bring to our attention. I will also demonstrate how these two ideas will also allow us to overcome the way in which existing considerations of this film have tended to place unnecessary limits upon the interest and importance of *Room at the Top*'s mise-en-scène. In this way, my reading of Clayton's film will offer the opportunity for further discussion. Chapter 4 is a detailed reading of John Schlesinger's 1963 film *Billy Liar*. I will demonstrate how the film's style and meaning might be fruitfully examined, and my reading will be particularly concerned to illustrate some aspects of the approach to mise-en-scène criticism outlined in John Gibbs's book *Mise-en-Scène: Film Style and Interpretation*. As this chapter will demonstrate, a British film like *Billy Liar* can sustain the kind of detailed aesthetic discussion that is usually reserved for films from other modes of cinema. My reading, then, will demonstrate that the style and meaning of a British film is worthy of sustained examination and discussion. John Schlesinger's 1962 film *A Kind of Loving* will be the subject of Chapter 5. Once again, this chapter will be centred upon a sustained reading. I will also aim to address some the specific criticisms that that have been directed towards this film. I will consider the concerns over narrative interruption that Andrew Higson has raised in relation to this film. I will also address the consternation that a particular camera movement found within the film caused Perkins in 'The British Cinema'. This is because Schlesinger, for Perkins, 'landscape-mongers in the most blatant and inept fashion'. Not only that, he also has 'no appreciation of the power of his décor'.[86] In keeping with the ethos underlying each of the chapters, my analysis of Schlesinger's film can be characterised by a positive evaluation which runs contrary to existing accounts from Perkins and Gibbs.

Chapter 6 will be concerned with Karel Reisz's *Saturday Night and Sunday Morning* (1960). My examination will centre on questions of causality. I will address the limitations of applying of David Bordwell and Kristin Thompson's ideas about cause and effect to an individual film. Accompanying this will be a further discussion of the ways in which the historical contextualisation of a British film, the kind of project espoused by practitioners of cinema history, limits the production of a more rounded examination of the film. As the chapter will demonstrate, and despite the best intentions of existing writers such as Aldgate and Richards, current accounts of Reisz's film refuse to get to grips with the detail of the film. Lindsay Anderson's *This Sporting Life* (1963) will be the subject of Chapter 7. As before, I will produce a sustained discussion of the relationship between the film's style and meaning. I will not only consider the fact that this film is the last in the series but will also allow the details of Anderson's film to formulate a further discussion about the processes and development of film criticism. In this way, the case I am making for a positive re-evaluation of these films will be complete.

I want to conclude here by considering Raymond Durgnat's views on the practice of critical preference. A practice of this kind, one that operates on the basis that 'Howard Hawks is better than . . .', for example, and one that can then substitute Hawks for Welles, or Ophuls, creates the unfavourable impression that 'vivid and insightful remarks or situations are a monopoly of a few prestigious individuals'. This and the tendency to summarise a period of film making by selecting 'the most distinguished films of the most distinguished directors' combine to create 'one of the principle distortions of film criticism'. This is not to say, however that the process of casting new light on critically unfashionable films is simply an exercise in archaeology because this, like the practice of critical preference, can be seen as just another convenience. It is simply the case that every generation 'has its own perspectives into the past, and needs its own criticism'. By way of an ending I am keen to appropriate Durgnat's words to mark the beginning of my examination. As he concludes:

> The chapters that follow differ from most British movie criticism also in concentrating less on evaluating the texture of films than on critical exegeses of certain themes, undercurrents and overtones. It is often assumed, though it has never been shown, that artworks not of the highest textural quality don't deserve thematic exegesis – that if they don't ring true to the highly sophisticated critic they can't ring true to anybody, and that what doesn't ring true can't have any meaning or subtlety.[87]

Notes

1　Louis Marcorelles, 'Conversation with Jean Renoir', *Sight and Sound*, Vol. 31, No. 2 (Spring 1962), pp. 78–83, p. 79.

2　Mark Shivas, 'Letter from London', *Film Culture*, No. 27 (Winter 1962/63), p. 21.

3　Pauline Kael, 'Is there a Cure for Film Criticism?', *Sight and Sound*, Vol. 31, No. 2 (Spring 1962), pp. 56–66, p. 57.

4　Peter Hutchings, 'Beyond the New Wave: Realism in British Cinema, 1959–63', in Robert Murphy, ed., *The British Cinema Book*, 2nd edition, London, BFI Publishing, 2002, pp. 146–152, pp. 146–147.

5　Hutchings, 'Beyond the New Wave', pp. 146–147.

6　Andrew Higson, *Waving the Flag: Constructing a National Cinema in Britain*, Oxford, Clarendon Press, 1995, pp. 269–270.

7　Julia Hallam with Margaret Marshment, *Realism and Popular Cinema*, Manchester and New York, Manchester University Press, 2000, pp. 45–51.

8　Samantha Lay, *British Social Realism: From Documentary to Brit Grit*, London and New York, Wallflower, 2002, p. 23.

9　R. Barton Palmer, 'What Was New in the British New Wave? – Re-viewing *Room at the Top*', *Journal of Popular Film and Television*, Vol. 14, No. 3 (Fall 1986), pp. 125–135, p. 128.

10　As Hutchings explains: 'Seen from this perspective, the predominately urban and industrial landscapes of British film realism, and the stories of the mainly working-class characters who populate them are revealed as vehicles for the expression of middle-class and patriarchal values' (Hutchings, 'Beyond the New Wave', p. 146).

Of course, as Hutchings continues, the basis for this suspicion was the earlier grouping of British realist films produced by John Grierson during the 1930s. This series of documentaries espoused a middle-class perspective that was apparently so pronounced that the changes in the British critical landscape noted by Hutchings caused them to be viewed as suspect for an excellent summary of the rise and reception of the British documentary movement (see Lay, *British Social Realism*, pp. 39–53).

11   Andrew Tudor, 'The Many Mythologies of Realism', *Screen*, Vol. 13, No. 1 (Spring 1972), pp. 6–36, p. 27.

12   As Lay explains: 'These film-makers were interested in extending the range of cinematic representation to include the working class beyond London to the industrial towns and cities of the north of England. They used unknown regional stage actors such as Tom Courteney, Albert Finney, Rachel Roberts and James Bolam, in ensemble casts. By situating their regionally authentic casts in regionally authentic locations, the British New Wave directors made new claims to realism, and made explicit through social realist fictions what was only implicit in documentary realist texts – that character and place were interconnected, and that environmental factors were largely deterministic of characters' fates and fortunes' (Lay, *British Social Realism*, pp. 5–19).

13   Neil Sinyard, *Jack Clayton*, Manchester and New York, Manchester University Press, 2000, pp. 11–17.

14   Anthony Aldgate and Jeffrey Richards, *Best of British: Cinema and Society from 1930 to the Present*, London and New York, I.B. Tauris, 1999, p. 186.

15   Jeffrey Richards, 'Rethinking British Cinema', in Justine Ashby and Andrew Higson, ed., *British Cinema: Past and Present*, London and New York, Routledge, 2000, pp. 21–34, p. 21.

16   See John Hill's *Sex, Class and Realism: British Cinema 1956–1963*, London, BFI Publishing, 1986, and Andrew Higson, 'Space, Place, Spectacle: Landscape and Townscape in the "Kitchen Sink" Film', in Andrew Higson, ed., *Dissolving Views: Key Writings on British Cinema*, London, Cassell, 1986, pp. 133–156.

17   As Alan Lovell notes, *Sight and Sound* was and is the subsidised magazine of the British Film Institute. It was set up 'to encourage the art of the film' and, as such, was in an ideal position to be a journal of film analysis, scholarship and theory. However, as he laments, 'Instead it became a magazine of film journalism about the contemporary cinema and involved in the apparatus of exhibition' (Alan Lovell, 'Notes on British Film Culture', *Screen*, Vol. 13, No. 2 (Summer 1972), pp. 5–15.

18   'The Critical Issue', *Sight and Sound*, Vol. 27, No. 6 (Autumn 1958), pp. 270–279, pp. 272–276.

19   Writing in *Film*, Peter John Dyer greeted the arrival of *Oxford Opinion* on the critical scene with hostility: 'Now the enthusiasm of such critics may seem invaluable to the cause of cinema; celluloid may be coming out their ears. But I wouldn't trust them with an inch of space in any magazine of mine. I wouldn't employ them because of their judgement, or rather

their lack of it; and because it follows that they will enjoy neither influence nor staying power' (Peter John Dyer, 'Counter Attack', *Film*, No. 26 (November–December 1960), pp. 8–9, p. 8).

20 '*Movie* Differences: A Discussion', *Movie*, No. 8 (April 1963), pp. 28–33.

21 David Bordwell, *Making Meaning: Inference and Rhetoric in the Interpretation of Cinema*, London, Harvard University Press, 1989, pp. 52–64. At this point it is also worth noting, as Pam Cook suggests, that *Movie*'s concept of mise-en-scène differed somewhat from that of its French counterparts, referring as it did to the overall formal organisation of films, their 'style'. As she continues: '*Movie*'s brand of mise-en-scène analysis is based on a deductive method whereby detailed description of films is seen to be the basis for criticism, a method which sees film criticism as a practical activity rather than as a theoretical project' (Pam Cook and Mieke Bernink, ed., *The Cinema Book* 2nd edition, London, BFI, 1999, p. 269).

22 John Gibbs, *Mise-en-scène: Film Style and Interpretation*, London and New York, Wallflower Press, 2002, pp. 62–66.

23 Bordwell, *Making Meaning*, pp. 29–31.

24 *Ibid.*, pp. 29–31.

25 Deborah Thomas, *Reading Hollywood: Spaces and Meaning in American Film*, London and New York, Wallflower Press, 2001, pp. 1–2.

26 *Ibid.*

27 As Cavell concludes: 'Then to explain how these appearances, significances, and matterings – these specific events of photogenesis – are made possible by the general photogenesis of film altogether, by the fact . . . that objects on film are always displaced, . . . (i.e., that we as viewers are always already displaced before them), would be an undertaking of what we might call film theory' (Stanley Cavell, 'What Becomes of Things on Film?', in *Themes Out of School: Effects and Causes*, Chicago, University of Chicago Press, 1984, pp. 180–183).

To further understand the relationship between style-based criticism and significance we might consider what Graeme Turner has to say. For him 'the notion of mise-en-scène is useful in that it allows us to talk about the way in which elements within a frame of a film or a shot composed of many consecutive frames, are placed, moved and lit. Since significance can be communicated without moving the camera or editing – for instance through a character moving closer to the camera, or throwing a shadow over another's face – the concept of mise-en-scène becomes an important means of locating the process through which such significance is communicated' (Graeme Turner, *Film as Social Practice*, London and New York, Routledge, 1988, p. 42).

28 Cavell, 'The Thought of Movies', in *Themes Out of School*, pp. 10–11.

29 Robin Wood, *Personal Views: Explorations in Film*, London, Gordon Fraser, 1976, pp. 10–12.

30 *Ibid.*

31 Penelope Houston, 'The Critical Question', *Sight and Sound*, Vol. 29, No. 4 (Autumn 1960), pp. 160–165, p. 164.

32 Ian Cameron, 'Introduction', in Ian Cameron, ed., *Movie Reader*, London, November Books, 1972, p. 6.

33   *Ibid.*
34   Jeffrey Richards quoting Ian Cameron, 'Rethinking British Cinema', pp. 21–34. Also, as John Caughie writes: 'Criticism tended to be neither very committed nor particularly rigorous. Within that context, in the 1960s, *Movie*'s attention to "style", to the way the film was constructed, to the movement of the mise-en-scène, its focus on "how" a film should be made, rather than "why" constituted and produced a radical shift in British film criticism' (John Caughie, ed., *Theories of Authorship* London and New York, Routledge, 1981, p. 49).
35   Charles Barr, 'Introduction: Amnesia and Schizophrenia', in Charles Barr, ed., *All Our Yesterdays: 90 Years of British Cinema*, London, BFI Publishing, 1986, pp. 1–30, p. 3.
36   Andrew Tudor, *Theories of Film*, London, Secker and Warburg, 1974, p. 123.
37   In fact, as Barr is led to conclude, it was the tradition of British film criticism that became more celebrated than the British cinema itself, creating the ironic situation where the international prestige of the former was sufficiently raised to lower the international prestige of the latter (Barr, 'Introduction: Amnesia and Schizophrenia', pp. 3–7).
38   V.F. Perkins, 'The British Cinema', *Movie*, No. 1 (June 1962), pp. 2–7, p. 2.
39   *Ibid.*, pp. 2–4.
40   Derek Hill discusses exactly this problem. As he writes, quoting John Osborne: 'The success of low budget films in France seems to have made little impression on distributors in this country. "I shouldn't think they've [production companies] even heard of the new wave," said Osborne gloomily. "It's easier far easier to find £500,000 for a film than £50,000, simply because half a million buys all the things the distributors consider a good investment, starting with top stars"' (Derek Hill, 'A Writer's Wave', *Sight and Sound*, Vol. 29, No. 2 (Spring 1960), pp. 56–60, p. 58).
41   Perkins, 'The British Cinema', p. 2.
42   *Ibid.*, p. 5.
43   '*Movie* Differences: A Discussion', pp. 30–31.
44   John Gibbs, *It was Never All in the Script: Mise-en-Scène and the Interpretation of Visual Style in British Film Journals, 1946–1978* (University of Reading, 1999, PhD Thesis), p. 135. The example of 'point-making' that Perkins uses in 'The British Cinema' is what he calls 'the first' love scene' in John Schlesinger's *A Kind of Loving* (1962). This is something I will examine in much more detail in my chapter on this film.
45   Perkins does offer *some* hope for the future of the British film. Karel Reisz's *Saturday Night and Sunday Morning* is seen as being 'preferable to the other new movies partly because its director does not attempt to palm himself off as one of the lads, and partly because he is less addicted than his colleagues to attempts at extraneous "style". Also he [Reisz] knows a little about how to use actors.' However, this faint praise is immediately followed by a damning examination of the film's fairground sequence and the conclusion that 'Reisz failed the test miserably'.
       Two other names are put forward as representing the 'hope' for a brighter future for the industry, Joseph Losey and Seth Holt. By this time Losey had made three films – *Time Without Pity* (1956), *Blind Date* (1959) and *The*

Criminal (1960) – but as Perkins ruefully notes: 'Losey is an American. He has, at least temporarily, left Britain. How much indigenous talent have we which could legitimately inspire hope?' Perkins answers this question by citing Seth Holt's *Taste of Fear*, made in 1961. Though Perkins is ready to admit that this film was not very good he is happy to predict that it might represent the future of British cinema. As he writes: 'To put it simply *Saturday Night and Sunday Morning* is a good film, and we can't imagine, on its evidence, that Karel Reisz will make a much better one. *Taste of Fear* is rather a bad film, and we can imagine Seth Holt making a masterpiece' (Perkins, 'The British Cinema', pp. 6–7).

46 Barr, 'Introduction: Amnesia and Schizophrenia', p. 4.
47 V.F. Perkins, *Film as Film*, Harmondsworth, Penguin, 1972, p. 62.
48 Cavell, 'The Thought of Movies', pp. 10–11.
49 Perkins, *Film as Film*, p. 59.
50 Hill, *Sex, Class and Realism*, p. 54.
51 *Ibid.*, p. 57.
52 *Ibid.*, p. 64.
53 Andrew Higson, 'Space, Place, Spectacle', p. 134.
54 Hill, *Sex, Class and Realism*, pp. 127–132.
55 Higson, 'Space, Place, Spectacle', p. 136.
56 Thomas Elsaesser, 'Between Style and Ideology', *Monogram*, No. 3, 1972, pp. 2–10, p. 7.
57 *Ibid.*, p. 7.
58 *Ibid.*, p. 7.
59 *Ibid.*, p. 5. For a further example of how this historical legacy has survived we might also consider what Geoff Brown has to say when he admits that 'for some the suspicion was growing that in abandoning the drawing-room for the kitchen sink British cinema had substituted one easy formula for another'. As Brown continues: 'Think British realism, and you think inevitably of kitchen sinks, factory chimneys, cobblestones, railway arches, bleak stretches of moor or beach, graffiti-lined council estates, people and landscapes placed in spare and striking juxtaposition. You also tend to think black-and-white: the perfect colour scheme for grey skies, smokestacks and poetic melancholy' (Geoff Brown, 'Paradise Found and Lost: The Course of British Realism', in Robert Murphy, ed., *The British Cinema Book*, London, BFI, 1997, pp. 187–197, pp. 188–189.
60 Perkins, *Film as Film*, pp. 58–62.
61 *Ibid.*, p. 78.
62 *Sight and Sound*, Vol. 30, No. 2 (Spring 1961), p. 100.
63 Ian Cameron, 'Attack', *Film*, No. 25 (September–October 1960), pp. 12–14, p. 13.
64 Elsaesser, 'Between Style and Ideology', p. 4.
65 Geoffrey Nowell-Smith, 'Movie and Myth', *Sight and Sound*, Vol. 32, No. 2 (Spring 1963), pp. 60–64, p. 64.
66 Penelope Houston, '*Room at the Top*', *Sight and Sound*, Vol. 28, No. 2 (Spring 1959), pp. 56–59, pp. 58–59.
67 David Robinson, '*Look Back in Anger*', *Sight and Sound*, Vol. 28, Nos 3 and 4 (Summer/Autumn 1959), pp. 122–125, p. 124.

68 Penelope Houston, 'Into the Sixties', *Sight and Sound*, Vol. 29, No. 1 (Winter 1959/60), pp. 4–7.

69 Peter John Dyer, '*Saturday Night and Sunday Morning*', *Sight and Sound*, Vol. 30, No. 1 (Winter 1960/61), p. 33.

70 Eric Rhode, '*A Kind of Loving*', *Sight and Sound*, Vol. 31, No. 3 (Summer 1962), pp. 143–144, p. 144.

71 'The Front Page', *Sight and Sound*, Vol. 31, No. 2 (Spring 1962), p. 5.

72 'The Front Page', p. 5.

73 '*Nowhere to Go*', *Sight and Sound*, Vol. 28, No. 1 (Winter 1958/59), p. 38.

74 'The Front Page', p. 55.

75 *Ibid*.

76 Perkins, 'The British Cinema', p. 7. Pam Cook reaches a similar conclusion in her discussion of the British critical climate of the period in question. *The Cinema Book*, p. 271.

77 Perkins, *Film as Film*, pp. 190–191.

78 *Ibid*. Though Perkins is writing some ten years from his 1962 article, the relevance of these later quotes can be found in the fact that there has been no real attempt on his behalf to modify his views on the British New Wave. Therefore, the time that has elapsed should have very little bearing on the use of these quotations.

79 Perkins, *Film as Film*, p. 191.

80 Tudor, *Theories of Film*, p. 34.

81 Wood, *Personal Views*, p. 78.

82 *Ibid*., p. 79.

83 *Ibid*., p. 79.

84 *Ibid*., pp. 80–81.

85 *Ibid*., p. 81.

86 Perkins, 'The British Cinema', p. 5.

87 Raymond Durgnat, *A Mirror for England: British Movies from Austerity to Affluence*, London, Faber and Faber, 1970, pp. 3–4.

2 From microscope to telescope: the films of Tony Richardson

I think it is no help at all for a film director to have had previous experience in the theatre – rather the opposite. Very few people have made the change successfully. The theatre is a literary tradition, and I have always had to fight to overcome a literary approach to film-making because of my work in it. The two roles are entirely different. In the theatre the director is in a solely interpretative position – interpreting what the playwright has written. However brilliantly he may do this, he creates nothing himself. In the cinema the director is the creative artist – ultimately responsible for what goes on the screen. A script which is of little worth in itself can be created into a great film by the director. There is no doubt, as far as I am concerned, that the cinema is the more satisfying medium. Making a film is, for the director, an entirely original act, from the moment of kicking a subject around, through the processes of shooting, editing, sound mixing – to the final master print. (Tony Richardson)[1]

The trouble was that what was 'unique' tended so quickly to turn into what was 'representative' – so that instead of reacting to what was extraordinary about the characters in the films, one found oneself anticipating what it was they had in common with those other films. (Alexander Walker)[2]

Sir – The praise that has been bestowed on such films as *Saturday Night, A Taste of Honey, A Kind of Loving*, shows how poor British films are. Like all serious films, these three are deficient in the only qualities that elevate films into the realm of art – imagination and depth. (George Camden)[3]

Critical position

Nowadays, for Peter Hutchings, writing on British cinema tends to lack what he calls 'evaluative judgements'. Films no longer tend to be viewed as good or bad but are often only seen as interesting. Potentially, this lack can be explained by a greater awareness of the contingency of value judgements and their relationship with broader ideological questions. At the same time, however, this is as much an issue of critical positions. As Hutchings continues, evaluative judgements do have the potential to undermine approaches concerned with establishing what a film's significance might be. Yet, this is useful because 'the undermining of interpretative authority opens up the interpretation itself to critical scrutiny.'[4]

It is true that the act of interpretation in (British) cinema still arouses certain suspicions. Using the details of a film as a starting-point for producing an interpretative reading is a process still tainted, to whatever degree, by the original desire to finger-print a film for direct evidence of individual authorial involvement that motivated practitioners of mise-en-scène criticism in the 1960s. Generally, this has meant that the study of British cinema has embraced other ways of discussing a film. However, there is still something to be said for evaluating individual films in detail. This is partly because films are not wholly defined by the context of their reception. They are also moulded by the context of their production. As Hutchings continues:

> Over-emphasising the importance of an audience's perception of cinema can make it difficult to grasp why films actually get made the way that they do. The other reason for focussing on an individual film is, of course, an evaluative one, and it involves identifying how the film in question deploys the resources of cinema in an imaginative, intelligent and distinctive manner.[5]

The key here is the question of detail.

The films of the British New Wave have acquired a fascinating status in relation to the history of British film criticism. 'The British Cinema' delivered the kind of evaluative claims that Hutchings calls for but it lacks the detailed investigation necessary for its claims to succeed. As we will see in the later investigation of *A Kind of Loving*, 'The British Cinema' does contain a brief discussion of one camera movement from the film. Also, *This Sporting Life* did generate two articles in later editions of the journal.[6] Yet *Movie*'s position in relation to these films lacks a sufficiently detailed examination of each film to allow their negative evaluation to remain unchallenged. Here, for example, is what Perkins had to say on Tony Richardson: 'Gratitude for the company's courage fades quickly when we are confronted with the conspicuous lack of talent in Woodfall's stock director, Tony Richardson. We would give quite a lot not to have seen *Look Back in Anger*, *The Entertainer* and *A Taste of Honey*.' Perkins felt that Richardson's films failed because by trying to ignore 'the distance between director and subject' they actually succeed only in emphasising it.[7] Sadly, there is no further discussion of how this failure might be best understood. Perkins does not make it clear what he means, and the original criticism has just been left to stand ever since. *Movie*'s hostility to these films came from the belief that they failed to deploy the resources of cinema with imagination or intelligence. Effectively, this has meant denying these films the right to be examined in the way that *Movie* examined other films. Yet, the kind of mise-en-scène approach espoused by *Movie* is the only way in which we might return to the kind of evaluative interpretation that is now needed. This is especially true when we also consider that *Movie*'s original objections were complicated by its relationship with *Sight and Sound*. When operating responsibly the process of film criticism needs to be an ongoing one and has to demonstrate a desire to revisit and reconsider existing critical positions. Only in this way can the process lose the linear sense of orthodoxy and evolve with a more enlightened and circular critical rhythm. As Hutchings is led to conclude:

> It seems to me that this kind of [interpretative] approach is indispensable to any evaluative claims for British cinema (and, despite all the new work being done on British film, evaluative claims are not being made nearly enough). It is also an approach that can provide a positive contribution to the historical methodologies that have helped to form the study of British cinema over the past two decades. Too often some of this historical work has contained implicit, unspoken value judgements about what makes a film interesting or good. It is surely better to bring these judgements out into the open, to make them explicit and discuss them.[8]

Four films

To this end, Richardson's films are the obvious place to begin. If we add 1962's *The Loneliness of the Long Distance Runner* to the list of films that Perkins passed judgement upon, in terms of output, at least, Richardson is certainly the director who contributed the most to this series of films. There is also something beguiling about the critical trajectory that these four films follow. This trajectory is marked by an initial optimism but ends with an air of pessimism and a sense of lost opportunity. This trajectory becomes representative of the New Wave as a series of films. These four films, then, provide the perfect opportunity for producing a series of introductory test-cases designed to demonstrate the potential of a broader re-evaluative project.

Accounts of Richardson's career are legion, and, perhaps owing to his personal access to the principal characters involved, Alexander Walker's *Hollywood, England* is the most useful here. Walker usefully describes the aims and objectives of 'Free Cinema'. He also examines Richardson's contributions to the theatre. Here, instead, I will begin by focussing on Richardson's desire to find innovation beyond the confines of the studio. As he explained at the time:

> The falseness, the stereotypedness, the staleness of British films is due to a refusal to approach a subject, the shooting of a scene, the use of a location, the design of sets, the casting of a small part, in a fresh and new way. There is constantly a premium on 'this was the way it was done last time' rather than on 'this is the way it has never been done before.'[9]

But it wasn't just the studios that left him exasperated. Richardson's experiences in television also cramped him creatively and, as Walker notes, 'kept him at a distance from his material'. Additionally, as Walker continues:

> it also cramped him physically, and this made a significant contribution to the feel of Richardson's films. The powerful 'physicality' they have comes partly from a talent for positioning actors in relation to their environment but it is also the response of a man whose own lanky, oddly disjointed and restless body with the scornful, dismissive gestures characteristic of him in the early days, made him continuously sensitive to his surroundings. Anderson and Reisz can both plan in their heads: Richardson prefers to start functioning when he gets himself to the scene of the action.[10]

Walker's observations give further weight to the claim that the British New Wave needs to be seen as less of a unified movement and more as a collection of individual films. Indeed, the description of Richardson's physical appearance gives a very clear sense of exactly how Richardson stood apart from the other directors he is always associated with. Walker mentions Anderson and Reisz but we can easily also add Clayton and Schlesinger to this list. With directors and their films standing apart from one another, the idea of a cohesive unified movement becomes harder and harder to sustain. Peter Wollen, for example, notes a similar difficulty in considering these films to be part of the same movement, and for Wollen this is especially problematic when they are compared with the French New Wave. As he writes:

> It has been argued that the 'Angry Young Men' films of 1959–63 were the 'British New Wave,' rather than the 'Jeune Cinéma Anglais,' as the French, who certainly ought to have known, dubbed it at the time. Yet surely to call these films New Wave is both inappropriate and misleading. First, the idea of a New Wave was intimately linked to the project of directorial 'authorship.' A good case can be made for Lindsay Anderson as a bilious but authentic 'auteur' (something he himself might deny in a fume of irascibility), but nobody has made a serious claim for the auteurist credentials of Reisz, Richardson, Schlesinger and others.[11]

Nor is it really necessary that they should. This is certainly not the intention here. Admittedly, I am interested in examining various aspects of the style and construction of Richardson's films but my reasons for doing this are solely motivated by the desire to stress the differences between the films. This emphasis upon their differences is crucial. This is not to be understood in terms of how Richardson's films all bear the hallmark of his input and thus arouse suspicion in the way that Hutchings suggests auteurist approaches have been known to do. Instead, the desire is to demonstrate that each of the New Wave films can sustain an analysis of the relationship between their style and meaning. Provided it is done with sufficient detail, an analysis of this kind is a useful way to understand the individual nature of each film. Irrespective of attempting to establish auteurist credentials, Tony Richardson is the most 'obvious' director to start with. This is certainly evident when we consider his initial championing by *Sight and Sound*.

A personal style?

David Robinson felt that Richardson's first film *Look Back in Anger* (1959), despite its faults, was important for the development of 'a style to the purposes of the piece'. Of course, as Robinson continues, there are problems with this including 'over-clever image cuts from sequence to sequence, an excessive fondness for dissolves [and] gratuitous bits of "social significance"'. Nevertheless, the film's 'sometimes strained, intellectual style' could be forgiven when 'for so long film-making has just been a business of illustrating scripts with moving pictures'. Robinson then highlights one prominent example of this new 'style', the camera's movement. As he continues: 'However exploratory, nervous, wandering, the camera movement is never obtrusive. We are not so much aware of a physical movement as of a turmoil and disturbance perfectly keyed to the action within the pictures.' As Robinson concludes:

> *Look Back in Anger* is a breakthrough – to a much greater extent, I believe, than *Room at the Top*, with which it must inevitably be compared. Here is a film which has something to say, and which says it without reference to conventional box-office values. It is a film in which a director has developed a personal style for the purposes of his theme.[12]

In a separate review, Penelope Houston draws attention to Richardson's efforts to translate a stage play to the screen. As she writes:

> Obviously a play as enclosed and concentrated as this one cannot be so extensively transferred to the open air without some risk of losing grip and control. But the attempt is to merge the real and the atmospheric: to make obviously, a film rather than a staged play. Much of the camera style is apparently designed to redress this balance. It aims . . . at the intensely intimate, with some emphasis on extreme close-up.[13]

The problem is, however, despite the fact that this idea of the film being 'intensely intimate' is an interesting one, that *Look Back in Anger* suffers from this emphasis on the extreme framing of its characters. Admittedly, as Walker suggests, the major importance of the film lies 'in the fact that it got made at all, in the period in which it was made, and in the appearance in the cinema of the talents that made it'.[14] Nevertheless, the biggest problem that this film faces is one of shot variety.

Ideally, as André Bazin suggests, if we are to understand the cinema as offering 'liberty of action in regard to space and freedom to choose your angle of approach to the action' then 'filming a play should give the setting a breadth and reality unattainable on the stage'.[15] The question becomes one of deploying resources. As Bazin explains:

> If the camera makes use of nature it is because it is able to. The camera puts at the disposal of the director all the resources of the telescope and the microscope. The last strand of a rope about to snap or an entire army making an assault on a hill are within our reach.[16]

Yet it is this movement from telescope to microscope that poses a problem for *Look Back in Anger* and there is a brief moment from the film that demonstrates this.

Alison (Mary Ure) has discovered that she is pregnant and is concerned that her husband Jimmy (Richard Burton) will be angry when he finds out. Needing some support, Alison has invited her best friend Helena (Claire Bloom) to stay with them while she is in town. Jimmy has always hated Helena and this means that her staying with them is likely to cause conflict. Helped by Cliff (Gary Raymond), a friend of the couple who has given up his room for Helena, Alison is preparing for her arrival. Quite understandably, she appears apprehensive. Jimmy has gone out and as we watch Alison getting ready for Helena's arrival we see that she is becoming concerned at the prospect of Jimmy coming home.

The dramatic intentions of the film have been clearly established at this point and the question the film poses here is a simple one: what will happen when Jimmy comes home? Expectancy hangs heavy and it is something of a relief, for the viewer, anyway, when we hear Jimmy's footsteps coming up the stairs. As she hears Jimmy approach Alison sits down at her dressing table. She sits looking into the mirror and the camera is positioned closely over her left shoulder.

1 Alison (Mary Ure) waits for Jimmy (Richard Burton) to return in *Look Back in Anger*.

The composition of this moment is a fascinating one. Alison sits on the right of the frame and her reflection can be seen on the left. This leaves a space in the mirror for Jimmy to enter, which he duly does. Seeing Jimmy in the mirror means that we can see him standing between the two views of Alison and the positions of the two characters now invite interpretation.

We can begin by considering that the two views of Alison indicate uncertainty. There are two ways that she can view the difficulties she is having with her husband. Either she tolerates his difficult behaviour or she takes steps to change her situation. This possibility for the different positions open to her is enhanced by the fact that the mirror usefully allows us to see both sides of her. Though she has her back to the camera we can also see her face reflected in the glass. Previously, Jimmy had caused Alison to burn herself on the iron and he now apologises to her. She tells him that there is no need. Having made a move towards conciliation Jimmy takes a step towards Alison. The film doesn't cut at this point, the mirror negates the need to do this. Instead, the camera readjusts slightly to ensure that Jimmy, though larger in the frame, is still visible in the mirror. Jimmy's movement means that he now looms over Alison. The couple do not look at each other. Jimmy then kneels and tells her that there is hardly a moment when he is not watching and wanting her. Alison stills stares ahead.

There is an intensity to this moment. Yet the angles of the composition here appear far too rigid. This rigidity can be linked to the positions the couple adopt in relation to each other – Jimmy being difficult and argumentative, Alison becoming numbed by his constant outbursts. We see evidence here of the strained relationship between husband and wife. But there is an additional problem, one that can be explained by taking this idea of being strained further.

The problem with this moment can be explained by the lack of significant camera movement. Richardson is keen to reflect the feeling of claustrophobia that comes from a bickering couple living in a very small flat, and the extremity of shot scale certainly contributes to what Houston called the 'intensely intimate' presentation. However, there is an air of studied suspension that impedes the dramatic flow, causing it to stagnate. Whilst lengthy pauses and carefully delivered lines help to demonstrate the skills of performance, they also contribute to the feeling that the tension here is overemphasised. This tension was first evident as Alison waited for Jimmy to return. However, once the conversation between them begins, the closeness of the camera and the deliberate delivery of the two performers combine with the (almost) static composition to exaggerate this tension rather than allow it to exist in harmony with other elements.

Finally, the camera has to move, following Alison as she turns towards Jimmy. This movement from left to right means that we no longer see her face reflected in the mirror. As she turns to face her husband this movement indicates a potential softening on her part. Perhaps Jimmy's declaration has removed the feeling of indecision that was suggested by the earlier composition? Jimmy explains how 'you get used to people' and the camera remains still. Jimmy eventually lays his head on Alison's lap and she cradles him in her arms. Once again the camera remains still but this stillness says less about the importance of their coming together and more about how the significance of their reconciliation is being conveyed. There is a certain solemnity here, one that appears to dampen the emotional charge of a man struggling to suppress his anger long enough to re-connect with his wife after he deliberately hurt her. The film cuts as we see Alison pull Jimmy up but this cut is followed by another close shot, perhaps the most extreme of all we've seen. Both faces fill the frame. The couple are about to kiss and as they do so the camera remains perfectly still.

It is hard to imagine how this opening exchange might have been filmed differently. Adopting a shot-reverse-shot strategy for the conversation would have changed the tone of the sequence, giving it a sense of movement when it is clear that Richardson was aiming to demonstrate a specific stillness. The problem is, however, that there is a very fine line between stillness and rigidity and this microscopic examination of a troubled relationship becomes impeded at this moment by the lack of a broader perspective. The emotional trajectory of this brief example has moved from two people standing apart from each other to two people coming together again and this movement is a significant one. Yet, the camera's continued proximity forces the emphasis upon this significance by failing to provide sufficient space for this emotional movement to be more subtly charted.

Following this thread leads to the belief that Richardson fails here in his efforts at redressing the balance between theatre and film. The strategy of extreme close shots works too much like the use of an insistent spotlight. Performers are clearly located within the narrative but their performances become overemphasised and the weight this strategy lends to their words appears to be too much. There *is* a sense of turmoil and disturbance, as Robinson rightly suggests, but the use of close shots means that there is just no respite. But does this makes *Look Back in Anger* a bad film?

The answer is no. There is something about effort and intent that prevents the film from being ranked in this way. Principally, it seems, the problem is related to Burton's performance. As Walker notes:

Had it been filmed eighteen months later, much about *Look Back in Anger* might have been different and probably better. The new wave of working-class or lower-working-class actors might have conferred a more class-conscious sharpness on Jimmy Porter: but they certainly would not have handicapped the character with the already established image of a film star like Richard Burton.[17]

Look Back in Anger is an interesting film for many reasons. It represents the beginning of Richardson's efforts to establish a new and separate position within the British film industry. The film also helped to generate a new series of critical debates about the development of a British cinematic style, or the lack of it. *Look Back in Anger* also became allied with other films trying to do similar things, Clayton's *Room at the Top*, for example. 'Interesting' is not necessarily a suitable evaluative term but this is not to suggest that the word should be seen as a negative criticism. As George Lellis was later led to note:

> Needless to say, the concept of making a movie by framing (often in quite the literal sense of the word) the dialogue which is at its core makes the film only as good as its script, much more so than is usually the case. In Richardson's early films this becomes a fascinating process to watch, for the scripts adapted from plays (*Look Back in Anger*, *The Entertainer*, *A Taste of Honey*) have strong characteristics of their own, and don't easily shake of their one-set conceptions and frequent rhetorical exuberance.

Not that this should necessarily matter. As Lellis concludes: 'There is, in any film, a point at which mistakes if pursued logically, can have not only integrity but fascination, and failures, if properly investigated, become more provocative than successes.'[18]

Irrespective of its flaws, *Look Back in Anger* is an important film for the fresh sense of optimism it generated in certain critical circles. This is evident in Robinson's enthusiastic review but there is further evidence in Penelope Houston's cinematic summary of 1959. As she declared:

> However and wherever we are going to do our film-making, one encouraging certainty remains. 1959 has been a year of intense vitality, an amazingly confident contrast to the uneasy 'fifties. The cinema has been killed off in the headlines several times during the past few years. The corpse has never looked healthier.[19]

Champagne and chips

For *Sight and Sound*, *The Entertainer* (1960) continued the good work that *Anger* had started. Penelope Houston optimistically declared the film 'a landmark in our cinema'. 'It was a brave film to make', she continued, 'and for all its limitations it has been bravely done.' As she notes:

> the level of conviction and concern, the savage humour with which a climate of desperation has been created, the whole effort to relate the immediate subject to larger context, are as rare as they are courageous. Anyone making

this kind of film in Britain is on his own, in the sense that he has no screen tradition to guide him.[20]

It is evident straightaway that unlike the undue weight that camera proximity and framing choices placed upon the intensity of emotional revelation in *Anger*, sufficient space is allowed here for the film's obvious emotional content to be revealed layer by layer. By adopting a broader palette of shot choice and camera distance Richardson manages to paint a (deceptively) simple picture of a complex character caught painfully between times. The film's subject matter also provides a clearer sense of the problems that *Anger* suffered from and *The Entertainer* aimed to overcome. To begin with, the problem with casting established performers in film versions of successful stage plays is evident. The question, as Alexander Walker notes, is one of balance, and the balance between Burton and *Anger* wasn't effectively achieved. When it came to the relationship between Richardson and Laurence Olivier this need for balance was evident in what Walker describes as 'the director's naturalistic preference' and 'the star's non-naturalistic technique'. As Walker continues: 'Richardson wanted to free the play from the stage; at the same time they also wanted to re-create Laurence Olivier's tour de force performance of Archie Rice, the stage "entertainer" of the title.'[21] By opting to broaden his shot choice Richardson manages to circumvent this problem successfully.

Stages in theatres occupy a privileged position in relation to the rest of the spaces available. The stage here is the site upon which Archie's struggles become clear for us all to see. Beyond the film, however, the idea of the stage remains relevant for what it reveals about the achievement of Richardson's first two films. Watching Archie performing reveals that the dimensions of stage can be altered. During the larger production numbers the stage is used to its full effect, providing a sense of depth and spectacle to proceedings. There are, however, more intimate moments when Archie is alone with the audience and here the lowering of the curtain foreshortens the stage's space and leaves very little room for manoeuvre. Using this idea to compare Richardson's first two films demonstrates that whereas *Anger* appeared content (or resigned) to foreshorten its dramatic space through the over-reliance on close shots, *The Entertainer* effectively deploys its spaces in a more rounded cinematic way. For example, despite the fact that the stage is an integral part of the narrative there is as much emphasis placed upon events backstage as there is upon those taking place in front of the curtain. The relationship between the film's spaces and its thematic concerns is more suitably realised than it was in *Anger*.

A further example of this is the glimpses of Archie provided from the wings. The camera's position at these moments is interesting because it occupies a place in between the theatre's primary spaces. From here, with Archie seen onstage, this idea of being positioned in between things applies to the character as well. There is a sequence towards the end of the film that is the perfect example of this idea. Additionally, because this sequence is not set in the theatre, it also reveals something useful about the further development of Richardson's stylistic outlook.

Archie has arranged to meet his daughter Jean (Joan Plowright) on a piece of waste ground that they both know. This patch of ground is located on a hill overlooking the seafront. The best chance of under-standing this character is when we see him in his dressing-room and the other backstage spaces of the theatre. These are the moments when he is not performing. This sequence on the waste ground offers a similar opportunity for insight. This sequence is the most important one in the film because this conversation is the central hub around which the film's spokes of dramatic revelation, tortured relationships and emotional intensity revolve with the same relentless whirl of the merry-go-round seen in the distance.[22]

Archie hasn't got long to spend with his daughter as he has to be elsewhere but the short time he spends with her goes a long way to revealing all we need to know about this man and his life. Unlike *Anger*, where dramatic revelation was continually overemphasised, the construc-tion of this conversation skilfully adds emotional weight to the situation without causing the sequence to become unbalanced. Archie begins by telling Jean that her mother left him when she caught him in bed with Phoebe (Brenda de Banzie), who later became his second wife. Jean was a baby at the time, he tells her. Archie follows this revelation by also revealing that he now wants to leave Phoebe and marry Tina (Shirley Ann Field), a contestant in a beauty contest whose father has promised to finance Archie's next show if he makes his daughter a star. Straight-away, there is a pattern emerging and Archie's romantic life has a pain-fully recurring feel to it. This much is evident from the dialogue alone, inscribed, as it is, with a sadness that makes us realise we are watching a man who can't stop making the same mistake. Yet, Richardson refuses to let this sadness overwhelm the conversation, choosing, instead, to let it contribute equally with the other elements present to the develop-ment of a more fully realised picture of Archie and the pathetic rhythms of his life.

The sequence begins with Jean already sitting down. Archie enters the frame by climbing to the top of the slope in front of her and behind him we can see the pier stretching out into the sea, a couple of desultory-looking fairground rides and various dilapidated buildings that accom-pany them. A merry-go-round slowly turns. From this perspective, the resort looks like it is out of season and as Archie approaches it is a simple enough task to establish a connection between this figure and this

2 Jean (Joan Plowright) discusses Canada with her father in *The Entertainer.*

3 The circular nature of Archie's life (Laurence Olivier) is revealed in *The Entertainer.*

landscape. Archie sits down to share champagne and chips with his daughter. Initially, as Jean mentions his opportunity for starting a new life in Canada, Archie sits at right angles to her and looks away. Archie tells Jean that he doesn't think much of the idea of moving to Canada, and his position within the frame lets us know that his view on the matter is at odds with his daughter's.

Archie is preoccupied and as he glances at his watch Jean asks him if he has to be somewhere else. Hesitantly, he replies that he does and his reply is the cue for a cut.

Jean is now shown in a close shot. She is positioned on the right side of the frame and the background behind her is out of focus. She tells her father that Phoebe has set her heart on starting a new life in Canada and as she looks up there is another cut to reveal Archie's reaction.

Ostensibly, this next shot is a simple mirroring of the previous one. Archie is framed in a close shot and the camera is positioned at a similar distance to the one of Jean. However, there are two important differences between these two shots. Firstly, Archie is positioned on the left side of the frame. Secondly, unlike with Jean, the background of the shot of Archie is in perfect focus.

The change in character position between the two shots is interesting for what it reveals about the difference of opinion between Archie and the rest of his family. Archie has no interest in leaving for Canada. This is despite the fact that he is a registered bankrupt with a fast-fading career. This lack of interest was suggested graphically by his sitting at ninety degrees to his daughter then confirmed visually by the difference of his position within the frame here. Were he also positioned on the right side then this would suggest the existence of some common ground between Archie and his daughter. The difference in backgrounds between these two shots is even more revealing. The direction of Archie's approach established a connection between him and the seafront and the sight of the seafront still visible in the frame here cements the relationship between Archie and this environment. Far from being obscured, the connection between character and landscape is perfectly realised here. Extending the comparison between the two shots says something further about the relationship between the characters and the framing.

As Archie approached Jean he asked her if she remembered a childhood incident that occurred on one of the rides we see behind him and his question imbues the view of the resort with a sense of the past. Archie, just like Jean, is positioned in the foreground of the frame. Nevertheless, there is a fundamental difference of significance between these two seemingly similar positions. Jean, the film earlier reveals, has a very modern way of looking at the world. This is evident from her work at a youth club and her involvement with civil protest. When she is talking about Archie moving to Canada with Phoebe, her position in the foreground indicates her relationship with the future. The blurred background in this shot represents the lack of importance that looking back to the past has for her. For Jean the only thing that matters is what there is to look forward to.

Archie, however, is unable to see things this way. Though he may be able to look forward – as his position in the frame suggests – he can only see as far as his next show. The composition of this shot makes it clear that for Archie the past, as represented by the view of the seafront we see behind him, binds him to this place. He is unable to break free from his surroundings. Instead, and just like the merry-go-round we clearly see behind him, the circular rhythm of Archie's life ensures that he is incapable of moving forward effectively to leave the past behind. Deriving this idea from the relationship between the characters and their framing is important because it allows the connection to be made between this moment and another that takes place at the end of the film. Connecting these two moments in this way offers a better understanding of the difference in achievement between Richardson's first two films.

Farewell performances

Following the thwarting of his plans to use Tina's father to finance his next show, Archie turns to his father Billy (Roger Livesey). Though Billy has been retired for a long time, Archie uses his reputation to secure a new deal with the theatrical agent Charlie Klein (Max Bacon). The proposal is for a nostalgic review that will feature Billy as the headline act and allow Archie to support him. Billy, however, dies in the wings, just before he is due onstage. Archie is told at the funeral that his only choices now are going to Canada or going to prison. Following this conversation the film moves to Archie's final performance. Considering his myopic approach to these matters, Archie doesn't yet know that this is the end.

The performance has started. The camera is positioned high in the circle and from this position the stage looks enormous. Archie stands at the back of the frame, performing in the tight circle of a single spotlight. The aim of this spotlight is to highlight the performance. Sadly, it also exposes the limits of Archie's life from here on in. As the earlier conversation with Jean revealed, Archie's life has always had a circular rhythm to it. Ultimately, as the spotlight makes explicit here, this rhythm has always forced him to operate within a limited circle of achievement. There follows a cut to another perspective. The camera is now positioned behind Archie and from this position the character's solitude is enhanced. Klein appears backstage and tells Jean that he is about to close the show. We then get another view of Archie, this time from the wings. As this succession of perspectives demonstrates, whichever way we look at it, Archie is finally finished.

Eventually Archie hears Klein's voice and looks offstage. He is finally aware that the show is to be closed. He tries to make light of this knowledge, joking in a close shot to the audience and as he does so we see that the camera's new position has shortened the circumference of the spotlight. The already limited aspects of his life are shrinking fast. A succession of three cuts follow, moving from the wings to Archie and then back again. A final cut returns to Archie and the framing is even tighter now. Over the space of these four cuts we have seen Klein leave angrily, Jean looks on sadly and Archie appear visibly choked by the news he has just heard. The rhythm of the editing is important here because it allows three significant reactions to be revealed without reducing the emphasis on Archie's position. At such a monumental stage in Archie's life it is only fair that he should say his goodbyes. Archie silences the orchestra with his hand and this gesture is the cue for another cut. The camera has returned once again to the back of the circle and the change in perspective causes Archie to appear alone and small in the distance. From here a proper sense of the enormity of what has just taken place. This is the end of a man's professional life and importantly the significance of this moment is not lost in the construction.

With the stage set, another cut returns to the entertainer. Archie remains defiant. 'I have a go, don't I, ladies?' he says. 'I have a go.' As Archie delivers his final lines he stands half in and half out of the spotlight before leaving. Just as he is almost swallowed by the darkness beyond the spotlight Archie turns once more, steps back into the spotlight and tells the audience how good they have been. Once again, this movement from broad views of the theatre to tighter more personal shots of Archie invites interpretation. Straightaway, the close shots here connect with the close shots we saw earlier. The view of Archie here is consistent with the view of the character seen earlier. This is still the image of a man trapped by his inability to see things the way they really are. In fact, standing alone on the stage in the full glare of the spotlight, there is no doubt as to the painful finality of Archie's position. The spotlight provides privileged access to the intimate final moments of a performer's career. The pained expression on his face is revealed when he hears that Klein is closing the show. All of this gives his final words to the audience an additional poignancy. Nevertheless, as moving as this epitaph is, the significance of this intimate view is overplayed if a broader view of the sequence's construction is overlooked. Naturally, standing alone in the spotlight, Archie is the film's central concern but unlike the example from *Anger* – where Richardson chose to over-accentuate the unfolding drama through the predominant use of extreme close shots – here Richardson portrays the tragedy of Archie's failure using a wider variety of camera positions and this strategy allows the emphasis to settle upon the images more effectively. Though the spotlight is insistent in its pinpointing the site of the tragedy – namely, Archie – the adoption of this more varied strategy reveals the pained and intimate expression of a failed performer and aids in understanding the tragedy without having to force the tragic nature of this image.

Once the curtain has been lowered for the final time Jean goes to commiserate with her father. As she touches him tenderly on the elbow the curtain rises again to reveal that the audience have all left now that the show is over. The camera is positioned behind them and the now-empty theatre is visible. With the lights on and the seats now empty the difference between foreground and background appears stable again. As Archie leaves the stage for the last time its importance has now been neutralised, losing its privileged position within his life. No longer separate, it is just another part of the building. As the end of the film reminds us, stages are significant only when they are in use. Otherwise, as this moment demonstrates, they are just so much empty space.

For Houston, Richardson was establishing a unique position for himself at the forefront of new developments in British cinema. As also suggested by Robinson's earlier discussion, Richardson was determined to develop a more personal approach to British film style, striving to prevent repetition through innovation.[23] It is a measure of *The Entertainer*'s achievement that it doesn't repeat the mistakes that hampered the dramatic flow of *Anger*. A large part of *The Entertainer*'s innovation derives from its adoption of a broader more varied shot strategy and this broader strategy is linked to the film's other innovation, the effective use of location. Richardson's use of the wasteland allowed connections to be made between the characters and the film's spaces. In turn, this facilitated a further connection between the film's spaces and its thematic concerns.

Inside and out

Look Back in Anger can best be characterised by the extremity of shot scale deployed to show the claustrophobic relationship between Alison and Jimmy. Sadly, however, a policy of this kind drastically limited the film's achievements. The construction of *The Entertainer*, on the other hand, demonstrates a willingness to move out from this extreme proximity. Not only is Archie's downfall realised through a broader range of shots, the film also manages to widen the perspective taken on Archie's downfall by the use of location shooting. By choosing to integrate the piece of waste ground into the narrative, Richardson was able to present a more rounded picture of the problems Archie faced in his life.

A Taste of Honey from 1961 is the next stage in this widening compositional development. As Terry Lovell notes in her discussion of the film: 'Shelagh Delaney's play was entirely set "in a comfortless flat in Manchester". While the film retains much of the original dialogue, it takes us out of this setting for the location sequences which give the film its most striking visual images.'[24] This sense of development is evident also in *Sight and Sound*'s review of the film. For George Stonier, *A Taste of Honey* was Richardson's best film since *Anger*. Not only that, Stonier also felt that this film was his most personal. For Stonier the film was a compelling demonstration of Richardson bringing 'all his skill to bear in casting, acting, atmospheric placing, the use, even the indulgence of location'.[25]

As the word suggests, Richardson's 'indulgent' use of location in this film has always caused a certain amount of critical concern. Perkins and

Elsaesser were particularly concerned with the way that films such as this one employed the locations they chose. Perkins feared for a lack of connection between character and environment.[26] For his part, Elsaesser believed that the use of location in a film like this had to be viewed as clichéd through its apparent overuse.[27] Lovell, too, concurs with this idea when she writes that 'the repertoire of images, narrative concerns and characters of the New Wave quickly became over-familiar, and its style soon lost its initial freshness of effect'.[28]

Lovell then suggests that each of the New Wave films 'has its shots of canals, street scenes, the pub, the fairground, the bus journey, the visit to the nearby countryside'. The implication is that despite a certain amount of interchange between these repeated images they still share a similarity of emphasis. This becomes complicated by the fact that Lovell appears to undermine herself when she is content to conclude that 'A Taste of Honey, above all the other films, gives priority to place'.[29] Other critics, too, have struggled with this apparent prioritising of place. John Hill, for one, suggests that an emphasis of this kind creates a disparity between place and action. This is because place doesn't provide 'the setting for narratively significant action'. Instead, 'it is insignificant action which provides the pretext for a visual display of place'.[30] For Hill, one explanation for this is as a means of inscribing a distance between these films and the overly contrived 'fictions' of Hollywood, with their tightly structured narratives and avoidance of residual elements. As he continues: 'By contrast, place in these films is accredited an autonomy and "integrity" outside the demands of the narrative, authenticating their claim, in doing so, to be more adequately "realistic" (and "outside" mere storytelling).' As Lovell concludes, citing Hill:

> The film's photography draws attention to itself. It does not create an unobtrusive backdrop to the narrative like the 'invisible' style of realism favoured by the French and British *auteur* critics, in which camera movement is subordinated to the demands of the narratives; and in which the mark of directorial 'art' is found in the mise-en-scène. Hill observes that the shots of the urban landscape in *A Taste of Honey*, as in other New Wave films, are redundant in terms of the narrative. They serve to slow down the action and oblige the viewer to pay attention to the film's pictorial beauty.[31]

There is a problem here, one that highlights the fundamental differences between the recurring tendency to view these films collectively and the desire to stress each film's individuality. Accounts such as Lovell's and Hill's depend upon isolating the film's use of space from its other elements. In the same way, for Lovell, Andrew Higson's discussion of these films 'centred on the representation of place in the New Wave, and on the films' use of exteriors rather than interiors'. As she continues: 'While frequently referred to in critical discussion of the New Wave, *A*

Taste of Honey is rarely analysed. When it is, the analysis centres on the sequences shot on location.'[32] The relationship between character and landscape is a prominent feature of this film. Yet, rather than pursuing this policy of isolation there is more to be gained from reincorporating the film's use of space into a more detailed discussion of its achievements. After all, the film's extended use of location is part of a deliberate desire to increase the possibility for achievement by extending the range of the setting. For too long the emphasis has always been on the idea of lacking integration, the impedance of narrative flow and, ultimately, of failure. In fact, *A Taste of Honey* successfully articulates a complex braiding of set, location and theme. For example, the film reveals a remarkable fascination with the idea of moving between interior spaces. Thematically, this is evident from the film's beginning, as we watch Helen (Dora Bryan) and her daughter Jo (Rita Tushingham) making their escape from their latest flat so as to avoid paying the rent. As the film unfolds, we see Helen leave Jo and set up home with her new husband Peter (Robert Stephens). This forces Jo to find somewhere to live on her own. Jo finds a new room and a chance encounter with Geoff (Murray Melvin) means that the two of them move in together. Eventually, whether concerned about her daughter's welfare or sickened by the drunkenness of her husband, Helen moves back into Jo's life, and her home. Helen's arrival forces Geoff to move out. In this way, the film's thematic concern with the movement between interior spaces is clearly demonstrated.

There are two problems that occur when it comes to discussing the film's use of interior and exterior space. To begin with, there is the tendency to view these two spaces as being completely separate. The other mistake is to compare the use of space in *Honey* with other New Wave films. Lovell, for example, demonstrates this when she writes:

> The economy of interior and exterior space in a film is organized in interesting ways when the protagonist is a woman rather than a man. The street and the public places of *Saturday Night and Sunday Morning* and *A Kind of Loving* are associated . . . with a dominant male sexuality that gains access to domestic interiors and sexual gratification, but ultimately is contained through marriage. Because private and public spaces are culturally gendered, they will be available for different sets of signification when the film centres on a young woman. Jo, like Arthur, moves between domestic interiors and the streets and countryside, but the two spaces are organized in this film less by gender than by generation.[33]

Lovell assigns different roles to public and private spaces, and this has the effect of separating their contribution to the film. It is preferable to avoid this separation and aim, instead, for a more detailed discussion of the relationship between all of the film's spaces and its thematic concerns.

The desire to do this is made even more compelling by the thought that the film is also interested in the idea of opportunity. This includes the idea of chances being taken, characters being denied the chance to do something, as well as the limiting of opportunity for a variety of reasons. There is, for example, a clear connection between this idea of opportunity, in its broadest sense, and the film's total use of space. The many shots of canals in the film are prominent in this respect. Unsurprisingly, shots of this kind have caused considerable critical concern. Nevertheless, the connection between the film's style and its meaning can be best understood through a detailed discussion that aims for integration, and in order for this to begin it is necessary to return to Lovell's listing of common features that all these films share.

Fairground failings

Lovell establishes a sense of uniformity by suggesting that the films of the British New Wave all contain certain recurring images. A more precise examination of the films suggests that a claim of this kind lacks the specific detail to make it more than just a dismissive observation. Nevertheless, Lovell's claim for a connection between *Honey* and *Saturday Night* does have some use, and this is because both of these films contain fairground sequences. Whilst we should be careful not to overemphasise the connection between these two very different sequences they are both still useful when it comes to the discussion of opportunity.[34]

For Arthur Seaton, the central protagonist in Reisz's film, the fairground represents the place where the opportunities of his life become drastically reduced. His affair with Brenda (Rachel Roberts), the wife of a colleague, has been revealed to her husband Jack (Bryan Pringle) and, in an understandable act of revenge, Jack has Arthur beaten up by two soldiers. Though the beating takes place outside of the fairground, Arthur is pursued and tries to make his escape by dodging between and behind the various rides and tents. He manages to get caught on various rides and the speed with which they spin only adds to the feeling that he will not get the opportunity to escape what is clearly coming to him. In this film the fairground in this film comes to represent betrayal, retribution, the inevitability of punishment and, ultimately, the curtailing of opportunity. On the other hand, the fairground in *A Taste of Honey* is revealed by the film to have a very different role.

Jo first meets Geoff when he comes into the shoe shop she works in looking for a new pair of shoes. Jo has already told her manager that she is going to view a new room. The room she views is a large one and she seems excited by the prospect of transforming the (interior) space into something hospitable. The sequence ends with Jo picking up a chair and the film cuts to reveal a street parade. This is the point at which Hill's concern over redundancy and the slowing of narrative action come to the fore. As he writes, describing the start of this sequence: 'there are eight shots, lasting a total of twenty-seven seconds, of a street parade and the assembled crowd of onlookers before the scene is motivated in narrative terms by a cut to Jo'. For Hill, the emphasis on place here, achieved through the deployment of 'establishing shots', occurs prior to the presentation of narrative action. The implication is that the emphasis created by these shots results in their redundancy.[35]

This is interesting because there is absolutely no sense of these early shots lacking suitable integration. Richardson is taking advantage of available resources but it seems perfectly logical to utilise a large event like this one when it comes to reiterating one of the film's most noticeable aspects, Jo's desertion by her mother and subsequent isolation which, in turn, leads to a determined attempt to become independent. This last idea is totally in keeping with Hill's description of 'an ideology of individualism cemented into the narrative form [of each New Wave film]'. For Hill this means that it is 'the individual's desires and motivations which structure the film's forward flow, the attainment or containment of these which bring the narrative to a close'.[36]

Admittedly, Hill's project is to outline similarities between each New Wave film but his observations are still useful. These shots of the parade can be justified thematically by linking them to Jo's enforced isolation. If, as Hill suggests, Jo's desire to be independent does structure the film's forward movement then the connection between these supposedly unmotivated shots and the rest of the film becomes a much closer one. The parade sequence was preceded by clear signs of Jo's new-found independence. She has found a job and somewhere for herself to live. Nevertheless, this new-found independence comes with an obvious price and taking the time to establish the size and scale of the crowds on the streets reveals more about the character's isolated position within this section of the film than it does about recurring compositional flaws characterising a whole series of films. This feeling of isolation is further enhanced by the fact the no one takes any notice of her. That is, of course, until she bumps into Geoff. Jo sees his shoes first, the ones she sold him and Geoff uses them to start a conversation. 'Are you by yourself?' he asks and follows this by suggesting that they go to the fair.

Like the parade, the sequence at the fair could be considered to be narratively redundant. There is a noticeable change of tone. The music on the soundtrack has a jazzier, jauntier feel to it and there is no audible dialogue between Jo and Geoff. The absence of voices here naturally places an additional emphasis on what we see. Yet, this sequence still needs to be viewed within the film's unfolding. Yes, there is the idea of an interlude here but, rather than separating the value of this moment from the rest of the film by suggesting its redundancy, it makes more sense to view the shots of the parade and the subsequent visit to the fair as demonstrating the thematic movement from Jo's lonely (and enforced) isolation to the beginning of her new friendship with Geoff. Huge crowds, after all, can be the loneliest of places but bumper cars are built to be shared. The integral thematic value of this part of the film is reinforced when we see Geoff walking Jo home and then being offered the chance to move in with her. The movement from isolation to friendship is made possible by the movement from Jo living alone to her sharing with Geoff.[37]

The value of this moment is further enhanced by the way in which Geoff and Jo met, and this allows the idea of chance encounters to be added to the broader consideration of opportunity. It was the fact that Geoff went into the shop where Jo worked and bought the shoes that meant they were able to recognise each other at the parade and, ultimately, live together. There is an alluring logic to this that allows the shots revealing this encounter to become successfully incorporated into the narrative's unfolding without impeding its flow. This logic can now be extended further by considering the way in which Jo and Jimmie (Paul Danquah) meet.

Early in the film we see Jo getting ready for school. She stands in the kitchen of the latest boarding-house she has been forced to move to by her irresponsible mother. Surrounded by stained walls and dirty net curtains, she appears agitated as she drinks her tea. This sense of agitation is aided by the composition here. Within the frame we see Jo standing on one side and the other half is dominated by a large steaming kettle. As we soon discover, Jo is unhappy with her mother for making her move again. Helen asks Jo why she is up so early and Jo replies that she now lives such a long way away from school that she needs plenty of time to get there. We also learn that Jo cannot wait to leave school anyway. Jo wants to find a job and somewhere of her own to live and this is motivated by a desire to become independent from her mother. As both mother and daughter talk about living their own lives the conversation demonstrates a simmering resentment.

Whilst at school, Jo acts the fool in the classroom and is forced to stay behind. As she finally leaves she falls down the stairs and grazes her knee. She starts her long walk home and her route takes her past the canals. Once again, just like the parade, the shots used to accompany her journey cause Hill considerable alarm. As he writes:

> What is striking is not so much the 'reality effect' as the artifice with which image and sound are organised. The shots are bound together by a soft and playful version of 'The Big Ship Sails', lingering dissolves (of three or four seconds each) bleed one shot into the next, careful compositions maintain a graphic continuity of line and mass.[38]

For Hill, this series of shots demonstrates a certain 'stylistic manipulation' which says less about the narrative action and more about the relationship between Richardson and Walter Lassally, his cameraman. Richardson's early films are noticeable for the desire to move away from the proximity of a single close shot and towards a broader treatment of the subject matter. However, this series of shots does fit neatly into the film's narrative unfolding. Jo is taking her time getting home because she is waiting for Helen and her lover to be out. Also, as we soon learn, Jo often walks this way home. This information gives a motivation to the route she takes. This series of shots can also be linked to the film's occupation with opportunity. The chance encounter between Jo and Geoff led to the opportunity for them to become friends and live together. Similarly, Jo's stroll past the canals causes her to bump into Jimmie again. Just like Geoff, Jo had already encountered Jimmie once before, when he helped her off the bus. Her second meeting with him, like her second with Geoff, neatly connects to this idea of opportunity.

Seeing that Jo has hurt herself, Jimmie takes her on board his ship and attends to her grazed knee. This gives the two of them the opportunity to get to know each other. Ultimately, Jo and Jimmie sleep together. Jo falls pregnant and the remainder of the film outlines the impact of her pregnancy on her, her mother and, of course, Geoff. Significant also, here, is the relationship between the canals, Jimmie's ship and their connection with the idea of opportunity. Seeing Jimmie's ship at rest is very moving. This is a ship that is designed to cross wide oceans but now stands moored in a narrow canal. The poignancy of the image is heightened when he tells Jo that there is no one on board. Unwilling to go home, Jo plays with Jimmie on the ship. As their relationship grows, so too does the possibility of experience. Indeed, as Lovell notes, Jo is already 'poised between childhood and womanhood' and the developing relationship with Jimmie presents her with an opportunity for sexual experience. However, as Lovell continues, the consequences of this opportunity are that she 'is precipitated into adult life by her affair with Jimmie and her pregnancy'.[39] It is these two different notions of opportunity that emphasise the position of the ship in the sequence. Being moved by this image becomes complicated by a more circular sensation once we come to understand the temporary nature of the situation. This empty ship is only waiting to be filled again and, once full, it will leave the narrow berth of the canal and go back to the open sea. This means that it is impossible for Jimmie and Jo to take their relationship any further. Yet, the thought of the ship's departure neatly coincides with thoughts of movement and opportunity.

Jo's second meeting with Geoff is entirely consistent with the film's concern to show its principal characters moving between interior spaces. In the same way, Jo's second encounter with Jimmie demonstrates the film's desire to link its characters with the external spaces it uses. This is evident in the succession of shots that follow Jo from her school to Jimmie's ship. This is also evident when considering the relationship between these spaces and the opportunities that meeting Jimmie presents Jo.

Lovell discusses the relationship between Jo and Jimmie by noting the association between the exterior spaces of the film and their lovemaking. As she notes:

> The few actual and attempted sexual encounters are not in the flat, but outside, from Jimmie and Jo's first kiss under a starlit sky on Jimmie's ship to Geoff's clumsy attempt to 'start something' on the hillside later. In the play Jimmie and Jo make love in the flat when her mother is away at Blackpool. In the film they begin to make love on waste ground and there is no indication that they move indoors to take advantage of Helen's absence and the availability of an empty double bed.[40]

Once again, Lovell is keen to establish a distinction between interior and exterior spaces. However, considering these spaces in relation to the opportunities they present allows us to avoid this separation and incorporate them, instead, into a more effective discussion of the film. For Jimmie, the ship represents the opportunity to move out of the narrow spaces indicated by the straight towpaths of the canals. His was only ever going to be a temporary stay anyway. For Jo, however, the ship's relationship with opportunity is a far more complicated one. Her encounter with Jimmie does offer the opportunity for sexual experience and, therefore, a sense of personal development. Yet, the temporary nature of their liaison means that this opportunity actually results in a curtailment of anything further. This is because falling pregnant prevents Jo from breaking free from the restrictions of her life. If the thought of Jimmie's ship crossing a wide ocean characterises the opportunities for movement that is available to him then the sight of this same ship moored in the narrow canal tells us something important about the limits of Jo's life. In this way, *A Taste of Honey* demonstrates a remarkable ability to incorporate its very deliberate use of space into a complex and moving examination of (the lack of) personal opportunity and the effect that chance encounters can have upon a person's life. Additionally, and contrary to existing critical opinion, this examination unfolds in such a smooth and efficient way that there is no threat to the narrative's coherence. However, Richardson's desire to continue extending his stylistic range had a very different effect on his next film.

The end of the road?

Considerable critical weight has been placed upon the idea that *The Loneliness of the Long Distance Runner* (1962) relied too heavily upon the kind of stylistic traits evident in the films of the *nouvelle vague*, and

Anthony Aldgate provides a useful summary of this tendency when he writes:

> At the time, it appears, British film critics were more inclined to pinpoint the similarities between the two and noted the extent to which the former [Richardson] seemingly drew upon the latter for stylistic inspiration, though whether the results were considered wholly beneficial for the development of a national cinema clearly remained open to question.[41]

'The British Cinema' exemplified the doubt Aldgate notes by crudely suggesting that British directors such as Richardson couldn't be compared with their European counterparts. Interestingly, and despite their initial differences, commentators such as Penelope Houston were closer to agreeing with *Movie* than critics such as Perkins would care to acknowledge. As Houston writes:

> *The Loneliness of the Long Distance Runner* makes what one assumes can only be conscious gestures in the direction of the *nouvelle vague*, with its speeded-up action, its frozen final shot, its self-consciously 'cinematic' emphases. But the echoes of *Les Quatre Cents Coups* also points the contrasts: where Truffaut's style grew out of his theme, Richardson's looks like the result of a deliberate act of will, so that the bits and pieces remain unassimilated.[42]

Here, Houston's suggestion of elements lacking assimilation is very close to Perkins's claims for a lack of effective integration. There clearly is a connection between Richardson and the *nouvelle vague*, as Aldgate explains:

> Tony Richardson, for his part, openly professed admiration for 'foreign' film directors and acknowledged their influence upon his work for the cinema. But, interestingly, it was Vittorio de Sica and Luis Buñuel he claimed to favour most – men from a generation of film-makers before the *nouvelle vague*.[43]

Nevertheless, whether directly influenced by Godard and Truffaut or not, *Loneliness* caused considerable critical consternation and nowhere was this consternation more deeply felt that in *Sight and Sound*.

Peter Harcourt's review opens with a weary resignation that borders on despair. Harcourt begins by complaining that in the process of adaptation 'the best elements in the original, elements that are inseparable from Alan Sillitoe's words, indeed the living breath of the story itself – all this has been lost' and replaced, for Harcourt, 'by an element of spite' which 'seems to be the basic impulse from which the film has been conceived'. The result of this is that the film lacks the ability to subtly evoke the sense of anything personal. Instead its vision 'has been narrowed to an examination of a social situation, and to the offering of an analysis which rings disquietingly false'. This results in 'confusion rather than an ambiguity of feeling, a confusion which finds its reflection in the style itself'. As Harcourt decides:

The film is in fact a series of clichés, depending for a response on the conditioned reflexes which we can be expected to bring to a set of recognisable types and incidents. There is no fresh observation of English society, nor any sense of an individual artistic response . . . There is an externality about the film's whole conception, so that unlike the story, it has neither a style nor a pulse of its own.[44]

Harcourt feels let down by what he sees as a 'generalised negative of rejection and hate'. For him, echoing the stance taken by Perkins, there was 'no organic relationship' between the film's style and the feelings of the central protagonist. The lack of such a relationship was only compounded by 'the picturesque bits of photography' which, similar to the accusations of 'landscape-mongering'[45] that were made by Perkins, looked just like 'inserted purple passages'. Harcourt was 'never made to feel that they have a meaning in relation to the chief protagonist'. All of these failings were symptomatic of an 'externality and uninventiveness of technique' that plagued so many of the new British films. Of course, as he concedes, there are the inevitable problems of economic pressures encouraging conventionality.[46]

Nevertheless, Harcourt felt that these existing problems were further compounded by an inherent 'sociological bias' and that it was this bias which contributed to the alleged distance between event and presentation in these films. This was because they appeared to be 'less concerned with the exploration of the intimacies of day-to-day living than with a pictorial demonstration of what is already known to be there'. All this leads Harcourt to conclude:

This is what life is like in Britain today (most of these films seem to say): look at our Establishment, our funfairs, our beaches; look at our Borstals and our ugly city lives. Yet why do we have so little feeling for the characters and so much against all that is ugly and wrong?[47]

Writing elsewhere, Penelope Houston echoed Harcourt's concerns over problems of dramatic integration when she suggested that 'It is not that the landscape itself becomes over-familiar, but that the film-makers have decided in advance exactly what they expect to find there'.[48]

Richardson's film is where the respective stands *Movie* and *Sight and Sound* made in relation to the New Wave converge once more. Supposedly clichéd and over-reaching, *Loneliness* marks the point at which the kind of critical optimism displayed by *Sight and Sound* for what Walter Lassally termed the 'clean, fresh and salty' new wave of British films evaporated.[49] Sadly, in re-evaluative terms, it is hard to disagree with the majority of the criticisms levelled at the film. However, rather than concentrate on the many 'flaws' already discussed, there is something new to be said.

The function of punctuation

Writing in *Film as Film*, Victor Perkins suggests that the concept of progress 'has a special significance for the movie which cannot be paralled in other forms'. As he explains:

> If we are to relate critical judgements sensibly to mechanical development, we must discover the extent to which an imperfect technology imposes artistic limitations; we must also assess the ways in which such limitations can aid or obstruct various kinds of artistic communication.[50]

The development of early film style was severely hampered by the limitations of the existing technology. Film stock was slow, lighting equipment clumsy and lenses primitive enough to limit the depth of focus. Nevertheless, mechanical limitations, as always, still encouraged inventiveness. Perkins cites D.W. Griffith's experiments with lighting and F.W. Murnau's revolutionary approach to camera movement in *The Last Laugh* (1924) as pertinent examples. As he continues:

> In the first thirty years of the movies, style was governed primarily by efforts to make the unsupported image do all the work. Filmmakers had to elaborate their portrayal of actions and reactions in order to achieve a comprehensible narrative. Some, like Griffith, were able to exploit this necessity so that the means employed to make the action clear became the means also of 'directing' its impact and significance. Applied without the skill or tact of a Griffith, however, elaboration tended to burden rather than support the picture. The presentation of events often became clumsy and repetitious. The momentum of the action could easily be lost in a strenuous pursuit of clarity by mediocre directors, or of effect and meaning by ambitious ones.[51]

For Perkins, the silent movie laboured if it went beyond 'elaboration at the level of pure action'. As he explains, the aspiration to subtlety might well be implicit in the choice of subject but was invariably undermined 'by the crude and laboured quality of the devices which made the subject comprehensible'.[52]

The relevance of Perkins's discussion can be found in his concern with the burden of elaboration. The development of style discussed is echoed by Richardson's desire for stylistic innovation. Of all the many stylistic flaws found in *Loneliness*, this burden of elaboration is most apparent in Richardson's reliance upon moments of silence. There are several examples of this in the film but two in particular stand apart as useful contrasts. The first of these demonstrates how the use of silence is effectively incorporated into the film. Unfortunately, the second example is indicative of the way in which, following Perkins, there is a 'crude and laboured' quality to Richardson's adoption of this device. Colin, the film's protagonist, played by Tom Courtenay, has undergone considerable domestic upheaval. His father dies early in the film and his mother (Avis Bunnage) receives £500 compensation from the factory where her husband was a labourer. She embarks upon a spending-spree and Gordon (Raymond Dyer) her 'fancy man', as Colin calls him, has moved in. Despite being unemployed, Colin now sees himself as the head of the family and is understandably perturbed by Gordon's presence. My first example begins with Colin and his friend Mike (James Bolam) sitting at home watching the new television Gordon brought into the house.[53]

Bored by the programme they are watching, Colin turns the sound down and the two friends enjoy supplying their own soundtrack. Their enjoyment is ended when Colin's mother and Gordon return home. An argument ensues between Colin and Gordon about whether the volume should be on or off. Gordon turns it on and Colin turns it off. Colin asserts himself by saying that he is the man of the house and this leads to a brief scuffle. Colin's mother gets involved. She reminds Colin that she owns everything in the house. Colin retorts by accusing her of moving her 'fancy man' in before his dead father was even cold. Stung by the accusation, she slaps Colin across the face and a heavy silence falls upon the room. In this example, the moment of silence that follows the slap fits perfectly into the unfolding logic of the film. Colin is understandably upset about Gordon's presence and his mother, despite her anger, can see this. From her perspective, the silence here can be best understood as representing the uncomfortable position between Gordon and Colin that she finds herself in. There is really not a lot she can say in reply to Colin's accusation. For Colin, on the other hand, this same silence becomes the logical conclusion of what it means to say too much, to vocalise something that is probably best left unsaid.

The silence here can be attributed as simply being the dramatic pause between important pieces of film dialogue. Nevertheless, its connection to the film's concern with domestic displacement offers the opportunity for it to be included into an interpretative discussion. Of principal interest here is the way in which Richardson chooses not to emphasise the silence. He simply allows it to fall naturally into the sequence and this allows the complicated domestic situation that Colin finds himself in to be coherently revealed without the need for undue elaboration. In this way, the silence becomes a useful way of punctuating the argument between Colin and his mother. This last idea is in keeping with Michel Chion's discussion of the same idea because, for him, the importance of punctuation, in the broadest sense, 'has long been a central concern of theatre directing'. However, as silent cinema developed from theatre, the function of punctuation began to change. As he continues:

> The silent cinema had multiple modes of punctuation: gestural, visual and rhythmical. Intertitles functioned as a new and specific kind of punctuation as well. Beyond the printed text, the graphics of intertitles, the possibility of repeating them, and their interaction with the shots constituted so many means of inflecting the film.[54]

For Chion, however, the advent of sound brought about a further change. This was because 'Synchronous sound brought to the cinema not the *principle* of punctuation but increasingly subtle means of punctuating scenes without putting a strain on the acting or editing'.[55] Sadly, however, as this next example demonstrates, Richardson's use of silence as punctuation can lack sufficient subtlety to prevent it putting a strain on the film's unfolding.

Physical exercise is a very important part of life at Ruxton Towers, the borstal Colin finds himself sent to after his conviction (for burglary). The borstal's governor, played by Michael Redgrave, places great emphasis upon this in his opening address to Colin and the other new offenders. Colin's athletic ability first comes to the Governor's attention during a football match. Colin scores a goal and the governor, impressed by his effort, comes to the changing-rooms after the match. He congratulates Colin and then leaves him to shower. 'It's often a moment like this that marks a big turning-point in a lad's life', we hear the governor tell one of the instructors. The film cuts to a close shot of Colin in the shower but the governor's voice can still be heard. 'It's not hard to guess', the governor continues, 'what sort of home life that lad had.' These words are followed by a noticeable silence on the soundtrack. During this silence the camera remains focused on Colin. He has heard what the governor has just said and his expression is a pensive one. After a reasonable pause, the film cuts to a shot of Colin's mother attending to the fire in her front room.

Straight away, the purpose of the silence here is understood. The governor's words act as a cue for the film to move back into the past to tell us something about Colin's domestic life. The silence, then, combined with the shot of Colin looking pensive, acts as the bridge between the film's present and its past, allowing these two tenses to be connected by the film. The concern is to do with the need for emphasis here. The governor's words provide a suitable opportunity for the film to move to a flashback. The camera remains focused on Colin's face. The combination of these two elements provides sufficient motivation for the film to enter the flashback to Colin's home life. If the film limited itself to these two elements then, just like the first example, the integrity of its unfolding would be retained. The use of silence here, however, places a further emphasis on the transitional sense of this moment and, as such, draws too much attention to the movement between tenses. Returning to Chion allows the silence here to be understood as a clear demonstration of Richardson's attempt to punctuate the film. Here, however, and unlike the first example, the silence places too heavy a burden upon the transition. This overemphasis returns us to Harcourt's earlier disappointment with what he saw as the film's preference for the brutality of the film's situation over concern for its characters. Alexander Walker, too, voices a similar concern when he observes that 'Far from granting the "Runner" his existential status through his own actions on the limited scale of resistance at his disposal, the film tries to justify those actions by crude references back to the society he comes from'.[56] Penelope Houston, too, concurs when she suggests that

> Richardson can do some things so well (the theatrical things, as might be expected from his background) that one wonders the more at the apparent failures of confidence in his own material which leads him into over-statement. He is a director who seems to do a good part of his thinking in capital letters.[57]

This idea of overstatement is an interesting one because, just like an athlete straining to achieve success on the track, Richardson appears too keen to achieve a winning result. Despite the deployment of every cinematic resource available to it, the film does have a curiously empty feel to it and appears drained by the effort required to stay ahead of the rest of the field. Just like Colin's undermining of the governor's desperate desire to win the cross-country race, the film's hollowness here outweighs any sense of victory.

The stylistic trajectory of Richardson's films mirrors the critical trajectory of the New Wave as a series. Early signs of promise and hopes of a distinctive style were soon forgotten as it became apparent that Richardson's desire to extend the range of his films resulted in his ultimately over-reaching. There is a distinctive movement away from the tight and narrow focus that characterised *Look Back in Anger*. *The Entertainer*, for example, even with its inserted outdoor sequences, manages to present a coherent picture of one man's downfall without disturbing the delicate balance between film style and thematic meaning. The same can be said for *A Taste of Honey*. It is certainly true that Richardson demonstrates a much greater willingness to move beyond the limits of the stage and embrace the ample opportunities for location shooting offered by the original play's locale. Yet, and despite the repeated critical belief that his use of locations destabilised the film's unfolding, Richardson's efforts here successfully incorporate internal and external spaces into a compelling and well-realised depiction of a young girl's struggle to find a position for herself within her world. By the time we get to *Loneliness*, however, it becomes clear that Richardson's desire to move his directorial innovations forward resulted in his over-reaching. Despite aiming to move beyond existing criticisms of this film by considering Richardson's use of silence it is clearly impossible to avoid agreeing with the disappointed conclusions reached by other critics. The delicate balance between style and meaning here is irrevocably damaged by self-consciousness and over-ambition.

It is perfectly clear that the films of the British New Wave can be successfully evaluated individually. It is possible to produce interpretative readings of individual films from this series. As these brief test-cases have suggested, we can come to consider the details of an individual film from this series without having to constantly rely on making comparative connections with other supposedly related films.

Notes

1 Ivan Butler, *The Making of Feature Films: A Guide*, Harmondsworth, Penguin Book Ltd, 1971, p. 98.

2 Alexander Walker, *Hollywood, England: The British Film Industry in the Sixties*, London, Michael Joseph Ltd, 1974, p. 463.

3 *Sight and Sound*, Vol. 32 No. 1 (Winter 1962/63), p. 49.

4 Peter Hutchings, *Dracula*, London: I.B. Taurus, 2003, p. 3.

5 *Ibid.*, p. 4.

6 See, for example, V.F. Perkins, 'The British Cinema', *Movie*, No. 1 (June 1962), p. 5. Also, Gavin Millar, 'This Sporting Life', *Movie*, No. 7 (February 1963), p. 33, and Ian Cameron, 'Against This Sporting Life', *Movie*, No. 10 (June 1963), pp. 21–22.

7 Perkins, 'The British Cinema', pp. 5–6.

8 Hutchings, *Dracula*, p. 4.

9 Tony Richardson, 'A Free Hand', *Sight and Sound*, Vol. 28 No. 2 (Spring 1959), pp. 60–64, p. 64.

10 Walker, *Hollywood, England*, p. 64.

11 Peter Wollen, 'The Last New Wave: Modernism in the British Films of the Thatcher Era', in Lester Friedman, ed., *British Cinema and Thatcherism: Fires Were Started*, London: UCL Press, 1993, pp. 35–51, pp. 36–37.

12 David Robinson, '*Look Back in Anger*', *Sight and Sound*, Vol. 28 Nos 3 and 4 (Summer/Autumn 1959), pp. 122–125, pp. 123–124.

13 Penelope Houston, '*Look Back in Anger*', *Sight and Sound*, Vol. 28 No. 1 (Winter 1958/59) pp. 31–33, p. 32.

14 Walker, *Hollywood, England*, p. 58.

15 André Bazin, *What Is Cinema?* Vol. 1, Berkeley, University of California Press, 1967, p. 86.

16 *Ibid.*, p. 103.

17 Walker, *Hollywood England*, p. 60.

18 George Lellis, 'Recent Richardson – Cashing the Blank Cheque', *Sight and Sound*, Vol. 38 No. 3 (Summer 1969), pp. 130–138, p. 130.

19 Penelope Houston, 'Into the Sixties', *Sight and Sound*, Vol. 29 No. 1, Winter 1959/60), pp. 4–7, p. 7.

20 Penelope Houston, '*The Entertainer*', *Sight and Sound*, Vol. 29 No. 4 (Autumn 1960), pp. 194–195, p. 194.

21 Walker, *Hollywood England*, p. 76.

22 Interestingly, this sequence was also one of several that were added when the play was adapted for the screen by Nigel Kneale. As Walker continues: '[Kneale] had also promised Richardson to take the play out of doors as much as possible – on to the pier, at the beauty-queen contest, into the caravan on the sand flats where Archie seduces the teenage winner – so as

to give the director all those opportunities he wanted for improvising scenes according to some felicitous accident of the location or the shooting set-up' (Walker, *ibid.*, p. 76).

23 Richardson, 'A Free Hand', p. 64.

24 Terry Lovell, 'Landscape and Stories in 1960s British Realism', in Andrew Higson, ed., *Dissolving Views: Key Writings on British* Cinema, London, Cassell, 1996, pp. 157–177, p. 169.

25 George Stonier, '*A Taste of Honey*', *Sight and Sound*, Vol. 30 No. 4 (Autumn 1961), p. 196.

26 Perkins, 'The British Cinema', p. 5.

27 Thomas Elsaesser, 'Between Style and Ideology', *Monogram* No. 3 (1972), pp. 2–10, p. 7.

28 Lovell, 'Landscape and Stories', p. 168.

29 *Ibid.*, p. 169.

30 John Hill, *Sex, Class and Realism: British Cinema 1956–1963*, London, BFI Publishing, 1986, p. 131.

31 Lovell, 'Landscape and Stories', p. 170.

32 *Ibid.*, p. 169.

33 *Ibid.*, p. 175.

34 Writing in 'The British Cinema' Perkins had this to say: 'The fairground sequence of *Saturday Night* is one of the set pieces of which the new directors are so fond, and is unutterably silly' (p. 6).

35 Hill, *Sex, Class and Realism*, p. 130.

36 *Ibid.*, p. 138.

37 I would also connect this idea of an interlude with a recurring positional pattern related to the two characters. We see this, for example, when the fact that they set up home together has a distinctly temporary feel to it. The moment when they go out to the country has a similar sense attached to it. Finally, there is also the moment when the two of them stand on a raft and discuss whether they have a future together. Each of these occasions feels like an interlude.

38 Hill, *Sex, Class and Realism*, p. 132.

39 Lovell, 'Landscape and Stories', p. 175.

40 *Ibid.*, p. 176.

41 Anthony Aldgate and Jeffrey Richards, *Best of British: Cinema and Society from 1930 to the Present,* London and New York, I.B. Tauris, 1999, p. 191.

42 Penelope Houston, *The Contemporary Cinema*, Harmondsworth, Penguin Books Ltd, 1963, p. 121.

43 Aldgate in Aldgate and Richards, *Best of British*, p. 192.

44 Peter Harcourt, 'I'd Rather Be Like I Am', *Sight and Sound*, Vol. 32 No. 1 (Winter 1962/63), pp. 16–19, pp. 17–18.

45 Perkins, 'The British Cinema', p. 5.

46 In addition, Harcourt felt that the freeze-frame that ended the film was clumsy and derivative and that the film's soundtrack suggested both 'confinement' and 'a mechanical response' (Harcourt, 'I'd Rather Be', pp. 18–19).

47 *Ibid.*, p. 19.

48 Houston, *The Contemporary Cinema*, p. 124.

49 Walter Lassally, 'The Dead Hand', *Sight and Sound*, Vol. 29 No. 3 (Summer 1960), pp. 113–115, pp. 114–115.

50 V.F. Perkins, *Film as Film*, Harmondsworth, Penguin Books, 1972, p. 47.

51 *Ibid.*, pp. 50–51.

52 *Ibid.*, p. 51.

53 Hill's reading of this film suggests that the television represents 'distaste for mass culture'. For Hill, this idea leads to a contrast between modern mass culture and traditional working-class culture, 'male' values and 'female' values (Hill, *Sex, Class and Realism*, pp. 153–154).

54 Michel Chion, *Audio-Vision*, New York, Columbia University Press, 1994, pp. 48–49.

55 *Ibid.*, p. 49.

56 Walker, *Hollywood, England*, p. 126.

57 Houston, *The Contemporary Cinema*, p. 121.

3 A cinema of surfaces: Jack Clayton's *Room at the Top*

> Let us then begin by examining the film in its general outline, as a shape, as a whole; and in setting ourselves such an aim, it will be observed, we are presupposing that a film is, in fact, a complete whole and does have a shape. This is the first thing we are entitled to expect of any work of art, that it shall have unity, and be a thing complete in itself which we can appreciate for its own sake, every part falling into place to create a satisfying pattern unmarred by redundancies, irrelevances or omissions. (Ernest Lindgren)[1]

> One cannot talk about a film meaningfully without finding some way of discussing the actual life of the film, which is in the movement of images and sounds. (Robin Wood)[2]

> Not so long ago, the director was an employee of a studio. He was given a script, went on the set, suggested what the camera and actors should do, and, when the shooting was over, put on his hat and went home, leaving his producer and editor to finish the job. These days, things are different. (Jack Clayton)[3]

A dark, disdained thread?

Julian Petley suggests that the vaunting and valorising of certain films must inevitably occur at the expense of dismissing and denigrating others. In the case of British cinema, this creates a division between realist and non-realist films and has resulted in 'a dark, disdained thread' of British films that have always been critically overlooked. One problem that has always dogged discussions of British films, realist or otherwise, has been the assumption that British films *appear* to be characterised by a 'signifying paucity, formal invisibility and concomitant stress on "content"'.[4] It was this 'appearance' that caused style-based critics such as Perkins to reject the British New Wave (almost) out of hand. From this perspective, the boundaries of Petley's 'lost continent' become further extended.

Admittedly, as Peter Hutchings acknowledges elsewhere, there is still 'unfinished business' when it comes to discussions of authorship and British cinema. Like him, however, I have no interest in supporting or disproving the auteurist method 'in general or in its specific application to British cinema'.[5] Nevertheless, following the discussion of *Movie*'s 'asymmetrical' view of British cinema, it is necessary to consider some further aspects of this method in more detail.

Hutchings outlines a series of possible responses to *Movie*'s stance on British cinema. Firstly, we might agree with their criticism and get on with writing about American film. We might attempt to redress this asymmetrical view by making a positive case for various British directors and thus 'advancing them up the histogram quality scale'.[6] A third option is to reject totally the critical method that gave rise to the histogram in the first place and find other ways of engaging with British film. As he explains:

> The proliferation of books and articles on British studios, genres, stars and audiences testifies to an increased critical awareness of the intertextual, the multiple contexts of reception, and the transindividual structures within which films get made. Within such a context, the auteurist method, and an associated ranking of directors on the basis of how good (or bad) they are, seems both unrealistic and elitist.[7]

The result of this is the 'tendency to locate directors in relation to various cultural and historical contexts'.

Robert Murphy, for example, among many others, places films such as Jack Clayton's *Room at the Top* (1959) within the broader cultural context of an artistic trajectory that started with the rise of Free Cinema.[8] Launched by Lindsay Anderson, Karel Reisz and Tony Richardson, six programmes of films were shown at the National Film Theatre between 1956 and 1959. Though not directly responsible for *Room at the Top* – Clayton had already been working in the film industry for some years – cinema history has chosen to view the documentaries of Free Cinema as one of the most obvious antecedents of the British New Wave. As Alan Lovell notes:

> The views of the world which emerge from Free Cinema films are recognisable, the result of preoccupations common among intellectuals in the second half of the 1950s. Broadly, these preoccupations were: a sympathetic interest in communities . . . fascination with the newly-emerging youth culture . . . unease about the quality of leisure in an urban society . . . and respect for the traditional working class.[9]

Adam Lowenstein further develops the cultural context surrounding Clayton's film by including literary developments from the same period, in particular authors such as Philip Larkin, Kingsley Amis and John Osborne. As Lowenstein continues:

> The jumble of elements comprising social realism in *Room at the Top* reflects the somewhat complex prehistory of the New Wave. In one sense, the New Wave grew out of 'The Movement', a literary circle of the early and mid-1950s that included Philip Larkin and Kingsley Amis . . . The Movement gained

a mythical dimension with the addition of the Angry Young Man, a figure brought to life in such plays as John Osborne's *Look Back in Anger* (first performed in 1956) and in literature like John Braine's novel *Room at the Top*, published in 1957.[10]

All of this translates into a more hybrid form of the traditional auteurist approach. This is because the desire to adopt such a form of film criticism bestows 'cultural importance and value upon either British cinema generally, or upon the particular areas of British cinema within which the directors are working'. Alternatively, we might use the figure of the director as a 'kind of heuristic device, a means of ordering, and making sense of, a particular sector of British film production'.[11] There is the immediate danger that the style and meaning of the New Wave films becomes less important than their position within a specific context. This helps to explain the continued critical emphasis on the conventions of social realism that we saw previously.

A continued emphasis of this kind has left the mise-en-scène of these films in a kind of critical limbo. Deciding that the realist conventions employed by these films have become overused and, thus, somehow detrimental to the films themselves, makes it increasingly difficult to account for the particular stylistic details of an individual film in a more positive light. It would be pointless for me to suggest that understanding a film through its position within a broader cultural context is not worthwhile because, as Robert Allen and Douglas Gomery explain, it is the difference between *explanation* and *explication* that lies at the heart of this discussion. Explanation is predicated on the fact that 'since its invention the cinema in American and most other countries has been used principally as a commercial entertainment form [and this has] affected the subject matter of films, the development of cinematic styles, and other aesthetic concerns'.[12] The importance of explanation can be found in the kind of questions it leads to. As they consider:

> Why, for example, did certain aesthetic styles emerge at particular times and not at others? Why did particular film-makers make the aesthetic choices they did and how were these choices circumscribed by the economic, social and technological context they found themselves in? How might a work have been read at a particular period and would these readings have differed according to gender or class?[13]

Explication, on the other hand, looks for examples of aesthetic significance in individual films. The danger here lies in the isolation of aesthetic considerations at the expense of context and other causal factors in film history. Nevertheless, when it comes to the British New Wave the balance between explanation and explication is historically such an asymmetrical one that there is considerable justification for choosing explication over explanation.[14] Indeed, as Penelope Houston remarked at the time:

> Writing about British films, it is said, one talks about what is done: writing about French or Italian films, one discusses how it's done. We are compelled, in other words, to put content before form, for the films have set out to investigate a social landscape rather than to make that discovery of a medium which a director such as Truffaut so rapturously communicates. Our film-makers travel as mass observers rather than as artists prepared to turn the landscape upside down if it happens to suit their purposes.[15]

The challenge is to give an account of a New Wave film, in this case, *Room at the Top*, to search for examples of aesthetic significance and then to integrate them into a sustained discussion of the film's style and meaning. Before this, however, it is necessary to consider a further problem that discussions of the New Wave tend to face.

A familiar luminosity?

The opening images of *Room at the Top* stand as one of the most familiar moments in the history of British cinema. Black and white images of industrial landscapes, railway stations and a young man arriving somewhere with a raincoat folded over his arm are instantly evocative of a certain time and place in the history of British cinema. Yet the delight of this evocation is tinged with an element of danger and this is because repeated meetings with moments like this one can give rise to an over-familiarity. The result of this is that the features that define these moments can attract a powerful critical contempt. This was certainly the case for Thomas Elsaesser, for example.[16] Nevertheless, a moment such as this one still shines with such a fascinating luminosity that this repeated dismissal becomes tiresome.

Indicative of a specific time and place, the danger is that images such as these become a form of cinematic shorthand, creating the impression that the British New Wave is as a cinema of surfaces, known to every-one, easily recognised but lacking in sufficient critical depth to make the films worthy of a serious, sustained study of their mise-en-scène.[17] Even still, it is possible that we can turn this idea of a shorthand to our advantage. In order to do this we need to take a closer look at the position Clayton's *Room at the Top* occupies within cinema history.

Returning to the chronology of New Wave films, we can see that *Room at the Top* is the first film in this cycle. From this position, bearing in mind Hutchings's discussion of how to deal with an auteurist approach to British cinema, the (almost) automatic response would be to deal with Clayton's film solely in terms of what it reveals about British cinema from this period. Yet, individual discussions of these films are better served when the film in question is considered in its own right. It is not enough just to account for the film's position within a specific time-line. A simple chronology, even when placed within a broader historical context, necessarily limits the significance of detail in single film. This is not its function. Yet, one way that we might start to free *Room at the Top* from its rigid contextual position is to be prepared to look beneath the surfaces of this cinema and investigate the more circular currents that flow within each of these films. In order to do this successfully we first need to take this idea of connecting similar surfaces a stage further.

Obvious connections?

In a perfectly logical step, Neil Sinyard is one of many commentators to have established a connection between *Room at the Top* and David Lean's 1945 film *Brief Encounter*. For Sinyard, synthesising the views of earlier critics, Clayton's film should be seen as 'a continuation and revitalisation of a great British film tradition that had been flagging during the 1950s'.[18] Not only that, *Room* 'plays against memories of Lean's masterpiece, whilst in a sense becoming the tragic love story of 1950s British cinema in the way that Lean's was for the previous decade'.[19] Finally, the connection between these two films is most obvious when 'the opening sound of the train whistle and the early setting of the station evoke fleeting memories' of Lean's film.[20] Setting aside a discussion of the film's tragic elements, I want to concentrate upon Sinyard's final claim.

Sinyard's claim for the most obvious connection here is indicative of the kind of approach outlined earlier. Linking Clayton's film with *Brief Encounter* allows the two films to be linked chronologically. Linked in this way, sequential logic will inevitably move the critic away from discussions of detail and towards debates about history and context. To develop a better understanding of the problems this causes it will be useful to make some connections of our own. We can suggest that the (surface) appearance of the opening sequence of Clayton's film connects with the end of *Billy Liar*. Certainly, within the New Wave series these two films stands as bookends, and Schlesinger's film (almost) ends with the eponymous hero, played by Tom Courtenay, standing on a platform at a railway station. In terms of a cinematic shorthand, the images of the train and Billy on the platform makes *Billy Liar* the next obvious link in the (artificial) chain we are creating. Now let's add another link.

There is a moment in *A Kind of Loving* when Vic (Alan Bates) meets his father as he walks to work. Vic's father works on the railway and as they talk we see trains passing behind them. Though Vic is not standing on the platform the sight and sound of a train spewing its steam into the air is enough for us to link this image with the others. We can also add a moment from *This Sporting Life*. Once again, we do not see Frank (Richard Harris) standing on a platform or boarding a train but the sight of him drunkenly stumbling home across a railway track is enough to make the connection. It is also possible to keep adding further links to this chain by looking beyond the New Wave. Richard Lester's *A Hard Day's Night* (1964) begins with images of the Beatles boarding a train bound for London. For a final link in this arbitrary chain we might include Mike Hodges's 1971 film *Get Carter*, which opens, like Clayton's film, with the main character aboard a train.

On one level, the artificiality of this chain suggests that there is little value to be had in making these connections. Images of trains, of railway stations, as well as characters starting out on journeys are not solely confined to British films. At the same time, however, would a chain of this kind be considered more critically substantial if we replaced the images of trains with those of cobbled streets, smoking chimneys or rolling moors? The next step would be to posit this chain of films within a broader cultural context. We could choose to consider the direction and destinations of the various train journeys we see. We begin, in Clayton's film, with a journey between two northern towns. This is followed by trains that leave the north of England and head for London in *Billy Liar* and in Lester's film. Finally, the train that Jack Carter (Michael Caine) boards in Hodges's film is one that leaves London and returns to the north. Contextually, the (surface) connection between these films could be reinforced by suggesting that they demonstrate a concern with postwar mobility.[21] This means we would have to work considerably harder to include the images found in *A Kind of Loving* and *This Sporting Life* but this wouldn't be impossible. As we saw with *A Taste of Honey*, Terry Lovell was happy to list all the images that the New Wave supposedly shared, even though only two of them contained sequences set at fairgrounds.[22] The merits of (artificially) linking this series of films in this way and then positioning them within a broader historical context does very little to facilitate a style-based discussion of an individual British film.

This discussion, then, like any of these train journeys, needs both a direction and a destination. This will be possible only if we are willing to dig deeper beneath the surface of these films, and this excavation will achieve two things. Firstly, *Room at the Top* will be freed from a strictly linear (or chronological) view of its importance. Secondly, it will demonstrate that an understanding of the film's thematic concerns may, on the surface, be very similar to those of another New Wave film but will, in fact, differ significantly once a deeper, more sustained investigation has begun. In order to understand the implications of these intentions, we only need to return to the chain of films we have created.

Considered solely at face value, it is readily apparent that there is little to be gained by compiling a list of films in this way. The principal connection between these films in this new chain is the similarity of their surfaces. Though they might be positioned within a linear chronology of British cinema there is little room for discussion when it come to the details of an individual film. Perversely, though, this list of artificially connected films still becomes the ideal point at which we might start to develop a new understanding of the relationship between cinema history and film studies. This is because, despite the apparent obviousness of their connections, there are, in fact, many differences between the films in this chain.

Brief Encounter has become synonymous with a particular form of sexual repression. Clayton's film, on the other hand, became famous, in part, for its X certificate and a 'fuller and more complex image of love'.[23] Thus, *Room at the Top* represented a major break from earlier presentations of sexual behaviour.[24] Furthermore, the main characters in Lean's film, played by Trevor Howard and Celia Johnson, are emotionally paralysed and unable to act upon their respective desires. Joe Lampton, on the other hand, is a character prepared to take decisive action and move towards the things he wants, rather than backing away. The opening of Clayton's film, then, becomes a demonstration of the distance Joe is prepared to travel in order to achieve his aims. Joe's arrival at Warnley also signals the possibility of new spaces to be explored. *Billy Liar* is a film that reaches its logical conclusion with Billy Fisher standing on a railway platform. Despite the obviousness of their connection, both as New Wave films and films with trains in them, there are a series of carefully nuanced thematic differences between the two films. If Clayton's film signals the sense of arriving somewhere new, as well as the hope and optimism that inevitably accompanies such a sense, then Schlesinger's film suggests a desire for departure.

Disillusioned by spaces that are too small and too familiar to him, Billy Fisher wishes to escape his home town and move to pastures new. You would imagine that the disillusionment he feels would be enough to make him leave but Billy is unable to act upon his desires and the film ends with him being left behind, unlike his friend Liz (Julie Christie). As the train leaves, the close of this film signals the end of a focus upon certain specific cinematic spaces. Moreover, this is accompanied by a correspondence between arriving somewhere, with the promise of hope and new discovery, and leaving somewhere behind.[25] The end of *Billy Liar* begins to reveal something more complicated hidden beneath its apparently obvious surface. Chronologically speaking, Schlesinger's film is seen as the last of the New Wave films and, therefore, as we see the train leaving for London something has clearly come to an end.[26] Yet, the departure of the train also suggests the idea of arriving somewhere else. We see this in *A Hard Day's Night*, which opens with the four Beatles on a train leaving the North behind and heading, like Julie Christie's character before them, for London. The impression is of a geographical shift being related to a new and different set of (potential) experiences. *Get Carter* shows Jack Carter leaving London and heading north to avenge his brother's death. This time, the geographical movement is reversed and the start of this film marks another change in direction. But how is all this relevant to our discussion of *Room at the Top*?

The obvious interplay between arriving and departing that character-ises the moments of these films presents a circularity (of theme). This stands in stark relief to the original simple linear account of their con-nection. Clearly there is more to the relationship between these moments than a simple description of their surface appearance would allow. This is despite their very obvious differences. Moving beyond an elementary summary of the chronological relationship between this list of films, we now reach the point at which my discussion of the style and meaning of *Room at the Top* can begin. Specifically, this must mean placing a critical importance on such things as beginnings and endings and then extra-polating a further series of themes from them; arriving somewhere new, for example, and the accompanying possibility of fresh experience. Departures, also, with desires, dreams and schemes that are successful or come to nothing. Questions of ambition, frustration, and disappointment. Desperation and the need to act. The definition of identity. In *Room at the Top*, matters of (personal) mobility co-exist with the problem of social paralysis. Just like the details of a single film, it is imperative that these themes are considered further. Yet, they also require a careful, sustained integration lest we run the risk of considering them only in isolation. Significant details should not be reduced to the level of mere description. Nor should underlying themes remain as simple assumptions.[27]

The challenge is twofold. *Room at the Top* needs to be freed from the strict chronology of cinema history. An examination of its style and meaning must overcome the trenchant demarcation characterising the relationship between film studies and the British New Wave.[28]

Arrivals and departures

Adam Lowenstein begins his discussion of *Room at the Top* by des-cribing the opening sequence in the following way:

> Joe [the principal character] sits and smokes in a railway carriage, with his shoeless feet elevated. He reads a newspaper which features 'Nottingham' in its front page headline, verifying the locale of the bleak industrial landscape passing outside the window. In a heavily symbolic gesture, Joe dons a new pair of shoes in preparation for his arrival at Warnley.[29]

Ostensibly, there is nothing wrong with Lowenstein's description. Joe, played by Laurence Harvey, has moved to another town to start a new job and the rest of the film will outline the events that befall him. Lowenstein acknowledges this idea when he concludes that the film begins with 'a journey that quite literally provides viewers with a well-marked road map to Joe Lampton's working-class identity'.[30] The problem is that Lowenstein's conclusion, this mapping of Joe's identity, follows a route from description to summary. But why should this matter?

The linearity of the description is unavoidable yet it does become problematic when it comes to conclusions. This is because Lowenstein uses his summary of the opening sequence to conclude that the film contains 'a telling insistence on maintaining spatialised class boundaries.' As he outlines:

> The [opening] sequence carefully defines Joe's class status by contrasting his comfort and sense of belonging in certain spaces (the train as it passes through the industrial environs; the outer office while the secretaries ogle him) with his awkward exclusion from others (the private office, where he cringes at his boss's suggestion that the people of Warnley are more 'civilised' than those of Dufton; the affluent world conveyed by Susan's clothing, car and boyfriend).[31]

From a simple (linear) description that summarises the opening sequence, Lowenstein makes a broader claim about the film's concerns and this is where the problems arise. Any discussion of Clayton's film might usefully begin by considering the spaces of the opening sequence. It would also be sensible to consider that these spaces might be understood in terms of the demarcation of boundaries, especially those of class. The concern with class issues that inform this film suggests that Joe's early movements are linked with the idea of social mobility. This is evident from a cursory examination of the film's opening. We see Joe starting a new job in a new town and expressing a desire to better himself. Yet there is a problem here.[32]

It would be foolish to suggest that *Room at the Top* is not interested in questions of class and social mobility. However, utilising a simple summary of a sequence as the basis for making a larger, more wide-reaching claim about *Room at the Top*'s concerns can only hinder the development of a more complete understanding of the film's construction. Approaching the film in this way allows the idea of (potentially) restrictive boundaries within the film to impose a similar restriction upon deeper and more sustained readings of the film. Limiting our understanding of the film's spaces in this way also makes it very tempting for us to impose these same limits upon the readings of other New Wave films.

In either case, there is no need for us to attempt a more sustained discussion of *Room at the Top*. We can satisfactorily summarise that Clayton's film is concerned only with one thing. However, the key to developing a more balanced discussion of the film's themes is to resist the urge to rely solely on description as a basis for making broader thematic claims. Instead, we need to develop an argument in which the critical emphasis is more evenly allocated. In this way, the issue of class boundaries does not have to be seen as the film's overriding concern but can be considered as one of the many elements that the film contains. Rather than isolate one aspect of the film through description and then rely upon this description alone to fashion a broader understanding of the film – in the example here, the issue of class but it could quite easily be smoking chimneys, terraced houses or train-related images – we need to aim for a more rounded account, one which strives, at all times, to achieve a more satisfactory balance.[33]

Positions and possibilities

Extending the logic of Lowenstein's account, we might infer that the film begins by suggesting that the linear flow of personal ambition is characterised by the idea of (social) mobility. Setting aside the issue of class, the narrative movement in *Room at the Top* is begun by Joe's initial desire to move *away* from Dufton, his home town, and move *forward* towards a new life with no intention of ever going back. As R. Barton Palmer writes:

> Spending his years as a POW studying accounting, Joe has made the leap from working class to the petty bourgeoisie. His rewards include a ticket out of Dufton, the unbearably grim factory town of his youth, and a white-collar job with local government in Warnley, a city also in the industrial north but one with an affluent middle class and the attendant cultural amenities.[34]

Once again, like Lowenstein, Barton Palmer is keen to view Joe's movement in terms of social mobility. Nevertheless, his observation also usefully emphasises the thematic importance attached to Joe's arrival. Thus, these opening images are a useful introduction to the prospects of opportunity, exploration and experience faced by Joe as he starts a new chapter of his life. Yet, we are still too reliant upon summarising the start of the film and this, in turn, reduces us to making assumptions about Joe's prospects. Indeed, *Room at the Top* offers far more than just a linear examination of one man's desire to get ahead. The film offers the opportunity for a more circular discussion of the many (potentially) conflicting concerns that new spaces and their accompanying experiences must inevitably generate. A reading of this kind will be possible only if we consider that a more measured and balanced discussion of the suspension of opportunity, experience and possibility is needed. Rather than just baldly introducing the film's concerns in its opening sequences, *Room at the Top* articulates its principal thematic concerns through a series of introductions. Though it might appear that these introductions simply establish Joe in his new environment there are, in fact, subtle shades of difference between each of them. This allows the development of a more refined understanding of what it means for Joe to start a new life in Warnley.

Room at the Top opens with Joe sitting on a train. Through the window behind him we catch glimpses of an industrial landscape, the purpose of which, as Lowenstein suggests, is to help establish the type of locations within which the rest of the film will take place. This view from the window becomes a visual clue to the film's setting. Though only a hint, at this stage, the brief glimpses of this industrial landscape help Lowenstein to decide that the train journey is, in fact, a useful metaphor for denoting Joe's working-class identity. Yet, it is still too early to make a definitive statement about what the film will be concerned with. We need more evidence and this is partly supplied seconds later when Joe walks out of Warnley station to find a taxi. Joe loads his suitcase and just before getting in he looks offscreen. This look is followed by a quick fade that reveals a frame full of smoking chimneys and dark, gloomy-looking factory buildings. We might consider this brief shot to be a visual confirmation of the film's locations and, hence, by relation, its concerns. This would certainly account for this shot's position within the opening sequence. This would also connect this shot with the glimpses of industrial landscape we saw through the window of the train. Thus, we are immediately introduced to the type of locations within which the film's narrative will unfold. This brief shot would also confirm Lowenstein's suggestion that the film is concerned with questions of working-class identity. But there is something rather more complicated occurring here, something that goes beyond the idea of this shot simply establishing setting and theme.

It is not clear whether this industrial view is the direct result of Joe's looking offscreen and this doubt is the result of both the camera's position and the perspective of the view within the frame. This doubt returns us to the accusations of 'inserted' shots that have always haunted the New Wave. Seen this way, this shot becomes nothing more than a gratuitous presentation of an industrial landscape from which we are 'forced' to infer that the film will baldly concern itself with class identities. The case for such an accusation would certainly be stronger if this shot was bookended by two simple cuts. The two fades, however, help to blur the boundaries of the relationship between the character's actions and this view of the factories and make it more difficult to actually define the status of this view. How else might we account for this brief shot of an industrial landscape occurring so early in the film? One way would be by considering George Wilson's discussions of cinematic point of view.[35]

With a sentiment that has a particular resonance here, the initial question is one of complacency. This is because particular moments from particular films have the ability to force us to reconsider the 'complacent' way in which we view them. Though Wilson chooses a moment from Orson Welles's *The Lady from Shanghai* (1948) as his example, *Room at the Top* demonstrates this tendency equally well. Wilson suggests that in order to make sense of even a short series of shots we need to establish a range of questions which will address the question of point of view. To do this we need to decide the degree to which each shot or series of shots provides direct objective information about the world of the film. We also need to pay attention to the shots related to the subjectivity of the characters contained within this world. In the majority of cases decisions of this kind are relatively easy to make but the potential for complication always remains.[36]

However, issues of local perceptual understanding are rarely answered by just considering the single series of shots that raised the issue in the first place. Therefore, it is necessary to relate the initial shot series to various other elements that can be found in the rest of the film. This is because, as Wilson writes:

> the film [in question] is best understood as deploying certain *global* strategies of narration within which the local perturbation, seen in a specified fashion, can be made to fit. These global strategies, especially in their more epistemic aspects, generate broad questions about how the film and its fictional world are to be apprehended and about how well we are situated to grasp whatever significance they may bear.[37]

Certainly, bearing in mind our earlier discussion of the all-too-obvious surface appearance of a film like *Room at the Top*, Wilson's concern for relating the global concerns of a film with more local concerns offers an ideal way in which we might come to a better understanding of this moment.

It is not easy to read the brief shot of the smoking chimneys as being strictly subjective. Despite the fact that it follows the shot of Joe looking around, this view cannot definitely be attributed to being from his point of view. Therefore, we might be inclined to say, that this shot 'provides direct objective information about the world of the film'. Seen this way, it is perfectly reasonable the insertion of such a shot is a perfect demonstration of the kind of stylistic fallibility that apparently plagued the British New Wave. This suggestion would be more acceptable if it was a simple cut that separated the shot of Joe looking and the shot of the factories. The fact that it is a fade which connects these two shots creates the possibility that there is a different relationship between them. In fact, what we have here is an interesting disjunction between a character's subjectivity and the film's objective presentation of its world. Thus, the 'local' and the 'global' fuse at this point to create a moment that 'forces' us to reconsider the way in which we might comprehend it. In order to do this I want to turn to Douglas Pye's discussion of some of the dimensions of cinematic point of view.

Pye starts by outlining various axes which orientate our perception of a particular film. Of most relevance in this example is the existence of the 'spatial axis'. In this way, 'the spatial position of the spectator in relation to the film's world is defined shot-by-shot, as the film progresses, in the views presented on the screen and their relationship to the sound-track'.[38] Leaving aside discussions of the film's soundtrack, it is this idea of the film's world which I wish to consider in more detail. As Pye continues:

> the spectator's position tends to change constantly but is stabilised by the conventions of continuity editing and dramatic structure, which enables illusions of coherent space to be created. The specific systems which a film develops in providing spatial access to the fictional world are the basis of this aspect of point of view.[39]

The shot of the chimneys that we were unable to associate fully with Joe's subjective view of his new surroundings can still be under-stood as a coherent part of the film's system. When combined with the conventions of continuity editing – in this case, the two fades that bookend this shot – we can read this view of an industrial landscape as being properly part of the film's provision of spatial access to its 'world'. In this way, we begin to overcome the objections of 'redundant' shot insertion.[40]

The problem is that it is impossible to develop a coherent argument about revelations of the film's world on the basis of a single shot. This is especially true when this shot has been artificially isolated from the context of the film's overall organisation. At best, a process of this kind might suggest a new line of enquiry but to pursue this line more effect-ively we now need to relate this shot to 'various other elements that can be found in the rest of the film'.

Faces, places and spaces

Joe's taxi takes him to the Town Hall and his arrival marks the point at which we can begin to develop a better understanding of the idea of social mobility. As Joe walks through the corridors, his shoes squeaking on the polished floor, he pauses to look through the first open door he finds, the council chamber. It is noticeable that the film does not cut to reveal the full extent of the spaces inside this chamber. In fact, the camera comes to rest behind Joe's shoulder in a movement which appears to downplay the significance of this room. This is interesting because the relationship between this civic space and the development of Joe's career is a crucial one. For this chamber is representative of all the authority, power and influence exerted in the world of the film. Yet, like the landscape through which the train passed, the importance of this space, and what it represents, is only hinted at by Joe's action. The possibility of the film's spaces being of thematic importance is introduced but still needs further confirmation.

4 Joe (Laurence Harvey) takes stock of his new surroundings in *Room at the Top*.

Joe reaches the Borough Treasurer's office and the film cuts as he enters. The camera is now inside the room and as Joe approaches a wooden counter the camera moves with him, stopping when he does. At rest, the camera is now positioned so that Joe stands on the right side of the frame. The receptionist, who recognises his name when he introduces himself, is positioned on the left side and the counter is now between them. Ostensibly, the counter acts as a barrier and is intended to keep Joe separate from the rest of the office but any sense of separation here is about to be removed by the editing pattern that follows. This process is started by the receptionist going to see if Hoylake, Joe's new boss, is ready to see him. As she leaves the counter there is a cut to a close shot of Joe. We see him follow the receptionist with his eyes before looking back at the counter. Another cut follows and this time we are shown exactly what Joe sees, the other receptionist, full in the frame and eyeing him hungrily. The camera only pauses here briefly before tracking sideways again to pick up the movement of a secretary walking across Joe's line of sight. The camera halts as the secretary reaches her desk. There is another secretary sitting here. She removes her glasses to get a better look at Joe. The film cuts back to another close shot of Joe.

Described in this way, this last paragraph does little more than give a simple linear account of a fairly typical, even unimaginative, pattern of editing. Like this, we have a description of the action similar to Lowenstein's earlier discussion. We might infer that this series of shots does little more than show us how physically attractive the character of Joe is meant to be to members of the opposite sex. However, simple linear descriptions will do little to further our more detailed cause. What else might we bring to this moment? Let's return to the first shot in this sequence.

With Joe positioned on the right and the receptionist opposite him, the wooden counter stands between them and has the effect of neatly dividing the spaces within the frame. This is an office, after all, and so the camera's objective presentation of another of the film's important spaces rightly suggests a rigidity of position that is perfectly in keeping with the ideas of formality and correct procedure in the work-place. We can connect the counter with the idea of social mobility because the counter and it all that it embodies – the straight-lined formality of the work-place – should be seen as the first of the many barriers Joe will encounter as he aims to improve himself. Yet, more work is needed here. Otherwise, the counter actually becomes an obstacle to a more detailed understanding of this moment. We also need to account for the more subjective shots in this sequence, the shots which reveal the exchange of looks between Joe and the women in the outer office.

The emphasis imposed by the close framing of a particular character is shared here between Joe and the receptionist behind the counter. In this way, flirtatious glances are not just given but also received. Despite the counter's obstructive position, this establishes a connection between the characters. With the counter's formal distance removed a similar connection is created between the spaces that the characters occupy. The formality of the work-place has become (momentarily) replaced by the more relaxed demonstration of mutual attraction.

If the replacing of formality with attraction does imply a movement then this idea can be developed further by considering the second significant movement made by the camera. As Joe approached the counter, the camera's first movement was an objective articulation of the film's dramatic spaces. In contrast, this second movement has to be seen as a directly subjective exploration of these same spaces. It follows, returning to Wilson, that linking these two movements will allow the interplay between the 'global' presentation of this moment's dramatic spaces and the more 'local' exploration of these same spaces by the characters to force us to reconsider this moment. Rather than just an additional confirmation of the (strictly) social mobility noted by Lowenstein, the idea of mobility itself now gains a more varied thematic sense. It becomes shaded, for example, by the potential for complication that accompanies expressions of sexual desire, as well as the possible movements and connections between characters on a more intimate level. As the film goes on to demonstrate, this is a very prominent theme. For the moment, however, it is necessary to compare events in the outer office with Joe's introduction to Hoylake (Raymond Huntley).

The receptionist returns to tell Joe that Hoylake will see him immediately, and as Joe enters the office the contrasts are immediately apparent. A formal austerity hangs over the room, helped by the heavy silence which replaces the sound of typewriters and chatter outside. As Joe sits

5 A formal distance between Joe and Hoylake (Raymond Huntley) is established in *Room at the Top*.

down the camera comes to rest behind his right shoulder. An impassive-looking Hoylake leans back and begins to outline the differences between Warnley and Dufton. 'I'm not surprised you wanted to leave Dufton', says Hoylake in an authoritative tone that is emphasised by his facing the camera. Joe's initial position, his back to camera, is in sharp contrast with his encounter with the women in the outer office. There, his face was prominent as he explored these new spaces with his eyes. Here, he appears faced with a more inflexible situation. We see this as Hoylake speaks and the film cuts to behind his shoulder.

Despite the fact that this shot allows us to view Joe's reaction it also ensures that Hoylake's desk is still visible between the two men and, as such, establishes a distance between them. 'You'll meet a better class of people here', Hoylake continues. His words are then given extra emphasis by a close shot of his face. The film cuts to Joe as he tries to defend his home town but the impact of his protests is undermined by another cut which returns to an unimpressed Hoylake.

The pattern of editing here outlines the meeting between the two men in a fairly unobtrusive way. Yet again, the question of social mobility becomes complicated by the construction of this encounter. The counter in the outer office, despite its position and what it was supposed to embody, offered little resistance when it came to establishing a connection between the spaces it was supposed to keep separate. Hoylake's desk, on the other hand, succeeds where the counter failed. As the film cuts between Hoylake and Joe, the desk is clearly visible between them.

The immediate result of this position is the distance it establishes between the two men. Considering the formalities of rank within the work-place, this is only right and proper. Unlike the counter, the desk, solid in the centre of the frame, ensures that a dignified distance is maintained between a clerk and his superior. To this end, the desk tells us something about Joe's professional ambitions by representing the divide that Joe will have to cross in order to improve his career. Thus, the issue of social mobility is brought sharply to our attention. But there is still more to say about this moment.

Returning to Joe's brief glimpse of the council chamber reminds us that Hoylake is a representative of such a civic space. Though not embodied with the same power and influence as a councillor, Hoylake is still indicative of the kind of attitudes that might be found in the council chamber. When combined with the rigid composition of the frames here, with both men kept separate, Hoylake's impassive dismissal of Dufton in favour of the more 'civilised' Warnley reveals a narrow-minded attitude toward a person's position within this world. This attitude we can infer, is representative of the local authority Hoylake represents. But it does not stop here. A further comparison between this scene and the previous one compounds this issue of social mobility even further.

The possibility for intimate exploration revealed by the series of flirtatious glances in the outer office added another dimension to our understanding of the film's spatial and, hence, its thematic concerns. By sharply contrasting with the fluidity of action that preceded it, the rigidity of Joe's encounter with Hoylake and the civic authority he represents adds a further complication. Social mobility, then, still remains the cornerstone of the film's opening sequences but, in relation to Joe's position, begins to evade the kind of simple definition offered by Lowenstein. The oppositions between personal exploration and the rigidity of a hierarchy, as well as the more fluid desire for connection and the immobility of formal distance, ensure that our introduction to Joe's arrival in Warnley requires much more than simple summary.

In both of these last two examples, it is the simplicity of the editing strategy that draws certain aspects of the film's thematic concerns to our attention. A more complicated and ambitious series of shots would be more likely to draw attention to the film's construction and thus leave the film open to adverse stylistic criticism. At the same time, the simple pattern of looks and reactions used here might leave the film prone to accusations of limited ambition and achievement. Yet, just like the earlier 'inserted' shot, the status of these two examples is not as clear cut as might be suggested. Just like before, there is another interesting conjunction, this time between the apparent simplicity of the editing pattern and the seeming complexity of the themes these patterns evoke. Unlike Lowenstein, who is content to conclude that this whole sequence is concerned only with mobility of the social kind, we can now see that things are not quite this simple and that there are several complementary aspects of this idea of mobility. Indeed, carefully accounting for this pattern of hints and confirmations becomes a way in which we might reconsider the relationship between *Room at the Top*'s style and the articulation of its themes. Though this discussion is concerned only with the film's opening sequences, it does suggest that a more detailed and multi-dimensional understanding of what it means to arrive somewhere new is the only way in which we might examine the mise-en-scène of *Room at the Top* and give it the critical justice it so clearly deserves.

Notes

1 Ernest Lindgren, *The Art of the Film*, London, George Allen & Unwin Ltd, 1948, p. 45.

2 Robin Wood, 'Ghostly Paradigms and H. C. F.: An Answer to Alan Lovell', *Screen*, Vol. 10 No. 3 (May/June 1969), pp. 35–48, p. 45.

3 Ivan Butler, *The Making of Feature Films: A Guide*, Harmondsworth, Penguin Book Ltd, 1971, p. 61.

4 Julian Petley, 'The Lost Continent', in Charles Barr, ed., *All Our Yesterdays: 90 Years of British Cinema*, London, BFI Publishing, 1986, pp. 98–119, pp. 98–99.

5 Peter Hutchings, 'The Histogram and the List: The Director in British Film Criticism', *Journal of Popular British Cinema*, No. 4 (2001), pp. 30–36, p. 30.

6 *Ibid.*, p. 31.

7 *Ibid.*, pp. 31–32.

8 Robert Murphy, *Sixties British Cinema*, London, BFI Publishing, 1992, pp. 10–11.

9 Alan Lovell and Jim Hillier, *Studies in Documentary*, London, BFI/Secker & Warburg, 1972, p. 142.

10 Adam Lowenstein, 'Under-The-Skin Horrors: Social Realism and Classlessness in *Peeping Tom* and the British New Wave', in Justine Ashby and Andrew Higson, ed., *British Cinema, Past and Present*, London and New York, Routledge, 2000, pp. 221–232, p. 226.

11 Hutchings, 'The Histogram and the List', pp. 32–33.

12 Robert Allen and Douglas Gomery, *Film History: Theory and* Practice, New York, Alfred A. Knopf, 1985, p. 75.

13 *Ibid.*, p. 76.

14 *Ibid.*, pp. 75–77.

15 Houston, *The Contemporary Cinema*, Harmondsworth, Penguin Books Ltd, 1963, p. 123.

16 Thomas Elsaesser, 'Between Style and Ideology', *Monogram* No. 3 (1972). See also Petley, 'The Lost Continent', pp. 98–100.

17 Terry Lovell makes a similar point in her discussion of Richardson's *A Taste of Honey*. As she writes: 'the repertoire of images, narrative concerns and characters of the New Wave quickly became over-familiar, and its style

soon lost its initial freshness of effect' (Terry Lovell, 'Landscape and Stories in 1960s British Realism', in Andrew Higson, ed., *Dissolving Views: Key Writings on British* Cinema, London, Cassell, 1996, p. 168). See also Andrew Higson, who defined surface realism as 'an iconography which authentically reproduces the visual and aural surfaces of the 'British way of life' in 'Space, Place, Spectacle: Landscape and Townscape in the "Kitchen Sink" Film', in Andrew Higson, ed., *Dissolving Views: Key Writings on British Cinema*, London, Cassell, 1986, p. 136. Also John Hill, who notes in a similar discussion: 'All too often, the mere display of the working class and sexual relationships on the screen is celebrated as a "Good Thing" in itself, irrespective of the way in which they have actually been dealt with by the films themselves' (John Hill, *Sex, Class and Realism: British Cinema 1956–1963*, London, BFI, 1986, p. 172).

18   Neil Sinyard, *Jack Clayton*, Manchester and New York, Manchester University Press, 2000, pp. 58–59.

19   *Ibid.*, p. 45.

20   *Ibid.*, p. 41.

21   This is exactly what Moya Luckett sets out to do in her 'Travel and Mobility: Femininity and National Identity in Swinging London Films', in Justine Ashby and Andrew Higson, *British Cinema, Past and Present*, London and New York, Routledge, 2000, pp. 233–245.

22   As she writes: 'Each of the New Wave films has its shots of canals, street scenes, the pub, the fairground, the bus journey, the visit to the nearby countryside' (Lovell, 'Landscape and Stories', p. 169).

23   See Tom Dewe Mathews, *Censored: What They Didn't Allow You to See, and Why: The Story of Film Censorship in Britain*, London, Chatto and Windus, 1994, for a more detailed discussion of this aspect of Clayton's film.

24   The quote is from Stuart Hall and Paddy Whannel's book *The Popular Arts*, cited in Sinyard, *Jack Clayton*, p. 59.

25   As Alexander Walker notes: 'That social and artistic changes take place around the same focal points is a hypothesis to treat with caution and, possibly, to despair of ever being able to prove conclusively; but what films like *Billy Liar* remind us of is the extraordinary power the cinema possesses, against all the odds, of anticipating as well as reflecting social change, so that the films seem to be at one and the same time prophecies of and metaphors for what is happening or going to happen' (Alexander Walker, *Hollywood, England: The British Film Industry in the Sixties*, London, Michael Joseph Ltd, 1974, p. 167).

26   David Robinson, for example, cites the arrival of *Billy Liar* as a turning point in the development of British cinema. As he writes: 'Maybe we always knew that swinging London was only a myth, the invention of *Time* and *Life* and the ad men. But Britain's swinging cinema was for a period a nightmare reality. Perhaps *Billy Liar* was the turning point? The original Waterhouse–Hall play seemed distinctly to belong to the realist cinema and theatre of the fifties, to the era of *Look Back in Anger*, *Room at the Top*, *Saturday Night and Sunday Morning* and (in itself indicating other new directions) *This Sporting Life*. John Schlesinger's earlier film *A Kind of Loving*, also belonged to this mood' (David Robinson, 'Case Histories of the

Next Renascence', *Sight and Sound*, Vol. 38 No. 1 (Winter 1968/69), pp. 36–40, p. 36.

27 Obviously, an approach of this kind might also go some way to counter the kind of negative evaluative claims we saw in Chapter 1, in particular those made by Elsaesser in 'Between Style and Ideology'.

28 In part, the impulse here is similar to the process of *re-emplotment* outlined by George Wilson. Of course, Wilson's project has an entirely different objective. Nevertheless, he usefully illuminates a core procedural element with the following description: 'We take an already familiar series of events, the members of which have seemed integrated into one kind of narrative, and argue that when they are re-ordered, re-weighted, and linked to still other events, they actually tell a different and, perhaps, better story' (George Wilson, 'On Film Narrative and Narrative Meaning', in Richard Allen and Murray Smith, ed., *Film Theory and Philosophy*, Oxford, Oxford University Press, 1997, pp. 221–238, p. 232). Further, as David Bordwell continues in his discussion of film interpretation: 'Neither causal nor functional explanation is the aim of film interpretation. Indeed, in a certain sense, knowledge of the text is not the most salient effect of the interpretative enterprise. It may be that interpretation's greatest achievement is its ability to encourage, albeit somewhat indirectly, reflections upon our conceptual schemes. By taming the new and sharpening the known, the interpretive institution reactivates and revises common frameworks of understanding' (David Bordwell, *Making Meaning: Inference and Rhetoric in the Interpretation of Cinema*, London, Harvard University Press, 1989, p. 257).

29 Lowenstein, ' "Under-The-Skin Horrors" ', p. 226.

30 *Ibid.*

31 *Ibid.*, p. 226.

32 We can continue this idea if we consider the relationship between a particular shot, or shot series, and the paragraph that describes it. As John Harrington writes: 'A shot, like a paragraph, offers both detailed information and an idea or mood. Any direct analogy between the shot and the paragraph, however, will quickly break down. The elements of a paragraph are met with one at a time. They are linear. The content of a shot is, for all practical purposes, available all at once' (John Harrington, *The Rhetoric of Film*, New York, Holt, Rinehart and Winston Inc., 1973, pp. 10–11).

33 Once again Victor Perkins is useful here when he writes that the act of description 'reduces the film narrative to verbal statement' and this reduction, in turn, causes the critic 'to assess the value and significance of the resulting form of words'. Rather, as Perkins concludes: 'In order to comprehend whole meanings, rather than those parts of the meaning which are present in verbal synopsis or visual code, attention must be paid to the whole content of shot, sequence and film. The extent to which a movie rewards this complete attention is an index of its achievement' (V.F. Perkins, *Film as Film*, Harmondsworth, Penguin, 1972, p. 79). Also, as Deborah Thomas notes: 'a film's meanings are thus not so much a set of propositions which can be readily detached from the film but rather a complex combination of themes and their simultaneous embodiments in a number of elements: the film's sound and look, its details of performance and camera

rhetoric, its structure and tone' (Deborah Thomas, *Reading Hollywood: Spaces and Meaning in American Film*, London and New York, Wallflower Press, 2001, p. 5).

34 R. Barton Palmer, 'What Was New About The British New Wave?', *Journal of Popular Film and Television*, Vol. 14 No. 3 (Fall 1986), pp. 125–135, p. 130.

35 George M. Wilson, *Narration in Light: Studies in Cinematic Point of View*, Baltimore, The Johns Hopkins University Press, 1986. Admittedly, Wilson's book is an astute examination of films from a particular period of Hollywood but, as we are beginning to see, the kind of examination advocated here can, on the whole, be extended to consider films from other national cinemas.

36 As Wilson warns: 'Every film necessarily controls and limits the character of the visual access that we have to its fictional events, and sometimes the precise nature of these limits and this control is both subtle and sophisticated. In any case, it is the various facets of this epistemic dimension of cinematic presentation which I wish to stress' (*ibid.*, p. 2).

37 *Ibid.*, p. 3. In effect, this is very close to the point raised by Perkins concerning the attention that needs to be paid 'to the whole content of shot, sequence and film' in order to avoid a reliance solely on 'verbal synopsis or visual code.' See note 33.

38 Douglas Pye, 'Movies and Point of View', *Movie*, No. 36 (2000), pp. 2–34, p. 8.

39 *Ibid.*, pp. 8–9.

40 As Pye is led to conclude: 'spatial point of view is almost invariably independent of any character. The specific spatial organisation of a scene, even when we closely share the location of a character, is seldom identified with the experience of the character.... The visual viewpoint of a character may be embraced through the point-of-view shot but the shots represent overall an independent view and our understanding of the film may depend on our recognition of that fact' (*ibid.*, p. 9).

4 Major themes and minor movements: composition and repetition in John Schlesinger's *Billy Liar*

Making a film is like going down a mine: once you've started you bid a metaphorical good-bye to the daylight and the outside world for the duration. Or you might describe it as a tempestuous love affair. I do not see how a director can make a satisfactory film unless he is deeply emotionally involved. I sometimes wish I could make a film with less agonizing and more exuberance, but if I did I imagine I should finish up even less content with the result than I am now. (John Schlesinger)[1]

Dream delivers us to dream, and there is no end to illusion. Life is a train of moods like a string of beads, and, as we pass through them, they prove to be many-colored lenses which paint the world their own hue, and each shows only what lies in its focus. From the mountain you can see the mountain. We animate what we can, and we see only what we animate. (Ralph Waldo Emerson)[2]

I think everyone knows odd moments in which it seems uncanny that one should find oneself just here now, that one's life should have come to this verge of time and place, that one's history should have unwound to this room, this road, this promontory. The uncanny is normal experience of film. Escape, rescue, the metamorphosis of a life by a chance encounter or juxtaposition – these conditions of contingency and placement underpin all the genres of film, from the Keaton and Chaplin figures who know nothing of the abyss they skirt, to the men who know too much. (Stanley Cavell)[3]

Ticket to ride?

Towards the end of *Billy Liar*, Billy Fisher, the liar of the title, played by Tom Courtenay, has arranged to go to London with his friend Liz (Julie Christie). He has bought his ticket for the late-night train but now faces a problem. Having spent the entire film telling everyone that he is leaving, Billy is faced with the possibility that he might finally have to go. The time for talking has now finished and Billy needs to act but as we watch it becomes increasingly clear that he cannot go through with his plan. Despite Liz's gentle protests, Billy gets off the train and hurries

6 Billy (Tom Courtenay) weighs up his options in *Billy Liar.*

to a milk machine on the platform. Billy inserts his money and as the cartons drop he looks over his shoulder. The camera moves closer as if waiting for a decision.

Alone in the frame, with just the vending machine for company, Billy stands with a carton of milk in each hand, apparently weighing up the decision of whether to leave or not. He shuts his eyes and breathes deeply. Behind him the sound of the train preparing to leave can be heard but Billy waits too long and the train heads off to London without him. He returns home and the film ends.

This ending neatly puts paid to Billy's plan to leave Bradford. With his grandmother dead and his parents in need of support, Billy's leaving appears to be the wrong thing for him to do. There is also the matter of the missing calendars and the petty cash he needs to sort out with his employers Shadrack and Duxbury. He has also managed to get engaged to two women at the same time. And he needs to make peace with his best friend Arthur (Rodney Bewes). Thus, Billy's emotional and social responsibilities conspire to thwart his plans and force him to miss the train and stay at home. But there is something troubling about the image of Billy standing by the milk machine, something that suggests we might be doing the film an injustice by settling for such simple conclusions. Is it possible that this moment is actually operating on a more complicated level, one that defies such clear-cut explanations? To begin to answer this question it is necessary to define a relationship to this image.

For Deborah Thomas the practice of film criticism aims to 'prise such details away from the whole through the explicitness of its linguistic descriptions, thereby bringing them and some of the issues they open up to our attention'.[4] But how is this process begun? John Gibbs offers an answer when he defines the concept of mise-en-scène. Gibbs begins by considering what the contents of the frame are, and the simple answer is that these include lighting, costume, décor, properties and the actors as well. Crucially, however, none of these things exists in isolation. As Gibbs continues:

The organisation of the contents of the frame encompasses the relationship of the actors to one another and to the décor, but also their relationship to the camera, and thus the audience's view. So in talking about mise-en-scène one is also talking about framing, camera movement, the particular lens employed and other photographic decisions. Mise-en-scène therefore encompasses both what the audience can see, and the way in which we are invited to see it. It refers to many of the major elements of communication in the cinema, and the combinations through which they operate expressively.[5]

Despite the critical necessity to be able to define the separate elements, as well as consider each element's potential for expression, it is important to consider these elements specifically in terms of their interaction. This is allied with the need to consider these elements 'by virtue of their context: the narrative situation, the "world" of the film, the accumulating strategies that the film-maker adopts'. With this interaction established it is also necessary to consider the idea of coherence, and Gibbs argues that we might see this in two ways. First, there is the idea of coherence existing *across* the work. Gibbs offers a visual motif as his example but this would include any other aspect of mise-en-scène which 'acquires significance through repetition.'[6] As he continues:

In each case, the subsequent appearance of the motif brings with it the weight of earlier associations. But coherence across a work would also apply to other aspects of the relationship between one moment and the rest, including consistency of tone and viewpoint, and the qualification that the individual element receives from its context.[7]

Coherence can apply between 'the different elements of a single moment' and the way in which these different elements 'interact to achieve significant effect'. This is vital because a convincing interpretation is entirely dependent upon the extent to which 'a coherent pattern can be established'. Ultimately, for the critic, it is not the individual elements of mise-en-scène that are significant in themselves, 'rather the relationship between elements, their interaction within a shot and across the narrative'.[8]

Of course, there are limits to such a 'synthetic' form of criticism, as Victor Perkins acknowledges elsewhere:

I have said that our only guide to the existence of a perceptible pattern or principle of organisation is the fact that it *is* perceived, in terms which allow for rational discussion. But it is common experience that a previously unobserved coherence may become apparent in the course of time or through increased familiarity with a work. If we *come* to perceive the pattern, it was presumably always available for perception. The argument spins away and leaves us continually looking over our shoulders at posterity with judgement in suspense.[9]

For Perkins, then, this means that a decision is required. We can start by choosing to define 'the perceptible by what we ourselves actually perceive or what can be demonstrated to us by others'.[10] We must also be prepared to demonstrate our critical humility by being willing to consider the arguments of others. Finally, we also have a duty to ensure that our standards are as clear and consistent as we can make them. This is because:

> we have to take account of our inability to discuss coherence of detail in anything but a very selective manner. The richer and more dense the pattern we find, the more conscious we shall be that time and space allow us to discuss only some representative parts. We have to be willing to show also why we regard particular flaws as crucial or particular achievements as typical.[11]

Caught?

With the camera holding the character in a close shot, it is a simple task to equate the edges of the frame with the apparently limited boundaries of Billy's life in Bradford. This allows a connection to be made between the character's position within the frame and his desire to escape the confines of life in his home town. Logic suggests that Billy is trapped in a situation that he cannot break free from. Alexander Walker reaches the same conclusion when he writes that:

> Escape is the theme of *Billy Liar*, but it is escape only into fantasy, not physical escape, that Billy achieves. He is trapped just as much by his dream-life as he is by industrial drabness, social conformity, unimaginative parents, and girl-friends who are either brazen flirts or chicken-brained dollies. He lacks the essential courage to get up and get out of his dull rut when his girl-friend sings him her 'Song of the South' and tries to entice him to hop aboard the early-morning milk train to London and put his dreams to the test with her.[12]

But there is more to say here. We can ascribe a sense of being trapped to this moment by combining the composition of this shot with our understanding of the film's thematic concerns. Yet the idea of escape, however important, is only part of the story.

On the right side of the frame we also see the bright light of the milk machine. We know that Liz is waiting off-left on the train and Billy is standing in the middle with his head bowed slightly, as if weighed down by the range of possibilities he is presented with here. The machine blocks one side of the frame. The left side is open and offers an opportunity for movement into the spaces beyond it, towards Liz, the train and, ultimately, London. But Billy's body is turned so that he has his back to the train. This is in keeping with the feeling of his being trapped suggested by the tight framing of the character. Equally, however, the unobstructed left edge also implies that things might not be too late. After all, all Billy has to do is turn around and get back on the train. In this way, this image defies a basic interpretation.

There is an element of ambiguity to what we see here and we, like the character, become suspended by this image, caught in two minds and unable to make a simple decision. Billy's desire to leave home is totally at odds with the reality of his situation and these conflicting interests only add to the ambiguity. All this means that we are actually offered an opportunity to revise our interpretation and question, instead, whether Billy is passively caught in the frame or has, in fact, actively placed himself in a position where his escaping Bradford becomes an impossibility. Either way, it is clear that the weight of Billy's dilemma roots him to the spot.

Billy's stillness is also interesting here because until now his life has been characterised by a certain freneticism. Our memory of the way in which he has raced from crisis to crisis means that his lack of movement here acquires a poignancy. But this is not all. Billy is also silent, and this is strange for a character who has talked himself in and out of a variety of situations since the film began. All around Billy we can hear whistling, drunken cries and the boom of steam trains getting ready to leave but these sounds serve only to emphasise the silence that has fallen upon him. Voices ring in the noisy night but somehow the frame containing Billy appears drained. Somewhere a telephone rings and its insistent sound echoes the station master's tone when he tells Billy that he hasn't got long. The soundtrack here makes us acutely aware of the fact that after a lifetime of talking this is one occasion when Billy has nothing to say. But his silence also reminds us of the fact that words are no longer needed here, it is action that is required and this charges the moment with expectation.

Having inserted his money, Billy looks over his shoulder before gently bending down to retrieve the milk from the machine. The camera moves with him, lowering as he does and then moves closer, as if waiting for a decision to be made. Initially, the camera's movement suggests an emphasis on the need for Billy to act decisively. Equally, however, the uncertainty about his intentions helps to undercut the emphasis, leaving us, instead, with the close and tender portrait of a character unwilling or unable to make a decision. The small movement of the camera here contrasts with the larger movement Billy needs to make in order to catch the train. But this movement, like the decision it is linked to, is something that we will not see. Instead, we are left with something more minor and decidedly less ambitious.

All in all, then, this single image has the potential to become a multi-dimensional representation of the relationship between the film's construction and its themes. Yet a single image, however compelling, is not enough to develop a detailed understanding of the interaction between a film's style and its meaning. In order to understand fully the position that Billy occupies in relation to his world we need consider the film more broadly. For this to happen successfully, it is necessary, as Gibbs suggests, to establish a link between this example and other moments in the film when the edges of the frame and Billy's position within it combine to offer us a cumulative insight into this character's situation. The purpose of this is to demonstrate that the most interesting insights into the reality of Billy's situation are to be found in a series of moments like this one on the platform when the bluster and disturbances caused by his stories have momentarily subsided and we are left just to watch as the full effects of Billy's contradictory existence are revealed.

This is important because, as we are about to see, the most interesting insights are revealed during moments when the film's conventions of construction are at their most obvious. The close framing of the character at the milk machine is one example of this tendency but others will be revealed. In this way, Gibbs's desire for interaction between elements of a film's detail will neatly dovetail with an ongoing discussion of *Billy Liar*'s mise-en-scène.[13]

A completer identity?

For Stanley Cavell 'to be human is to wish, and in particular to wish for a completer identity than one has so far attained; and that such a wish may project a complete world *opposed* to the world one so far shares with others'.[14] Of course, though Cavell does not make this explicit, a distance must inevitably exist between the world you share and the one you wish for and, for Billy, just such a wish involves just such a distance. For, living where he does, in Bradford, and working where he does, as an undertaker's clerk for the funeral directors Shadrack & Duxbury, Billy is haunted by a deep-seated frustration which leaves him feeling far from complete. He dreams of moving to London and becoming a scriptwriter for the comedian Danny Boon (Leslie Randall), and this dream is representative of the distance that exists between Cavell's two worlds.

This ambition indicates a way forward for Billy, the first step in closing the distance between where he finds himself and where he wants to be. Yet, as the film unfolds, we come to understand that Billy's life, in fact, doesn't move forward in the linear way that one might expect. In conventional narrative terms, *Billy Liar* operates in a perfectly logical way. Notwithstanding the occasional excursions into Ambrosia, the fantasy world that Billy rules in his head, events in the film lead to subsequent events with the usual causal flow you would come to expect from a fiction film. Yet the reality is that Billy's life has a decidedly different feel to it and this is because as the film unfolds the end result is that Billy never appears to be moving forwards. To understand this idea it is necessary to trace the route through the film that leads to the image of Billy standing by the milk machine.

It is Saturday night and the local dance hall is the place to be. Unable to disentangle himself from the lies that he tells, Billy has arranged to meet Rita (Gwendolyn Watts) and Barbara (Helen Fraser), his two fiancées. As the sequence opens they are both standing outside the Locarno. Rita eventually gets tired of waiting and goes inside but Barbara remains outside and Billy has to sneak past her by borrowing a crash helmet to disguise himself. Billy appears pleased that his deception was successful but the privacy that this disguise affords him is only temporary. With Billy inside, the film cuts to reveal a shot of the dance floor. The camera is positioned on the floor and tracks slowly from right to left. The frame is filled with the bodies of people dancing and as the camera moves we see the band performing.

Because of the camera's close proximity to the assembled dancers, the importance of this initial camera movement might be overlooked. This is because it is immediately followed by a cut which serves to locate Billy within the crowd and, ostensibly this first movement does little more than reveal the nature of the Locarno's spaces. We would be extremely suspicious if we did not see people dancing in a dance hall. Yet, this initial camera movement is followed by two others, and a consideration of the three of them together offers an interesting insight into the action that is about to unfold. The establishing shot of the dance floor is followed by one that tracks Billy as he walks along its edge. The crowds on the dance floor were introduced by a camera movement moving from right to left. When the film cuts to locate Billy the camera moves again but this time its direction is reversed. As Billy walks the camera now moves with him from left to right and this reversal shows him to be moving in a different direction to the people around him. A couple walk past him and their movement suggests that Billy is out of step with his surroundings. There then follows a brief shot of Rita dancing close by. Preoccupied with the rhythm of the music, she doesn't see Billy. Nevertheless, the problems that her presence will eventually cause for him are hinted at by Billy's reactions. He carefully creeps around a pillar so as to avoid her.

The film cuts and we see what he has seen: Liz sitting upstairs looking over the balcony. Spotting Liz gives Billy the opportunity to go upstairs and get away from the dance floor. With the camera now behind Billy, we see him start to climb the stairs. As he heads for the balcony the camera remains still. Shadrack (Leonard Rossiter), Billy's boss, and his wife enter the frame and as they move towards the dance floor the camera starts to follow them. This third movement, like the first one, is from right to left.

Considering this part of the sequence at face value allows us to understand that the crowded spaces of the dance hall are about to become an important arena within which the effects of Billy's lies will be painfully revealed. This is revealed by the way in which Billy is forced not only to enter the Locarno in disguise but also to creep along the edge of the dance floor. Seeing Rita dancing and knowing that Barbara is still waiting outside adds an air of inevitability to the opening of the sequence. It will only be a matter of time before the two of them become known to each other and the consequences of their meeting will be played out in the most public of ways. Shadrack's arrival is important for the further emphasis it places on the fact that the Locarno is full of people who know Billy and his business. But our knowledge of all of these things should not prevent us from understanding that the film's construction of this sequence is doing much more than just baldly clearing the way for the inevitable drama to come.

Here, the film is skilfully establishing the spaces necessary for the action of the sequence to occur in whilst simultaneously commenting upon the thematic reality of Billy's situation. The three camera movements found in this part of the sequence are significant for the insight they offer into Billy's relationship with his world. Considered individually, the first movement introduces the spaces of the sequence, the second positions Billy within these spaces and the third indicates the presence of other characters with particular narrative importance. However, when they are considered together, Billy's desire to try and separate himself from the routines and movements of his life in Bradford is subtly brought to our attention by the repetition of camera movement and the differences in direction that characterise them.

The repetition of composition

The film joins Billy on the balcony. He smiles as he walks towards Liz. The camera is positioned behind her and as Billy approaches we can see that the balcony is also busy. Billy sits down and the film cuts again. The couple sit at either edge of the frame framed in a close shot. With Billy positioned on the right and Liz on the left, the dance floor below is still visible between them. As Billy and Liz begin to talk they lean in towards each other but even these actions are not enough to block our view of the dancers below. Though the couple obviously share an intimate affection for each other this introductory part of their conversation clearly lacks privacy. Billy acknowledges this when he tells Liz how many people here know him. As if to echo this, the film cuts to another shot of Rita dancing below them. We return to the couple but this time, however, the camera is positioned on the other side, between the couple and the dance floor. There then follows a series of five brief shots that need to be examined in more detail. Here is a simple outline:

[1]   Extreme close shot – Liz on the right side of the frame, Billy's head partly visible

[2]   Extreme close shot – reversed this time. Billy's face fills left side of the frame, back of Liz's head visible

[3]   Same as [1]

[4]   Same as [2]

[5]   Same as [1]

The extremity of the close shots in this series gives the conversation a feeling of privacy. The editing here offers an intimate exchange between two people keen to catch up on each other's news. These shots ensure that only Liz and Billy are visible in the frame and this intimacy is encouraged by the camera's position between the characters and the dance floor. For the moment, at least, the rest of the dance-hall has been excluded. The editing here does intervene by adding an element of artificiality to this intimacy but this serves only to reinforce the problems Billy faces in terms of privacy.

One interpretation of this moment would be to consider that this series of extreme close shots adds an unnecessary dramatic weight to the conversation. After all, the nearness of the characters to the camera appears to impose the film's wish that Billy and Liz talk privately at this moment. Thus, we might consider *Billy Liar*'s style here to be heavy-handed and lacking sufficient subtlety when it comes to dealing with its characters and their concerns. As we saw with *Look Back in Anger*, this caused considerable problems. Here, however, the film is carefully articulating Billy's situation in a much more sophisticated way than first appears. There is an additional emphasis here, one that draws attention to the difficulties Billy has in avoiding the many people who know him but this is only half the story.

This shot series is ended by a cut that returns the camera to its position between the couple and the dance floor. Though our view has been widened, the camera's position maintains the feeling of privacy. Ostensibly, then, this new composition does nothing more than mirror the framing which preceded the five-shot part of the conversation. As before, Billy and Liz are positioned at either edge of the frame. This time, however, their positions are reversed. In itself, this is not particularly remarkable. Yet, as the conversation continues, Billy's new position within the frame offers a valuable insight into both his character and his motivation.

This next part of the conversation begins with Billy telling Liz that the comedian Danny Boon has offered him a job in London. This is not true because Billy has already spoken to Danny and much to Billy's regret, the best that Danny could offer him was the off-hand suggestion that he contact his office if he was ever in London. Nevertheless, Billy tells Liz that he now has the chance to go to London, and at this point the film cuts to another series of alternating close shots. Once again, here is the series in more detail:

[1] Extreme close shot of Liz on the right of the frame. 'Well?' she asks Billy. 'When are you going?'

[2] Extreme close shot of Billy on left of frame. 'Soon', he replies. 'As soon as I can manage.'

[3] Same as [1] – 'Why do not you go now?'

[4] Same as [2] – 'It's difficult.'

[5] Same as [1] – 'No it's not, it's easy. You get on a train and four hours later there you are in London.'

[6] Same as [2] – 'It's easy for you, you've had the practice.'

[7] Same as [1] – Liz doesn't reply.

The first thing to notice is the difference in shot length. In the first series there was a uniformity of length and this gave their conversation an even tone, with the emphasis on an equal exchange of news and information. Here, however, the shots are no longer the same length as each other. This series also contains two extra shots and both of these things give this next part of the conversation a completely different feel. We also need to be aware of the repetition of composition here.

In both series Billy is positioned on the left and Liz on the right. In the first five shots Billy's position was the natural consequence of the change in the camera's position and was remarkable for the apparent privacy that this position offered the character in relation to the dance floor below. Here, however, the repetition of this position tells a different story. The conversation now has a different tone. Liz challenges Billy by suggesting how simple it would be for him to make the break. As she tells him, all he has to do is get on the train and go. In Billy's complicated life, however, nothing can ever be so straightforward and this is reflected in his response to her prompting. He is not ready to go, he tells her, and it is at this point we realise that there has been a subtle shift in the importance of Billy's position within the frame.

In the first shot series the emphasis was on the opportunity for an even and intimate exchange between the pair of them. The various elements of the second series combine to create a very different impression. Consider, for example, the transition between shots 5 and 6. As Liz explains how simple it would be for Billy to leave, the film cuts before she finishes talking. The sound of her words bleed into the next shot of Billy (shot 6) and draw further attention to both his response and his position in the frame. The directness of Liz's question surprises him and, combined with the weight of her words, we now understand that Billy has been placed on the spot.

Here, the repetition of the film's composition offers the most refined reflection on the reality of Billy's situation. The moment's more obvious elements, like the dialogue and the extremity of scale created by the close shots, also have a significant part to play. Yet, it is the small differences between two seemingly identical editing strategies that offer the best insight because the repetition here achieves two important things. Firstly, the film gives another useful indication of the nature of Billy's situation. Secondly, and more importantly, the effective working relationship between the film's construction and the expression of its thematic concerns is perfectly illustrated. My discussion here has relied upon a consideration of the relationship between the frame and Billy's position within it. However, this aspect of the sequence is not something to be considered in isolation and the claims made are in keeping with Perkins's call for a 'selective' discussion of the 'representative parts' of a film's detail.[15]

It's a wonderful life?

The privacy shared by Billy and Liz is only short-lived. The dance hall is just too public a place. Yet, surprisingly enough, Billy is not disturbed by the intrusion of one of the many people he is trying hard to avoid. This will follow. Instead, it is the sound of the band starting another number that distracts him. The band play the opening bars of 'Twisterella', a song that Billy co-wrote with his friend Arthur, and the sound of this song initiates the next part of the sequence. Events are about to escalate with a causal ferocity as Billy is forced to confront the more public aspects of his life.

It all begins when he spots Shadrack and his wife approaching his table. Desperate to avoid them, Billy hides in a photo-booth before heading back downstairs. As he reaches the bottom of the stairs he bumps into a forlorn-looking Barbara. She is understandably upset at having been left outside but Billy convinces her that they were supposed to meet inside. Billy is keen for them to dance but Barbara is unable to co-ordinate her feet properly and gives up.[16] She suggests that they go for a drink instead but on the way they pass Rita. She, like Barbara, is upset at having been stood up. Billy attempts to talk his way out the situation but the two girls start fighting over the engagement ring they have both worn. Billy takes advantage of the confusion and slips away. The film cuts and we see him, once again, walking down the edge of the dance floor.

This sequence began with the dance hall being defined as the site for future drama. We saw a variety of people who have been affected in one way or another by Billy's stories and were left in no doubt that something was bound to happen. We have also seen how the film presented the struggle that Billy was bound to face here, one between the private facts of his life and their likely public exposure. The many tangled lines of Billy's life are about to culminate in a moment of excruciating exposure.

As Billy walks down the edge of the floor the band finish playing 'Twisterella'. His movement here echoes the first time we saw him in the Locarno. This time, however, there is nowhere left for him to hide. The bandleader announces that the last song they played was written by two local lads, Fisher and Crabtree. Arthur, already on stage, is presented to the audience and he spots Billy. The band leader calls for a spotlight and Billy is caught in its glare. There now follows what appears to be a cruel parody of the two shot series considered earlier. Let's begin by considering the shot breakdown:

[1]   Long shot of the dance floor. Camera positioned on balcony looking down on to the nearly empty dance floor. The beam of a searchlight crosses the floor and locates Billy.

[2]   Close shot of Billy looking sheepish.

[3]   Close shot of Liz. She rolls her eyes in mock bewilderment as the band-leader tells everyone about Billy's new job in London.

[4]   Medium shot of Rita and Barbara looking upset and dishevelled.

[5]   Close shot of Billy's cynical colleague, Eric Stamp (George Innes). He shouts 'Billy Liar'.

[6]   Medium shot of the balcony. The spotlight shines straight at the camera and on either side we see people looking down and clapping.

[7]   Long shot of the dance floor. It is empty this time, except for Billy caught in the spotlight.

[8]   Close shot of Billy. He looks uncomfortable and places his hand over his face.

With the camera looking down from the balcony, this series begins with a long shot of the dance floor. With no music, people have stopped dancing and are making their way to the side. The spotlight finds Billy and forces him to reluctantly take centre-stage. The camera's distance here is in stark contrast to its previous closeness to Billy and our memory of the earlier part of this sequence makes Billy's isolation here all the more difficult to watch. This is because the camera's new position has removed the intimacy we earlier experienced as we watched him flirting with Liz. Also, the construction of the earlier part of this sequence has primed us to expect Billy's eventual exposure, and now that it is happening this new distance ensures that we are not spared the full extent of the situation's cruelty.

From this position the camera now acts as an additional spotlight casting its own beam, sweeping the room, picking out the pertinent people and revealing their reactions accordingly. The characters that we see in the shots that follow have all been personally affected in one way or another by Billy's stories and from this starting-position the camera is able to unite them across the various spaces of the Locarno. This helps to explain the succession of reactions that follow this first shot. First we are given a view of Billy's reaction. In an extremely close shot we see him reluctantly acknowledge the band-leader. This is followed by a shot of Liz. She rolls her eyes with mock surprise when Billy's 'good' news is announced. We then see the reaction of Rita and Barbara. Dishevelled in a medium shot, Barbara sobs, Rita's mascara has run down her cheek. Billy's work-mate is next. Framed, once again, in a medium shot, the cynical Stamp is enjoying the spectacle and hurls abuse at Billy. This is followed by a shot of the spotlight itself.

Through the light's glare we can see people looking down and applauding. This shot helps to reinforce the camera's position in relation to the action below and is followed by another long shot of Billy alone on the dance floor. This shot series concludes with another extremely close shot of the hapless Billy. Notwithstanding the importance of the rest of the shots in this sequence, it is two close shots of Billy that are of most interest and this is because they are the next vital elements in this unfolding pattern of framing and character position.

An immediate connection can be made with the shot that concluded the second part of the conversation with Liz. Liz's line of gentle questioning combined with the editing strategy to place Billy in a position where it felt as if he would have to make a decision about his future very soon. Here, beneath the cruel glare of the spotlight, the public exposure of Billy's fanciful ambitions only adds to this idea that it is time for him to act. In one sense, it doesn't appear that he has any choice. Whether true or not, the whole world now knows about his 'job' with Danny Boon and causally, at least, the film now needs to move this situation forward towards some kind of resolution. But there is more to say here.

The public nature of this spectacle adds an element of cruelty to what we see. It was only a matter of time before Billy's lies would be revealed for what they were but the way in which he is now exposed is painful to watch. This final image returns us to the poignant image of Billy standing by the milk machine and the repetition tells us something about the human propensity for sadness, loneliness, and quiet desperation.

Billy and Liz leave the dance hall and go for a walk in a park. They find a secluded spot and sit on a bench. After the noise and humiliation of the Locarno the park seems a perfect place to escape to. It appears that they are on their own and Billy tells Liz about Ambrosia, his 'imaginary country'. Liz perfectly understands Billy's need to daydream and explains that she does it herself. There is a tenderness to this conversation. Billy and Liz start to talk about maps, models and marriage. Out of the spotlight and apparently safe among the shadows they begin to kiss and finally it appears that Billy has found the privacy and affection he has been looking for. But as the previous sequence has shown us, Billy's private desires have an unfortunate habit of being revealed in the most public of ways. Stamp and two friends have followed the couple and are hiding in the bushes listening. Unable to contain themselves, they start to laugh and it seems that there is just no avoiding further humiliation.

The idea of one man's heartfelt desires being so cruelly exposed is a powerful one and it impossible not to feel sorry for Billy here. This episode in the park merely compounds the sadness experienced when the terrible position that he finds himself in is considered. The film seamlessly combines its chosen methods of construction with an effective articulation of its thematic concerns. Perhaps this is what makes its portrait of a man so completely at odds with his surrounding such a powerful one. In the history of narrative film, of course, images of emptiness and thwarted dreams, of failed plans and unrealised ambitions are nothing new but there are still moments, from time to time, when the sheer tragedy of what we see heightens the impact of a particular image. To this end, the dramatic revelation of Billy's predicament brings to mind the situation George Bailey (James Stewart) faces in Frank Capra's 1946 film *It's a Wonderful Life*. Though worlds apart in terms of ambition, intention, reception, style and performance, both films feature characters whose private struggles with the day-to-dayness of their existence are revealed in the most public and painful of ways.

Like the incident with the spotlight in *Billy Liar*, Capra's film perfectly captures the dreadful sense of what it is to be surrounded by people but still be entirely on your own. Consider the uncomfortable moment when George suggests to Gloria Grahame's Violet that they go walking barefoot in the mountains and the private, heartfelt nature of such an innocent suggestion is cruelly exposed by a mocking crowd who have gathered round the couple. This is a heartbreaking moment but, as *Billy Liar* demonstrates, impressive insights into the precariousness of human relationships are not the sole preserve of Capra's film.

Twist or stick?

In the pleasing succession of positions that echo the straight lines of a railway track the film finally places Billy into the square frames of a train carriage. He has bought his ticket and met Liz. They are sitting on the train waiting for it to leave for London. This moment provides a useful contrast with the two conversations in the dance hall. During the second of those conversations we came to understand that Billy's position on the left of the frame represented a position of possibility and opportunity. But this position also carried with it a requirement that Billy should act upon his ambitions.

With the first shot here showing Billy sitting on the left, we can deduce that sitting on the train means that Billy is taking the opportunity offered to him by Liz. However, we can immediately see a change in the demeanour of the two characters. Liz appears perfectly comfortable and settles down for the long journey by taking her scarf off and getting out her cigarettes. Billy, however, is decidedly ill at ease. Previously, we saw the couple lean in towards each other and fill the frame with their animated affection for each other. Now there is an uncomfortable tension.

A group of musicians get on to the train and their arrival adds a further contrast between the two moments. Previously, Billy and Liz talked while the people around them were (temporarily) excluded. Now, the film chooses not to separate the couple from their surroundings. As the musicians joke about leaving Bradford and going home, their presence gives the spaces of the carriage a sense of vitality. Liz is perfectly comfortable with this. Indeed, one of the musicians leans into the frame and flirts with her. For Billy, however, their presence makes his discomfort all the more noticeable. Lacking the courage of his convictions, Billy uses the excuse of getting them both a drink to get off the train. With Billy gone, Liz turns her head to watch him as he hurries to the milk machine. The shot that follows is the most important of this section. This is because the film does not cut to show us Billy's progress from Liz's point of view but offers us, instead, a view of Billy from beyond the guard collecting tickets. In this way, Billy runs towards the camera and moves further away from the train and as he grows bigger in the frame we come to understand the special relationship that exists between the film's themes and its construction.

The camera here has remained behind and its position welcomes Billy back to the reality of his world. As it does so, the illusory nature of Billy's ambitions comes sharply into focus. Despite the calls continually made within the film for upheavals and movements that require Billy to make major changes to his life, the film actually constructs an alternative view of Billy's potential for mobility, one that is characterised by much more minor movements that find their expression in both the camera's mobility and the position of characters within the frame.

So far, I have described two moments from the film that are significant in terms of what they tell us about Billy and his situation. Despite its position towards the end of the film, the image of Billy standing by the vending machine provides a perfect starting-point for an investigation into the position he occupies in relation to his world. It would be easy to suggest that this image represents the bind that the character finds himself in in relation to his dream of leaving for London. Certainly, Billy's position within the frame can easily be read in this way. This reading is strengthened by the knowledge of the narrative events that have led to this point. Yet we must also avoid the temptation to overload the significance of a single image. This image defies such a one-dimensional interpretation and offers, instead, a variety of possibilities. The question is whether Billy has passively allowed himself to become trapped or has actively placed himself into a position whereby his leaving Bradford becomes unlikely. It is the ambiguity of this image that has led us to look for other moments in the film when a consideration of Billy's position in the frame offers us an insight into the problems he faces.

Billy's conversation with Liz at the dance hall is remarkable for the way in which the composition of the framing offers a better understanding of the film's concern with questions of personal movement and escape. The camera's position played a prominent role in developing this understanding. The film here relies on the camera's closeness to the characters to convey the sense of someone struggling with issues of personal constraint. There is no doubt as to the difficult task Billy faces to free himself from the routines of his daily life. However, the film also offers the possibility for a more nuanced insight in Billy's problems. This is revealed in the repetition of a series of shots.

The first series cuts evenly between Billy and Liz as they swap their news with each other. The gentle rhythm of the editing here allows us to concentrate on watching two people flirting comfortably with each other. In this way, little attention is paid to the positions of the characters in the frame. Yet, seconds later, another conversation begins and this time the positions of the characters within the frame offer a vital insight into the way the film will unfold.

The composition of this conversation is the same as the previous one. The film still cuts back and forth as the characters discuss moving to London but the serious nature of this conversation means that everything has changed. The gentle rhythm has been replaced by a more uneven one and this is reflected in the difference of tone. Liz has decided to leave for London and her directness in pressing Billy to make a similar decision creates an imbalance in the composition. In the first series, the film waited for the framed character to finish speaking before cutting. This time, Liz's words bleed between the frames and place extra emphasis on Billy's response. The extreme close shot of Billy that ends the second series suggests that Billy has now been placed firmly on the spot. This much is evident when Billy gets on the train. The time has come for him to make the break but he is unable to do so. Rather than looking forward to starting a new life Billy is actually looking to get back to his old life. Yet, to ultimately understand the relationship between Billy's creative ambitions and the lack of decisive movement in his life we need to return to the busy dance floor in the Locarno.

It should come as no surprise, especially to those of us who have tried it, that the Twist is one of those dances, unlike the Conga, say, where you stay in (virtually) one place. You may move from side to side but, as we saw from the crowd on the dance floor, the Twist lacks a specifically forward movement. While Billy and Liz talk about moving on and moving forward in the first sequence we saw, the song 'Twisterella' – the song Billy tells Liz he helped to write – hints at something else, namely his staying roughly in the same position. As the rest of the film unfolds, this song stands as a subtle reminder that Billy's artistic aspirations will always leave him standing still. These aspirations may be energetic, as this dance demonstrates, and they may also be (partially) realised but, as the moment by the milk machine reveals, Billy's creative aspirations will never generate sufficient momentum for his life to move forward the way that he would want it to.

If the role of Liz in the film and the train's forward movement combine to represent one of the film's major themes, that of moving on, then, conversely, Billy's life can be characterised by more minor movements like the one we saw across the width of the frame during the first conversations we watched. Though a lateral movement like this might place him in a position of possibility it will never offer the opportunity for his life to move forward.

Dance halls in films have always offered people the opportunity to dance and flirt, to have public arguments and intimate conversations. Similarly, railway stations in the cinema are always the places where people set off for pastures new, return home in triumph, or are left standing on the platform. This is especially true in the case of British cinema, where David Lean's *Brief Encounter* (1945) established the railway station as *the* place for unfulfilled love and tragic endings. Yet, the spaces and places of *Billy Liar* are vital and fully integrated components in this film's specific examination of the sometimes contradictory and often problematic relationship between one man and the world in which he lives. Where else other than a dance hall could the potential for public self-expression co-exist with the possibility for an intimate and personal conversation? What better place to demonstrate that the joy of moving on co-exists with the pain of being left behind than at a railway station? As John Gibbs continues in his discussion of working with a film's mise-en-scène:

> To be able to relate our sense of the meanings of a film back to the movement of the camera, a use of colour, or the organisation of décor and character is one of the reasons why a mise-en-scène approach makes for a most satisfying criticism to write and read. One of the great pleasures and advantages of a mise-en-scène, or a more generally style-based, approach is that it enables you to anchor your understanding of a film, and to support your arguments with evidence. It gives us a way of sharing and communicating enthusiasm for a film, and for making an interpretation persuasive.[17]

Notes

1 Ivan Butler, *The Making of Feature Films: A Guide*, Harmondsworth, Penguin Books Ltd, 1971, p. 84.

2 Ralph Waldo Emerson, *Self-Reliance and Other Essays*, New York, Dover Publications Inc., 1993, p. 85.

3 Stanley Cavell, *The World Viewed: Enlarged Edition*, Cambridge, MA, Harvard University Press, 1971, 1974, 1979, p. 156.

4 Deborah Thomas, *Reading Hollywood: Spaces and Meaning in American Film*, London, Wallflower Press, 2001, p. 5.

5 John Gibbs, *Mise-en-scène: Film Style and Interpretation*, London and New York, Wallflower Press, 2002, p. 5.

6 *Ibid.*, p. 26.

7 *Ibid.*, p. 40.

8 *Ibid.*, p. 41.

9 V.F. Perkins, *Film As Film*, Harmondsworth: Penguin Books, 1972, p. 191.

10 *Ibid.*, pp. 191–192.

11 *Ibid.*, pp. 192–193.

12 Alexander Walker, *Hollywood, England: The British Film Industry in the Sixties*, London, Harrap, 1974, p. 165.

13 It is worth noting here that the film also offers insights, at regular intervals, into the private world of fantasy where Billy habitually retreats. These excursions into Ambrosia – the imaginary land that Billy rules over – are clearly signposted as fantasy and have their own special status within the narrative. Thus, you might say, the film is studded along its length with a series of insights, some extremely obvious and other less so, which help to contribute to our understanding of Billy's life and the relationship with his world. For the main part, my discussion will avoid these more demonstrative moments and concentrate, instead, on the less obvious ones.

14 Stanley Cavell, *Themes Out of School: Effects and Causes*, Chicago, University of Chicago Press, 1984, p. 181.

15 Walker, *Hollywood, England*, p. 165.

16 For me, the sight of Barbara being unable to dance says something about her (lack of) sensuality.

17 Gibbs, *Mise-en-scène*, p. 98.

5　The critical forest

As much as I remain dedicated to the cinema, however, I cannot pretend it is culturally self-sufficient. The best criticism will continue to be the criticism that is richest in associations. There are all kinds of gaps and blind spots to be explored. The danger is that a methodological orthodoxy will stifle all individual initiatives in the scholarly sector, and only widen the gap between showbiz and academe. (Andrew Sarris)[1]

Our aim is to provide people with the means for making their own judgements. We try to explain what we see in a film in order that a reader may measure this against his own experience of a film, and make his own judgement, rather than providing him with a ready-made judgement. (Ian Cameron)[2]

My belief is that an understanding of mise-en-scène is a prerequisite for making other kinds of claims about films and, whatever argument you want to make, whatever the motivation for your discussion, a sense of how style relates to meaning needs to be central to your enquiry. (John Gibbs)[3]

The 'interrupted' narrative?

A Kind of Loving opens with a shot of two rows of dirty-looking terraced houses. A group of children play football on the ground between the houses and as with the industrial spaces that were visible through the window as Joe Lampton rode the train into Warnley, a real sense of the film's locations is established straight away. As the title-music begins, three children break off from their game and begin to run across the frame. The camera follows them from right to left and as they run past the last house on the end of the terrace a patch of waste ground opens out before the camera. The rear view of another row of terraced houses now lines the back of the frame. The three children run in the foreground. Two washing lines fill the middle of the frame and the composition here gives the frame an effective and easy balance. The children pass the end of this terrace and the waste ground opens out even further. In the distance we can see two streets, one that runs across the centre of the frame and the other running at right angles, flanked by further rows of houses and stretching off into the distance. As the children head towards the nearest road a large church comes into view. Two cars and several groups of people are also visible. An ice-cream van drives into the frame and we now see other children running from elsewhere, all heading towards it. The tune the van plays is audible on the soundtrack. Just as the children reach the van, the film cuts. In the next shot, the camera is positioned close to the van. We see a pair of women walk across the frame and their conversation informs us that a wedding is taking place in the church. This explains the reasons for the cars and the gathered crowd. The van fills the left side of the frame and the three children run behind the two women to reach it. Though the camera has moved, the church, the terraced houses and the crowds are still perfectly visible in the frame. There then follows another cut and this time the camera is positioned amongst the crowd outside the front door of the church. Though the church and its door loom large the frame still contains the same elements as before. Behind the gathered crowds we can still see the ice-cream van. Behind the van another row of terraced houses is visible in the far background.

I want to begin by asking: what are we meant to make of these images of urban scenery? One interpretation would be that the film's opening uses real locations in exactly the kind of way that critics like Perkins so despised. The terraced houses, in particular, would appear to support this view and could easily be considered to be the kind of directorially ostentatious yet stylistically shallow use of location that was so vilified in 'The British Cinema'. Andrew Higson later developed this idea further when he suggested that the problems experienced when watching a film such as *A Kind of Loving* can partly be characterised as reading shots of this kind in terms of ambivalence or redundancy. As he writes:

> The ambivalence, the potential redundancy of the image, this 'something more' is rarely wasted in the classical Hollywood film. While mise-en-scène is predominately organized in the interests of clinching narrative significance, it is also developed as something fascinating in itself, a source of visual pleasure, a spectacle.[4]

This is because the movement between narration and description becomes 'transformed into the pull between narrative and spectacle' and the sense of New Wave spectacle is derived from 'a tension between the demands of narrative and the demands of realism'. As Higson continues:

> Landscape and townscape shots – that is, expansive shots of rural or urban scenery – must at one level construct a *narrative space* in which the protagonists of the drama can perform the various actions of the plot. Narratives require space in which they can unfold. But because the British New Wave films were promoted as realist, landscape and townscape shots must always be much more than neutral narrative spaces. Each of these location shots demands also to be read as a real historical *place* which can authenticate the fiction.[5]

And this is where Higson's tension reveals itself. As he continues:

There remains a tension between the demands of narrative and the demands of realism, however, with the narrative compulsion of the film working continually to transform place once more back into space. This tension can be transcended when landscape and townscape shots are incorporated into and as the movements of the narration itself. In these cases, place becomes a signifier of character, a metaphor for the state of mind of the protagonists in the well-worn conventions of the naturalist tradition.[6]

However, shots of this kind in the New Wave films – termed by Higson an 'iconographic cliché' – can also be read as *spectacle*, as a visually pleasurable lure to the spectator's eye, and which allows them to 'cut against narrative meaning and flow'.[7]

Of course, Higson is extremely careful here. Pursuing his own claims for ambivalence, he boldly asserts that the British cinema is not usually noted for its visual pleasure. Nevertheless, certain images – like the shot of the terraced houses – 'still hold the eye'.[8] And here is the point at which Higson's assertions begin to cut against the flow of his own argument. In part, this is due to the assumptions he is willing to make on the role of spectacle in these films. As he writes, following John Ellis:

> The experience of narrative is in part the feeling that something is missing from each image we are offered. Since the whole story is not yet complete, since this particular image cannot tell us the whole story, we want to move on, to explore further, to see the next image, and the next, until we have found what was missing and the story is complete. With spectacle, on the other hand, the spectator is confronted with an image which is so fascinating that it seems complete, with nothing missing. Consequently, the desire to move on, to see the next image, is much less urgent.[9]

The question is, then, for Higson, in what sense can an image of this kind – what he describes as 'That Long Shot of Our Town from That Hill' – 'be incorporated into the narrative space of the film?' For Higson, this question can be answered the following way:

> Although these images are coded as spectacular, they can still be clawed back into the narrative system of the films according to the logic of point-of-view shots and establishing shots. They each offer a general shot of the city, establishing economically, the overall space in which the action takes place.[10]

However, a shot of this kind (apparently) creates a 'disjunction' of character and place and this, in turn, raises questions about the 'potential incoherence of point-of-view'.[11] A film like this one, Higson argues, uses the point of view of the central character inhabiting a 'full' environment as the focus for its organisation. This is achieved by 'the narrative centrality of the characters, by the use of optical point-of-view shots and [in certain cases] by various forms of interior monologue':

Thus we are encouraged to empathise with the characters rather than be aware of the camera and the way in which it presents those characters to us. But there are always certain shots which seem to trouble this sense of a perfect fit. They seem to draw attention to the fact that we are watching a film, and that the story-teller views things from a particular perspective.

For Higson, then:

> It is this ostentation which problematizes the vision of the 'kitchen-sink' films. The overwhelming 'visibility' of certain shots precisely as *views through the camera* troubles the coherence of a film which is organised around the point of view of the central protagonist. Hence the sense of doubt which lingers over the status of That Long Shot of Our Town from That Hill.[12]

Higson does not explicitly discuss this part of Schlesinger's film – he uses a later example which we will consider in due course – but we can extend his ideas to other shots that could be read as having a similar interruptive role within the narrative. The question is, though, when I watch these opening images, do I really consider them as 'spectacle'? Does my desire to see what will happen next become suspended by my wanting to gaze at these particular images? I am not sure that this really is the case. Neither am I convinced that shots like these early ones do create problems for the narrative as a result of their 'visibility'. After all, the film has only just begun and I find it impossible to believe that this view of the terraced houses – seen through a camera positioned on a hill – is such a problematic one. We have not even been introduced to the film's principal characters. Clearly, then, the underlying question here is one of viewpoint. In particular, I would argue that a concern for the potential 'damage' to the film's coherence that a shot like this might cause is wholly dependent upon our willingness to align ourselves with the critical trajectory that stemmed from Perkins's original criticisms of New Wave style. But we do not have to be so willing to accept this point of view. The problem is also compounded by the tendency to view these films as a single entity that all share the same features and, thus, the same faults. This is something else that we need to move away from. After all, in terms of the approach to film criticism that I am advocating it would be ludicrous to suggest that the most effective way to write about the style and meaning of John Ford's *Stagecoach* (1939) and George Stevens's *Shane* (1953), for example, is to emphasise the fact that they both use prairie landscapes to help over-contextualise their narratives and overemphasise their settings. (Of course, these are both westerns, which might suggest that I am keen to claim that the British New Wave should be considered a genre of British cinema. This is not the case. Perhaps, then, we might substitute David Lynch's *The Straight Story* (1999) for one or other of these examples.) Anyhow, whatever way we decide to look at it, it is the individual details of the particular film and not those features that it might share with others that need to be addressed. Only in this way can we avoid the same kind of assumptions that 'The British Cinema' made in the first place. In turn, by relying less on establishing features that bind these films together we come to understand moments of style like the opening shots here as being interesting only when considered in relation to the patterns and manner of construction which characterise the rest of *A Kind of Loving*. It is critically myopic to isolate one feature of a film's construction and then use it to construct an argument about the whole film without considering other aspects. There is an assumption of sameness that is at fault here, one that has been allowed to exist (almost) unchallenged since these films were first made. In fact, extending Higson's logic, there is a further tension at work here, one between the assumption that landscape and townscape shots of the kind described really have the sort of visual hold on us that Higson suggests and the further assumption that realist conventions and their use are the still the most fascinating thing about the films of the British New Wave. The idea here is that allegations of corruption derived from the repeated used of realist conventions, allegations that have been used to denigrate the style of these films, now extend to existing critical discussions of these conventions. The task is, then, to demonstrate how to account for the various elements present within the frame without insisting on emphasising one of these elements at the expense of the others present. I will also show how this affects our understanding of the rest of the film.

The logic of equality

I now want to return to Douglas Pye's discussion of cinematic space and point of view. As I demonstrated in my reading of *Room at the Top*, Pye's approach is a useful tool for reconsidering the style of these films. As Pye continues:

> Because they are so often misrepresented or overlooked, it is worth drawing attention in particular to the relationship between the spatial location of the characters and the views taken by the camera. Thus, we could share the locations of a character if both space and time were signified as continuous and the camera stayed in close proximity to a character throughout. Even in such a hypothetical case though, the spectator would be likely to share the location of the character without sharing her perception of space – we generally look *at* the character more than *with* her – and the moment-to-moment spatial relationships between camera and character could still be infinitely varied. Characteristics of visual style, both the use of the camera (scale of shot, camera position, camera movement, lens, shot length) and editing, need to be considered here.[13]

The key here is this idea of characterising elements of the film's visual style to reconsider the relationship between the film and the spaces it unfolds in. My description of the film's opening shots suggests an emphasis upon the equality of the various elements we see within the frame, and this is important for three reasons. Firstly, an equality of this sort allows the film's location to be revealed without an undue emphasis being placed upon its revelation. This then allows the landscape we see revealed to be evenly integrated into the film's narrative movement. Secondly, this sharing of emphasis then creates a sense of connected space. Consider the position of the church in the shot series. As we are about to discover, this is where the film's central couple Vic and Ingrid, played by Alan Bates and June Ritchie, are about to meet for the first time. This is because Christine, Vic's sister, is getting married. Nevertheless, despite its importance to the narrative, the church is not isolated from its surroundings. Instead, the emphasis here is more evenly distributed, with the church existing in an organic relationship with the other elements of the location chosen. We can also say the same for the other elements seen in the frames here – the rows of terraced houses, for example. Their continued presence obviously establishes the setting for the film's subsequent unfolding but they do not appear to be isolated or over-emphasised within the frame. Thirdly, this sense of logical connection can then be extended to the film's style. It is the children running across the wasteland that motivates the camera's movement. As the camera follows them, their running into the broader spaces around them gives us a more nearly complete view of the environment. The continuous shot also allows the church and the crowds to come into view naturally. The length of the shot and the lack of a cut here ensures that this revelation of space and the elements it contains are smoothly revealed within a perfectly reasonable logic of construction. Even when the film does cut, this logic is continued, with the children, the van, the church and the crowds all perfectly visible within the same frame of the next two shots. In this way, the film's opening avoids the kind of directorial heavy-handedness that Perkins *et al.* felt blighted the film. Instead, its opening effectively establishes an equal relationship between the film's setting, the camera's movement and the narrative's unfolding. Of course, returning to Pye's observations, we have not considered the role of the characters in this pattern. This is something we will consider in due course. For the moment, however, it is concerns over specific aspects of 'style' that have been characterised as interrupting the forward flow of the New Wave narrative. This is and will remain a matter of interpretation but the act of film interpretation itself is as much dependent upon the distribution or redistribution of critical emphasis as it is on anything else. The next question is: where does this new discussion of the film's opening lead us? To answer this we need to return, once more, to 'The British Cinema'.

The critical forest

Victor Perkins reserved special scorn for Schlesinger's debut feature film. Describing the film as inept and prone to blatant landscape-mongering, Perkins then chooses to demonstrate this by highlighting a moment from the film. As he writes:

> An example: the first 'love' scene in *A Kind of Loving* is filmed mainly in a medium shot which shows us the boy and girl necking in a park shelter. On the walls behind and to the side of them we see the usual graffiti of names and hearts. The setting makes, in this way, a fairly obvious but relevant comment on the action. But Schlesinger has no appreciation of the power of his décor; he destroys the whole effect by moving his camera to take the actors out of the shot and isolate the inscriptions in meaningless close-up. As if he hadn't done enough damage he continues the movement until we come to rest on a totally gratuitous detail: a poster forbidding mutilation of the shelter.[14]

Perkins is perfectly entitled to describe the film in this or any other way. This is one of the prerogatives that accompanies the act of writing film criticism. The problem is the way in which Perkins's self-confessed peevishness has never been reconsidered but, instead, has become an accepted way of thinking about this film. For example, writing forty years later about the same moment, John Gibbs is keen to reinforce Perkins's original criticism by justifying his accusation in the following way. As Gibbs continues:

> Such a camera movement inevitably draws attention to the director. This is not what Perkins is objecting to per se, he is bemoaning the heavy-handed manner with which Schlesinger guides the spectator's attention. Here the camera movement offers a commentary on the action but one in which the integral relationship between décor and action is sacrificed to make a directorial point.[15]

Gibbs is willing to align himself with Perkins without being prepared to return to the details of the moment. For an exponent of mise-en-scène criticism like Gibbs this is a real problem. A further problem arises when we actually consider what Gibbs is saying. For example, is the relationship 'between décor and action' really sacrificed so that Schlesinger can make a point? What kind of point is Schlesinger trying to make? Is Schlesinger's manner here is really as 'heavy-handed' as Gibbs is keen to stress? Is it true that Schlesinger has 'no appreciation of the power of his décor'? Are these questions really those that we should be asking? Is this just more evidence of the tendency to downplay the critical significance of the New Wave films? Where is the evidence needed for these criticisms to be sustained? Finally, is it the detail or the director that is more important here?

I consider the relationship between décor and action here to be a useful area of study but I am reluctant to make an interpretative claim about directorial intention. All too easily, claims of this kind smack of a critical callowness or else are smothered by a cloying over-appreciation that clouds discussion of the film in question. The question of motivation here is more about the critic than the detail or the director. For a perfect example of this consider what happened when *Film as Film* was reviewed by the British journal *Screen*.

Sam Rohdie begins by noting that Perkins's book was not the theorisation of *Movie* itself. However, the relationship between this critic and this journal is not one that can be easily overlooked. Perkins was a founding member of *Movie*'s editorial board and 'The British Cinema' was written on behalf of the board. His ideas connect him with other *Movie* critics and 'in its rationalisation of certain central *Movie* concerns of the 1960s' *Film as Film* 'only makes sense in the context of the *Movie* tradition'.[16] Notwithstanding the ideological intrigue with which this journal later became synonymous, Rohdie concludes that the closeness of this relationship was partly to blame for what he saw as a narrow and limited approach to the study of film. Rohdie was suspicious of Perkins's willingness to exclude considerations of 'the immediate present (Godard) and the distant past (Eisenstein)' and this led him to conclude:

> What appeared in the mid-1960s as new, an innovation, ends now as Romantic parody. The strain of Perkins's conservatism is evident in the rhetoric of the prose, a kind of incantation. It is no easy task to exclude the last decade of cinema, to ignore modern theory and to reject most of the past.[17]

Movie's critical project, despite its editors' protestations and talk of witness stands not judgement seats, was one of rejection and exclusion. Yet, stung by Rohdie's criticism, Perkins responded by suggesting that he was not trying to establish a theory of the cinema 'whose criteria will comprehend *La Règle du Jeu*, *Othon*, *The Bugs Bunny Show* and *The Modern Coal Burning Steam Locomotive*'. His project was much more modest and sensible and to demonstrate this Perkins concludes the defence of his approach with the following statement:

> The Hollywood film of the late 1950s and early 1960s is not an isolated freak; a theory which provides the tools for its understanding and judgement will function equally effectively for most of the films I have seen by Antonioni, Bresson, Chabrol, Dwan, Edwards, Feuillade, Griffith, Huston, Ince, Jewison, Kazan, Lubitsch, Mizoguchi, Nichols, Ophuls, Pabst, Quine, Renoir, Sirk, Tati, Ulmer, Visconti, Welles (Dammit), Young and Zeffirelli. My choice of illustration for my argument does more than 'reflect areas of my own enthusiasm and knowledge.'[18]

Does it though? In this new alphabetical addendum to the original *Movie* histogram there is still no room for Anderson, Clayton, Richardson, Reisz or Schlesinger and this makes me wonder whether Perkins is being a little disingenuous here. If Perkins's project is not to prescribe a theory that can be applied to 'the cinema' why does he then feel the need to produce a further list of directors he considers might be suitable for his attention? It is perfectly reasonable that personal responses to the cinema must inevitably include decisions about what will and what will not be watched, considered and examined.[19]

It is the range of Rohdie's criticisms and the problems with Perkins's response that are interesting here. Just like the earlier contradiction which informed Perkins's stance on the British New Wave, the problems here only add to my disquiet. We can link *Movie*'s original critical project to the calls for conservation made by Andrew Sarris when he asked why 'should anyone look at . . . the trees if the forest itself [Hollywood] be deemed aesthetically objectionable?' Despite the many critical projects embarked upon by pioneers such as *Movie*, it has always been that all the paths cut led to the same few clearings. The result of this has meant that whilst certain critics and commentators appear content to attend to the style and construction of their favourite trees – Hitchcock's sequoias, for example, the cherry blossoms of Mizoguchi or even the trees that grow in Vienna's Prater Park – significant other parts of the forest, starved of sunlight and dying in the deep shadows cast by the 'topmost' trees, have suffered ever since from a lack of detailed responsible analysis. To this end, it is now time for a new path to be cleared.[20]

A perfume named 'Desire'

It all begins with Vic catching the eye of Ingrid at his sister's wedding. They both work for the same company, Dawson Whittakers Limited. He is a draughtsman and she is a typist. There is an obvious attraction between them – we see this later in the staff canteen – and Vic finally gets his chance to talk to Ingrid when they find themselves on the same bus home. He breaks the ice by asking to borrow the bus fare and though the conversation is awkward at first he finally plucks up enough courage to ask her out on a date. They meet at the local cinema and the early stage of their relationship betrays all the classic signs of a burgeoning romance. Surrounded by people kissing, the atmosphere of the cinema is charged with an air of sexual possibility but it is not until Ingrid drops her glove that the couple properly touch. From here, Vic takes a chance and slides his arm around her shoulders. With the physical tension between them reduced, they start to flirt more openly. Vic admires her perfume. Ingrid tells him it is called 'Desire' and that she only wears it on special occasions. With the warmth growing between them

Ingrid moves closer to Vic and they share their first kiss. Buoyed by the success of their first date they arrange to meet again but this time Ingrid is accompanied by her best friend Dorothy (Patsy Rowlands). The awkwardness of their first date is now replaced by the inconvenience of a third person being present and Vic reacts angrily. Dorothy walks between them and generally gets in the way. Vic cuts a lonely figure as Ingrid and Dorothy buy toffees and window-shop. Finally, irritated by Dorothy's gossiping, Vic insults and then threatens her. With Dorothy now in tears and Ingrid unhappily caught between the two of them, Vic furiously walks away.

The couple do not see each other for some time but while Vic is having lunch at his sister's flat his brother Jimmy hands him a note from Ingrid. No longer angry, Vic is desperate to see Ingrid and leaves without eating. Ingrid is waiting in the local park and the couple talk over each other in their excitement. The park is on the top of a hill overlooking the town and as they begin to walk together the camera is positioned discreetly behind them. Just as it did with the church, the camera's movement here allows an aspect of the film's location – a public shelter – to come naturally into view. The length of the take also gives us a good view of the town in the distance. There is nothing extraordinary about its appearance here. This part of the film is shot on location, after all, and it is perfectly reasonable to see the town in this way at this moment. Far from being spectacular, seeing the town in the distance gives a sense of the ordinary, the commonplace and the usual to proceedings. Vic and Ingrid turn towards the shelter and only then does the film cut. The camera is now inside the shelter and this allows the couple to be framed in the doorway. As they enter the camera moves back, clearing a space for this intimacy to begin.[21]

Ingrid sits down straight away but Vic stands in the doorway. There is always an apprehensiveness to moments such as these, a brief pause when we want something like this to happen but do not always know quite how it should begin. It is clear from her expression that Ingrid feels the same way and both characters pause, poised and about to act upon their feelings for each other. This pause is also interesting because it gives us a chance to note the interior of the shelter. Clearly visible on the wall are the inscriptions of the many other couples who have come together here and the sight of this establishes a connection between the couple and their surroundings, a connection which is at once special but also very ordinary. Though this is the first time that Vic and Ingrid have found themselves in this position the décor demonstrates that they are not the first couple to take advantage of the shelter in this way and, once again, we get a sense of something natural and commonplace about to occur. Vic finally sits down and the film cuts again. As in the bus when they first met and the cinema where they first kissed, the couple sit side by side facing the camera. It was the dropping of a glove that initiated their first kiss in the cinema, and as Ingrid removes her glove here we can read this as a signal for what is to come. The camera certainly takes this as a cue and begins to move slowly forward.

Vic puts his arm around Ingrid. She nuzzles closer. The camera's position allows their bodies to fill the width of the frame. Ingrid explains that she did not want Dorothy to get in the way and as she apologises Vic's hand comes to rest on her shoulder. Slowly, it seems, the layers of their disagreement are melting away. They lean together and kiss. Vic begins to unbutton her coat. Another cut places the couple's faces at right angles and full in the frame now, Vic kisses her face and her neck and her ears while Ingrid continues to explain how she feels. Their lips meet again and this time there is a power to their passion. There is another cut and it is Vic who faces the camera now. With his eyes closed we can see that there is an equality to their attraction, an intensity that they evidently share.

A description of this kind is useful for gaining a sense of the feelings that Vic and Ingrid share, but it does little to help counter Perkins's criticism of this moment. We need to do more than just describe the actions of a boy and girl 'necking'. Adopting a more-rounded approach to the elements of this moment requires us also to consider the relationship between the actions of the two characters and the film's soundtrack.[22]

As we watch the couple we hear them tell each other how sorry they are and these are the ordinary sounds that you would expect to hear from lovers who have argued and are now trying to make amends. Likewise, we hear the rising sighs of Vic and Ingrid as the passion between the couple grows. They pull each other closer and kiss with a greater intensity but as they do so we suddenly hear footsteps on the soundtrack. Surprised by the sound, Vic and Ingrid spring apart. The film cuts to a brief shot of an embarrassed man walking past the shelter with his dog. Behind him, we get to see another shot of the town in the distance.

This interruption is interesting for several reasons. In this situation, the shelter is just too public a place for the couple to achieve real intimacy. Clearly the privacy offered by the camera's position in the doorway was only going to be a temporary one. Nevertheless, this moment offers a compelling insight into the relationship between the couple and their environment. When they first met in the park we saw the town stretched out in the distance before them. As they walked together the camera followed behind them and the shelter came into view. All of this occurred without a cut. When the film cuts here we get another view of the town in the distance. Looking out from the shelter, as if from the point of view of the couple, we still get to see the frame of the doorway.

Once again, a connection is made between the couple, the shelter and the broader view that surrounds them. Returning to Higson's earlier concerns over the status of such shots and the views of landscape they contain, I find little evidence of ambivalence or redundancy here. Nor do I find myself unduly concerned about the supposed tension between narration and description. In fact, I would question whether the issue of this tension is really that pertinent any more. After all, the use of locations in other modes of cinema is rarely questioned and/or criticised to the same extent as it has been in relation to the British New Wave. To this end, I certainly do not share Higson's concerns for visually arresting images working against the flow of the film and thus preventing us from understanding narrative meaning. In fact, the movement of the camera combines with the lack of a cut here to include the view of the town in such a way as to demonstrate its complete connectedness with the other elements found in the frame here. This means that there is little, if any, evidence of disjunction and incoherence. Though the use of locations might contrast greatly with previous methods of British film making, I get absolutely no sense of doubt or disquiet about the relationship between views of the town seen in *A Kind of Loving* and the film's unfolding. Rather, returning to the action, I find that this idea of complete integration actually offers us a clearer understanding of the relationship between Vic and Ingrid. This idea of integration is also evident when we consider the role the public shelter plays in the couple's courtship.

Despite the camera's proximity to the couple, the shelter does not represent an opportunity to escape the world they live and get on with the business of being alone together. Vic and Ingrid enact their rituals of courting and kissing firmly integrated within their environment, with all the potential for interruption that accompanies them. The shelter is not a privileged space where the couple have been transported by the film in order to consolidate their relationship away from the pressures and expectations of their everyday lives. Instead, it sits in the park where they meet. The park is in the town where they live. Like this, the relationship between the characters and their environment is made even more concrete. But there is something more here, something else of vital importance to our reading the rest of this sequence. The idea of the integration of elements here suggests that the presence of the footsteps on the soundtrack adds another dimension to this relationship between the couple, their environment and the film's construction. This further dimension is what will allow us to move beyond Perkins's facile dismissal of this moment.

With the embarrassed man having passed, the film cuts back to the couple. We see them catch their breath and can feel the disappointment that comes with the interruption of passion. They resume their kissing and as they do the camera begins to move slowly to the right. As the camera leaves the couple we get to see more graffiti scratched into the wood. The camera continues to move. We see more graffiti and then a sign which says that the shelter should not be defaced. The camera moves further to the right to reveal yet more graffiti. The film then cuts back to an extreme close shot of Vic and Ingrid caught up in the throes of passion. The joy on Ingrid's face is clearly visible over Vic's shoulder.

This is the camera movement that caused Perkins and Gibbs so much consternation. Gibbs bemoaned the heavy-handedness of the movement and Perkins felt this view of the graffiti and the sign to be totally gratuitous. Both believed that this moment of the film's style destroyed the relationship between the décor and the action taking place. But neither critic takes the soundtrack into account here. From both of their descriptions you would assume that the film was silent here and that the movement of the camera was the only thing of interest. Yet the film has already established a connection between the actions of the couple, the environment within which these actions take place and the manner, including the soundtrack, with which these actions are revealed. This means that when the camera moves away from the couple they are both still clearly audible off-screen. We hear Vic tell Ingrid how he is crazy about her. We also hear her sigh. With the connection between the couple and the environment, or décor, already established, this camera movement doesn't 'detach' itself from the action as Perkins and Gibbs would like to think. Both critics are wrong here. The soundtrack ensures that the camera movement is still linked to the couple. In fact, far from becoming isolated by virtue of its alleged over-prominence, this movement also acquires a thematic importance which integrates it still further into the importance and achievement of this moment. It does this by commenting on the routines and rituals of courtship. Seeing the graffiti makes us consider how many other couples have sought the shelter of this shelter and used it to snatch a brief moment of privacy. Hearing the sounds of pleasure on the soundtrack heightens the significance by making us consider other occasions when sounds of passion might have been heard here. Far from sitting clumsily on top of the moment, detaching itself from the film's unfolding, or being intrusive in any way, the camera movement is blended seamlessly with décor, character and theme.[23]

Writing in 'Moments of Choice', Perkins is keen to point out that editing and camera movements are specific decisions through which the direction of a film can alter viewpoint. For him, quite logically, this is part of a broader strategy whereby 'selection and sequence' are the keys to altering this viewpoint. Editing, for example, the cutting from one object to another, asserts 'continuity across a chopped-up time and space'. This is clearly evident in A Kind of Loving. In our opening example, the continuity of space and location between the church and the environment it is situated in remains intact, even when the first long take ends and the film cuts to change the camera's position. But we can strengthen our argument here if we consider the effect that moving the camera can have. As Perkins notes: 'To shift the frame via camera movement, on the other hand, is to impose an order of perception on objects which exist in a continuous time and space so that they could, in principle, be seen all at once.'[24] This idea is the perfect way in which we might come to reconsider the film's construction. For, far from destroying the relationship between objects in the frame – either through the overemphasis of a single element at the expense of others present or detaching the décor from the action – the camera's movement in these two examples imposes an order of perception in exactly the way that Perkins describes. Of course, as we should know by now, this is still a question of interpretation. Indeed, as Perkins continues:

> the expressiveness of a film style is so much a matter of balance, of what happens when you put together, in a particular way, a posture, a facial expression, an off screen voice and a camera viewpoint. At the very centre of the director's job is this task of co-ordination.[25]

Considering the fact that the views Perkins expressed in 'The British Cinema' have never been properly addressed, it is high time we reconsidered these criticisms ourselves and refused to recycle them without question. In this way, the critic's task, like the director's, also becomes one of co-ordination. The fundamental point about postures and viewpoints of any kind is that they exist to be reconsidered. Some clearly are but with others the emphasis is still waiting to be redistributed.

Notes

1   Andrew Sarris, 'Film Criticism in the Seventies', *Film Comment*, Vol. 14 (January/February 1978), pp. 9–11, p. 11.
2   '*Movie* Differences: A Discussion', *Movie*, No. 8 (April 1963), pp. 28–33, p. 33.
3   John Gibbs, *Mise-en-scène: Film Style and Interpretation*, London and New York, Wallflower Press, 2002, p. 100.
4   Andrew Higson, 'Space, Place, Spectacle: Landscape and Townscape in the "Kitchen Sink" Film', in *Dissolving Views: Key Writings on British Cinema*, London, Cassell, 1986, pp. 133–156, p. 135.
5   *Ibid.*, p. 134.
6   *Ibid.*, p. 134.
7   *Ibid.*, p. 135.
8   *Ibid.*, p. 135.
9   *Ibid.*, p. 135.
10 *Ibid.*, p. 138.
11 *Ibid.*, p. 149.
12 *Ibid.*, p. 150.

13   Douglas Pye, 'Movies and Point of View', *Movie*, No. 36 (Spring 2000), pp. 2–34, p. 9.

14   V.F. Perkins, 'The British Cinema', *Movie*, No. 1 (June 1962), pp. 2–7, p. 5.

15   John Gibbs, *It was Never All in the Script: Mise-en-Scène and the Interpretation of Visual Style in British Film Journals, 1946–1978* (University of Reading, 1999, PhD Thesis), p. 135.

16   Sam Rohdie, *Screen*, Vol. 13, No. 4 (Winter 1972/3), pp. 137–143, p. 141.

17   *Ibid.*, p. 143.

18   V.F. Perkins, 'A Reply to Sam Rohdie', *Screen*, Vol. 13, No. 4 (Winter 1972/3), pp. 146–151, p. 149.

19   As Janet Staiger notes in her discussion of film canons: 'In purely practical terms, a scholar of cinema cannot study every film ever made. Selection becomes a necessity and with selection usually comes a politics of inclusions and exclusions. Some films are moved to the centre of attention; others, to the margins.' And, for Staiger, there are several reasons for this movement. To begin with, there is the issue of efficiency. This can be defined as the institutionalising of a certain set of texts so that any subsequent referencing of them is both 'economical and brief'. Even with the best of intentions, this issue is immediately problematic because, as Staiger continues 'selection for efficiency and practicality can too easily slide into a politics of denigration and of exclusion that is based on the mistaken notion that those films regularly chosen are necessarily unique or superior'. Then there is the issue of 'order'. This is also a problematic process with, once again, an element of assumption involved. As Staiger continues: 'Another rationale for selection relates to a worthwhile goal of putting some order into the apparent chaos of so many films. Grouping, classifying, and finding typicality are long-honoured and traditional pursuits in the acquisition of knowledge. Hence large numbers of films are more easily handled if certain generalizing characteristics are determined. The idea of "Renaissance painting" or "realist drama" or "American horror films" provides a grip on a large and historically specific group of objects. Yet, very often, only a select set of works are given as examples of a group with these becoming not merely typical instances, but exemplaries. Logically, once the characteristics of a grouping are developed (noting, of course, the philosophical and logistical problems of such an act), any item in the set ought to be equally valid as an object of analysis' (Janet Staiger, 'The Politics of Film Canons', *Cinema Journal*, No. 3 (Spring 1985), pp. 4–23, pp. 8–10).

20   Of course, Sarris, like Gibbs, is describing critical approaches to Hollywood films. Nevertheless, in the light of the subsequent rediscovery and stylistic examination of this particular cinema his sentiments appear easily transferable (Andrew Sarris, *The American Cinema: Directors and Directions 1929–1968*, New York: E.P. Dutton & Co., Inc., 1968, pp. 20–22).

21   Characters framed in this way are important moments in cinema history – think of the framing of Ethan Edwards (John Wayne) at the end of John Ford's 1956 film *The Searchers*, for example – and Charles Affron notes the influence that such a moment can have on our understanding of a film when he writes: 'The doorway and its variant portals, gates, and French windows are the cinema's most insistent configurations of affect. A threshold

that invites crossing, the doorway is both vibrant with the dynamics of entrance and exit, and informed with the tread of our own experience. The range of that experience, from the habitual departures and arrivals through the front doors of our workaday lives to the rites of passage, initiations, and ceremonies enacted under ornamental canopies and aisles of crossed swords, is captured on the sills of cottages and cathedrals. Whether routine or mysterious, these traversals resonate with our sensorimotor responses and our memories. The modes of access to where we live, work and worship are privileged within the decorum of cinema' (Charles Affron, *Cinema and Sentiment*, Chicago, University of Chicago Press, 1982, p. 44). And in this case, of course, also where we love. For the camera's position here invites us to witness the couple crossing the threshold to a new intimacy.

22 As Douglas Pye continues in his discussion: 'In many (possibly most) cases, access to diegetic sound seems to correspond to the spatial relationship that the camera defines between the spectator and the action – the closer the camera is, the more easily we can hear the sound created in the fictional world; the further away the camera is, the more likely it is that the diegetic sound will be obscured or inaudible. In these cases, image and sound enact the same spatial relationship to the action, with our access apparently governed by the physical properties of sound that operate in our ordinary lives' (Pye, 'Movies and Point of View', p. 9).

23 In fact, the camera movement does something else here. In part, it also articulates the difficulties that courting couples such as Vic and Ingrid face when it comes to being alone together by artificially creating a brief moment of privacy for them.

24 V.F. Perkins, 'Moments of Choice', in A. Lloyd (ed.), *Movies of the Fifties* (London, Orbis, 1982), pp. 209–213, p. 213.

25 *Ibid.*

6 Straight lines and rigid readings: Arthur Seaton and the arc of flight

There is a passage of D.H Lawrence (it occurs in *Lady Chatterley's Lover*) that [F.R] Leavis was fond of quoting: 'It is the way our sympathy flows and recoils that really determines our lives. And here lies the importance of the novel properly handled: it can lead the sympathetic consciousness into new places, and away in recoil from things gone dead.' One can make the same claim for criticism 'properly handled': its function should equally be to 'lead the sympathetic consciousness into new places,' and that involves a constant readiness to change and modify one's own position as one's perception of human needs changes. (Robin Wood)[1]

Our judgements concerning the worth of things, big or little, depend on the *feelings* the things arouse in us. Where we judge a thing to be precious in consequence of the idea we frame of it, this is only because the *idea* is itself associated with a feeling. If we were radically feelingless, and if ideas were the only things our mind could entertain, we should lose all our likes and dislikes at a stroke, and be unable to point to any one situation or experience in life more valuable or significant than any other. (William James)[2]

A radio is not a louder voice, an aeroplane not a better car, and the motion picture (an invention of the same period of history) should not be thought of as a faster painting or a more real play.

All of these forms are qualitatively different from those which preceded them. They must not be understood as unrelated developments, bound merely by coincidence, but as diverse aspects of a new way of thought and a new way of life – one in which an appreciation of time, movement, energy, and dynamics is more immediately meaningful than the familiar concept of matter as a static solid anchored to a stable cosmos. (Maya Deren)[3]

Assumptions

Saturday Night and Sunday Morning ends with Arthur Seaton (Albert Finney) and his fiancée Doreen (Shirley Ann Field) sitting on a hill over-looking a new estate that is being built. Arthur's behaviour throughout the unfolding film has been characterised by a certain irresponsibility but, following an unwanted pregnancy and a beating from two soldiers, the implication is that Arthur will now submit to a more responsible future by marrying Doreen and living in one of these new houses. The film actually closes with him and Doreen walking down the hill and we never find out what happens to them in the future. Nevertheless, the connection between this character's behaviour and the events that befall him is seductive enough to make us want to speculate on the type of future he faces. Speculation of this kind is further fuelled by the idea that Arthur's rebelliousness has somehow been contained. This is the conclusion that John Hill reaches in his discussion of what he calls the 'new wave' narrative.

Hill reaches this conclusion by drawing on Tzvetan Todorov's concept of the passage in a narrative 'from one equilibrium to another'. This passage begins with a stable situation that is disturbed and thus becomes 'a state of disequilibrium'. Eventually, the original equilibrium is restored but now it is somehow different from the original situation. For Hill, the narrative of a film such as Reisz's loosely adheres to this model, with the film's central disturbance 'usually a socially or sexually transgressive desire'. Moreover, as Hill continues, this movement from disequilibrium to a new equilibrium is not random but patterned in terms of a linear chain of events. Typically, it is individual characters who become the agents of this causality. For Hill, this link between the film's causal chain and its central characters is essential when it comes to considering the ending of a film in question. As he explains:

> Implicit in the structure of the narrative, its movement from one equilibrium to another, its relations of cause and effect, is a requirement for change. But, in so far as the narrative is based upon individual agency, it is characteristic that the endings of such films should rely on individual, rather than social and political change. As a result, the resolutions characteristic of the working-class films tend to conform to one or other of two main types: the central character either *opts out of society or else adapts and adjusts to its demands.*[4]

Following Hill's logic, the question we should be asking is whether the film's ending signals Arthur's opting-out of society or his adjusting to its demands. If we were to view the film's causal logic as the best source for an answer then we would have to say that Arthur is adjusting to society's demands. But I wonder if it is really as simple as this. How can we reach a definitive conclusion about the film on the basis of such a general approach? The problem is the line of argument that Hill is choosing to follow.

Doubts and hesitations

Using words such as 'loosely', 'typically', 'should', and 'tend', Hill draws on the understanding of narration in the fiction film developed by David

Bordwell and Kristin Thompson. They, like Hill, place a particular emphasis upon the idea of causality. However, the template proposed by Bordwell and Thompson is not without its own conceptual problems. For example, here is Bordwell writing in *Film Art*:

> The number of possible narratives is unlimited. Historically, however, the cinema has tended to be dominated by a single mode of narrative form. In the course of this book we shall refer to this dominant mode as the 'classical Hollywood cinema' — 'classical' because of its wide and long history, 'Hollywood' because the mode assumed its definitive shape in American studio films. The same mode, however, governs many narrative films made in other countries . . . This conception of narrative depends on the assumption that the action will spring primarily from *individual characters as causal agents*.[5]

Straight away we need to be clear here. There is no denying the importance of causes and effects to the unfolding of a film, but the generalising tendency that stems from Bordwell's insistence on the idea that 'causality is the prime unifying principle' is problematic. Note, in particular, the use of 'tended' and 'assumption'. As he continues:

> The classical Hollywood film presents psychologically defined individuals who struggle to solve a clear-cut problem or attain specific goals. In the course of this struggle, the characters enter into conflict with others or with external circumstances. The story ends with a decisive victory or defeat, a resolution of the problem and a clear achievement or non-achievement of the goals. The principal causal agency is thus the character, a discriminated individual endowed with a consistent batch of evident traits, qualities, and behaviours.[6]

Bordwell's template lacks a suitable precision to make anything other than extremely general claims about individual films. Is it enough to say that the end of a fiction film can be characterised by victory *or* defeat, achievement *or* non-achievement? Or, like Hill, that a character opts-out *or* conforms? The vagueness troubles me here. An approach of this kind only takes us as far as classifying the ending of all 'New Wave' narratives in one of two ways. This is not enough when it comes to accounting for the differences between one film and another. The problem is in the methodology. As Douglas Pye explains in his discussion of the Bordwell model:

> The phrase 'Classical Hollywood Cinema' has itself achieved widespread currency among film critics and theorists. In effect, it has become a shorthand carrying the illusion of shared assumptions — we all know what that is. Whether we do is clearly another matter, but Bordwell, Staiger and Thompson's codification — by far the most detailed we have — shows every sign of becoming what it clearly intends to be: the standard reference point. It is therefore of particular importance to register doubts and hesitations.[7]

My hesitation, like Pye's, is derived from the fear that an insistence on causality is too general to be practical. This would not be a problem if we were content to categorise films as types, emphasising the features they have in common, as Hill does with the endings here. Yet, when it comes to being more specific, an approach of this kind is extremely limited. This is especially true when it comes to developing a better idea of a film's manner and meaning, for example. As Pye continues:

> in *The Classical Hollywood Cinema*, style is delineated as a matrix of formal conventions which govern articulation of time and space around a narrative dominated by coherent causality and consistent, goal-orientated characters. Beyond reference to story events and characters, the relationship between style and meaning is set aside.[8]

The result of this is that such a tendency will result in a complete underestimation of a particular film's complexities.[9] Elizabeth Cowie reaches the same conclusion in her discussion of Bordwell's model. With all possible deviations included within the definition itself, and every exception proving the rule, the church, for her, is 'so broad that heresy is impossible'.[10]

Hill's project differs greatly from my own, concerned as Hill is with providing an analysis of these films 'in relation to the social and economic context of their production'.[11] Nevertheless, to demonstrate the differences of detail that distinguish this film from others it is necessary to formulate a more specific understanding of the film's ending. One possible solution is to consider the approach outlined by Jeffrey Richards and Anthony Aldgate.

Context and history

Writing in 1983, Jeffrey Richards calls for an approach to British cinema based upon a 'contextual cinematic history' and an approach of this kind, Richards suggests,

> deals not in pure speculation but in solid research, the assembling, evaluation and interpretation of facts, the relating of films to the world, the search for an understanding through the medium of popular films of the changing social and sexual roles of men and women, the concepts of work and leisure, class and race, peace and war, the real determinants of change and continuity in the real world.[12]

Particular emphasis is placed 'on the exploration of the context within which a film was produced' and for Richards this involves three main lines of enquiry. We need to analyse a film's mise-en-scène to discover what the film is saying. The film must also be placed within the context of its production. This enquiry is ended by a consideration of reaction and reception. As Richards explains: 'To some extent, all three strands are interwoven, for popular cinema has an organic relationship with the rest of popular culture, and popular culture as a whole plays a part in the social and political history of its time.'[13]

It is critically counterproductive to consider any aspect of a film in isolation, and the idea of interwoven strands seems to concur with this. As Richards concludes: 'When all this evidence has been taken into account, we hope to show how feature films can be used to illuminate the history of this century at various key points.'[14] However, this approach demonstrates a degree of incompleteness when it comes to 'looking at the structure and the meaning of the film, as conveyed by the script, visuals, acting, direction, photography and music'. This is because the emphasis on the strands is not evenly distributed and returns us to the sense of asymmetry that *Movie*'s histogram originally created. To understand this we need to consider this approach in greater detail.

Aldgate's discussion of Reisz's film is based upon his asking: what is there to gain 'by seeking to place *Saturday Night and Sunday Morning* in its "proper" historical context'. Aldgate aims to do this by considering the film's ending. For him, the conclusion gives the whole narrative an attractive ambiguity and this does seem like an extremely good place to start. However, Aldgate's discussion falls some way short of actually considering this ambiguity in greater detail. He immediately downplays any interest that it might have in relation to the film's structure and meaning and thus unwittingly demonstrates the limits of this approach. As he writes:

> In certain circumstances, of course, this [ambiguity] can be said to indicate a rich and dense artistic text, in short, a 'classic', which is precisely the status that some have accorded to the film of *Saturday Night and Sunday Morning* in the British cinema. And it cannot be denied that the film has many admirable and enduring qualities. But in this case the ambiguities were hardly the result of any creative input; they arose from the contingencies of its production.[15]

To illuminate his argument, Aldgate chronicles the difference of opinion between scriptwriter and director. Aldgate cites a difference of opinion over the final fate of Arthur Seaton (Albert Finney), the film's central character. Alan Sillitoe's purpose 'was to show that Arthur had indeed changed since the beginning of the film and that he was in many ways the same person'. By contrast, Reisz 'is reported to have viewed the ending of the film as a surrender.'[16]

However, as Aldgate acknowledges, Reisz later felt that he wasn't 'too keen' on the stone-throwing ending and for Aldgate this imbues the ending with an ambiguity. My interest in following what appears to be a well-trodden path is to take a closer look at Aldgate's conclusions and question whether they properly satisfy the criteria of the contextual-cinematic approach advocated here.[17]

Context and reception

Does an approach of this kind really 'analyse what the film is saying'? Aldgate acknowledges that the film displays an ambiguity which *might* be interesting but he is more interested in the possibility that this ambiguity is derived from the interaction between the intentions of the scriptwriter, the director and the British Board of Film Classification. For Aldgate this means that the film's richness in other areas, certainly in the structure and the meaning of the film – a central tenet of the approach he and Richards espouse – becomes overlooked by recounting the story behind the making of the film. Here, context undermines or, in fact, nullifies the importance of the film's specific detail. There is a clear inequality of emphasis here. The problem is that all 'this evidence' has not been taken into account. If an approach is based upon three central and seemingly equal tenets then why should one of them suffer disproportionately in terms of attention? Would not it be far simpler just to remove the first of these tenets from the approach? The end result – Aldgate's discussion of *Saturday Night and Sunday Morning* – would certainly lose its imbalance. My criticism of this approach is completely arbitrary but, as Aldgate acknowledges in the revised version of *Best of British*, this is not a problem. As he explains:

> To better understand the precise points at issue in dealing with mainstream British cinema down the years, it is probably useful to adopt a chronological approach to its historiography. However arbitrary it may sometimes appear to divide a broad expanse of time into shorter discrete periods, this at least offers a twofold advantage in allowing for detailed comparison between differing methodologies and interpretations as applied to specific filmic examples, while also retaining a broad overview of contrasting reactions to the major sea changes affecting British cinema generally (not to mention social changes at large).[18]

Even here Aldgate is not completely certain. The best he can suggest is that it is 'probably useful' to adopt such an approach but when presented with the chance to apply an interpretation to a specific film example – in this case the ending of Reisz's film – his desire to maintain 'a broad overview' prevents him from doing so. The specific details of a film's manner and construction appear less important than the detailed establishment of the context that surrounds it.

This surprises me because the contextual-historical approach is keen to remove the distance between film studies and cinema history. As Richards suggests in 'Rethinking British Cinema':

Neither camp has an exclusive monopoly of wisdom. Both are needed. Both are valuable. Recently there has been a rewarding convergence between the two approaches, as cinema historians have taken on board some of the more useful and illuminating of the theoretical developments, such as gender theory, and the Film Studies scholars have been grounding their film analysis more securely in historical context.[19]

The problem is that the balance between these two camps has never been properly reconsidered. Scholars of film (studies) such as Perkins can aggressively deride the British cinema for not containing sufficiently interesting detail to make a study of its mise-en-scène worthwhile. Proponents of (cinema) history such as Richards and Aldgate over-rely upon context to ensure that British films are suitably cocooned in a historical discussion so as to be preserved from sustained stylistic investigation. The time is right for us to be more radical here and less defensive. Consider, for example, the rest of Richards's discussion. As he continues:

> Criticism is of course inevitable and desirable, but it is best delivered in a spirit of gentleness and good humour. For we are, when all is said and done, all colleagues in the wider struggle against the enormous condescension of the likes of François Truffaut who famously declared the terms British and cinema to be incompatible.[20]

Also:

> A regular criticism of Cinema History is that it is devoid of theory. As an empiricist of many years standing, I feel that it is worth pointing out to the proponents of that argument that empiricism is a theory and one that is longer established and more thoroughly tried and tested than some of the more fashionable but short-lived theories of recent years.[21]

This defensiveness raises two interesting points. Firstly, it is not clear from this declaration whether we are all involved in the struggle against the same critical condescension. A critic like Perkins would happily agree with Truffaut and be more inclined to condescension than he or she would be to defending British films from claims of incompatibility with the medium itself. Neither is it clear whether the struggle Richards claims we are involved in is even against the same opponents. I am not convinced that 'French linguistic theories' have done the kind of critical damage to British films as have those assertions that a British film lacks a mise-en-scène suitable for sustained discussions of style and meaning. This defensiveness surprises me because Richards takes the opportunity to rephrase and re-emphasise the three concerns of his approach. As he reiterates:

> The empirical cinema historian deals for the most part not in mere speculation but in solid archival research, the assembling, evaluation and interpretation of the facts about the production and reception of films. Particular emphasis

is placed on establishing and exploring the context, social, cultural, political and economic, within which the film was produced. The empirical cinema historian has three main concerns. The first is to analyse the content of the individual film and ascertain how its themes and ideas are conveyed by script, mise-en-scène, acting, direction, editing, photography and music.[22]

I have repeated only the first concern here because what is of more interest is this continued insistence upon examining the mise-en-scène of the film in question. This is the second time that Richards has called for an analysis of a film that 'ascertains how its themes and ideas are conveyed' but it is obvious that questions of context and reception have a higher priority. This is disappointing because, despite acknowledging the influence that *Movie* has had upon British film criticism, Richards is unwilling to go any further. An empirical approach of this kind would certainly be suited to re-evaluating 'The British Cinema's' prominence in the chronological history of British film criticism. This would be as much a study of context as it would be of reception and would further define the opponents against whom scholars of British film are struggling. But Richards chooses not to do this directly. The best he can manage is the hope that this might happen one day. As he writes:

> It is perhaps a measure of the way in which Cinema History and Film Studies have evolved in the last thirty years that it now would be perfectly possible to read a journal article or hear a conference paper entitled 'Issues of gender and genre: the cases of *An Alligator Named Daisy*, *Above Us the Waves* and *Ramsbottom Rides Again*'.[23]

Richards's use of the word 'possible' here alarms me. Like Aldgate's earlier use of 'probably', the reticence is there for all to see and becomes indicative of a disavowal. Despite calling for the discussion of a film's mise-en-scène to be included, it appears that such a discussion has no real place in the contextual-historical approach. To address this imbalance properly it is necessary to return to the film's ending.

The qualities of framing

As Arthur and Doreen sit on the hill, the camera is positioned behind the couple and the estate stretches out in the distance behind them. When we first see Arthur and Doreen together they are positioned very close to the camera. Doreen fills the foreground of the frame and leans back over her shoulder to talk to Arthur. He is positioned on the edge of the frame, half-in and half-out of the shot. The estate is partially obscured by the couple but a construction sign is visible and reveals that these are new houses that have not quite been finished. The initial composition here is cramped and slightly awkward. Knowing the narrative events that have led to this point – including Brenda's unwanted pregnancy with Arthur and the beating he receives as a result of this affair being discovered – it is tempting to conclude that Arthur is being forced to settle down in order to avoid getting into further trouble. Following the causal route espoused by Bordwell and Hill makes this conclusion almost inevitable. This conclusion is ostensibly endorsed by the film's construction here.

Arthur tells Doreen that he would be happy to live in an old house but she wants a new one, 'with a bathroom and everything'. Doreen's desire for a new house combines with her central position within the frame to create the impression that she is perfectly happy to have her future outlined in this way. Arthur's initial position, however – half-in and half-out of the frame – does not necessarily give the same impression. Before this consideration threatens to interrupt the causal line Arthur stands up and the camera rises with him. Arthur is now clearly contained within the straight edges of the frame and the composition appears to support the theory that the film's causal trajectory has forced Arthur into this position. Arthur, for Hill, at least, is finally adjusting to society's demands. His position, like Doreen's, is defined by the boundaries of the frame. This idea is further aided by the view of the new houses behind him. Character and landscape appear fused at this point. Arthur then turns to throw a stone in the direction of the houses. Doreen asks him why he threw a stone and he tells her that he does not know. He also tells her that it will not be the last one he throws.

This new exchange between them is revealed in a series of alternating close shots, and the tightness of the framing seems to contradict this final expression of personal freedom. (In fact, this brief series of close shots can be used as further evidence of Arthur's 'adjusting' by appearing like a succession of photographs. You can almost picture them framed and sitting on the mantelpiece of the new house they will move into.) With all the evidence in place, the causal chain that has led Arthur to this point is completed when he takes Doreen by the hand and the couple walk down the hill towards – you would imagine – their future life.

Straight lines and rigid readings

Using a causal template to account for the passage between Arthur's initial irresponsibility to the 'conformity' that closes the film is very attractive. *Saturday Night and Sunday Morning* appears to fit perfectly within the Bordwell/Hill causal model. After all, the film is concerned with a man who works in a factory and spends his working hours operating a lathe on the production-line. As we can see from the film's opening sequence, the repetitive nature of the many jobs on the shop-floor of the bicycle factory leaves very little room for self-expression of any kind. Arthur makes a point of comparing himself with other older workers who, he says, have been ground down in a way that he means to avoid. As we watch it becomes apparent that Arthur is being paid per item he produces, and the process of counting the finished items, as well as counting down the amount left until he can finish for the day, makes his job as repetitive as any other. There is further evidence of this when the factory siren finally sounds for the end of the day.

The film cuts to a view of the factory from outside. The camera is positioned high above the ground and this position allows us to watch the workers leave. Men and women enter the frame from various points and slowly the frame begins to fill. The interest in this moment can be found in the direction taken by the workers, all moving in the same direction at the same time. This journey from work to home, like the one they make in reverse, from home to work, becomes a metaphor for the rigidity and repetition that governs their lives. In addition, this daily routine is characterised by a uniformity of direction, a linearity that is specific to a life structured in this way. This is certainly the case for Arthur. Our introduction to Arthur is accompanied by a voice-over in which he asserts his rebellious nature but, as we soon discover, Arthur enjoys the money too much to make a proper stand against the bastards trying to grind him down. Arthur's rebellion is limited to working well within himself so as not to be further exploited than he already is, getting as drunk as he possibly can on a Saturday night, sleeping with the wife of a colleague and shooting his nosy neighbour with an air-rifle. Seen this way, it is little wonder that the character's path across the narrative seems as linear as the production-line he works upon. As the film ends, the trajectory of Arthur's life can easily be defined in this way, with a straight line from work to marriage to buying a house to having children and watching television. Ultimately, then, the film's ending might easily be understood as Arthur being unable to break free from the straight lines of the rigid routine that have come to frame his life. This is the simplest way in which we might come to understand the film. As always, however, rigid readings are prone to problems.

In a separate discussion of film style, Bordwell and Thompson turn to the subject of framing. As they write:

> Sometimes we are tempted to assign absolute meanings to angles, distances, and other qualities of framing. It is tempting to believe that framing from a low angle automatically 'says' that a character is powerful and that framing from a high angle presents him or her as dwarfed or defeated. Verbal analogies are especially seductive: A canted frame seems to mean that 'the world is out of kilter.'[24]

If this was the case every time, they argue, 'individual films would thereby lose much of their uniqueness and richness. The fact is that framings have no absolute or general meanings.' As they continue:

In *some* films, angles and distances carry such meanings as mentioned above, but in other films – probably most films – they do not. To rely on such formulas is to forget that meaning and effect always stem from the total film, from its operation as a system. The context of the film will determine the function of the framings, just as it determines the function of mise-en-scène, photographic qualities, and other techniques.[25]

Applying this discussion to the film's ending helps to cast considerable doubt upon the conclusions reached. Admittedly, the context of the film will determine the function of the framings but if the discussion of this film is to successfully emphasise its difference from the other New Wave films then the need is to avoid assigning absolute meanings to the qualities of framing here. This also means that following the causal line taken by Bordwell and Hill is not the best way to achieve this. However tempting it may be, the conclusions reached by such an approach are just too rigid and lack the flexibility to include the possibility that the film ends with an element of ambiguity.

Returning to the contextual-historical approach is one way in which we can start to break free from the rigid causal interpretation of the film. Aldgate's discussion of the film makes the claim for the film being open-ended. However, because Aldgate is unwilling to develop his investigation of the film by examining its mise-en-scène the strength of the claim for the film's ambiguity is significantly weakened. The principal reason for this is the lack of a personal engagement with the details of the film itself. Aldgate's discussion of the film's ending involves his considering the views of both the script writer and the director but it does fall short of engaging with the film's mise-en-scène. This would not matter apart from the fact that an engagement of this kind is supposed to be central to his approach. The contextual-historical approach appears to be as limited as the straight lines followed by Bordwell and Hill. The 'containment' of Arthur Seaton stands as a useful metaphor for certain tendencies in the history of British film criticism. Whether bound by an adherence to linearity, tightly framed by a discussion of context alone or, in the case of 'The British Cinema', simply rejected out of hand, the distance that exists between British film studies and the history of its cinema is still far wider than Richards believes. This is not to say that all is lost. Indeed, it is the very ambiguity that Aldgate's discussion touches on but does not explore that will reduce this distance.

Throwing stones

This sequence begins with the camera placed on the side of a hill overlooking a new housing estate. In the distance, on the right side of the frame, we can see a man and a woman walking down the hill. Though they are too far away for their faces to be visible it is their direction which is the most interesting. The camera begins to move slowly to the left and as it does so the broad expanse of the estate is revealed. Following a minor positional adjustment, the camera comes to rest on Arthur and Doreen. Arthur's position within this initial composition places him half-in and half-out of the frame and hints at an uncertainty but this uncertainty is immediately dispelled by the subsequent tighter framings of Arthur. Now, however, I want to consider the range of Arthur's positions within the frame more carefully.

Doreen is keen to live in a house like the ones being built because she says so. Arthur is not so keen and his initial position can be used to strengthen this claim. However, this position is not maintained for the rest of the sequence. As Arthur stands up it is immediately followed by a much more conventional framing of the character, one that places him *within* its straight edges. This is where the sense of Arthur's containment comes from. This sense is heightened by the closer tighter shots that characterise their conversation and is apparently completed when Arthur takes Doreen's hand and they head off down the hill. Yet there is the possibility that the film's ending is not as tightly framed as we might think. The relationship between the characters' positions in the frame and the unfolding of the narrative that has led us to this point is, in fact, coloured by a variety of subtle possibilities that prevents us from making any kind of absolute claims about this crucial part of the film.

Following their brief exchange about the age of the house that they would prefer to live in, Arthur stands up, and this action is interesting for three reasons. Firstly, and rather obviously, as he stands, the camera moves up with him. Secondly, more importantly, this double movement, of camera and of performer, frees Arthur from the frame he shared with Doreen. Thirdly, and most significantly, this reconfiguration of positions places Arthur clearly *within* the straight edges of the frame. But what are we meant to make of this? At this point the emphasis is now on Arthur's position within his world but care is needed when articulating this emphasis. Earlier, I suggested that this new framing denotes the moment at which Arthur's containment is signalled once and for all within the film. Now, however, bearing in mind the warning about using the frame to make statements about the character, I do not want to be so definitive.

A closer inspection of the composition here reveals that Arthur occupies the right-hand side and the rest of the frame is filled with a view of the estate behind him. The frame is divided equally between these two elements and this is what makes this moment so interesting. One reading of this would consider this a compositional ploy to effectively merge Arthur with his life-to-come by placing an equal emphasis on the character's initial position and the new position he will eventually move into. Alternatively, the arrangement says something about the weighing-up of options. Arthur is faced with choosing the path of responsibility that leads down the hill, the path of irresponsibility that is likely to lead to more beatings and more domestic dramas or a further direction that will involve both of these paths somehow running in parallel. Either way, and this list is certainly not meant to be exhaustive, the film's manner and construction here is sufficiently interesting to allow the equal suspension of several (potentially conflicting) ways of viewing the film's ending. We should not be concerned with the accusations of subjectivity that might be levelled at this list. As Raymond Durgnat asks us to consider:

> Suppose a film ends with the camera tracking back from the lovers embracing alone on the beach. This may mean 'how tiny and unprotected they are' or 'how frail and futile their love' or 'the whole wide world is theirs' or 'this is the moment of destiny' (for plan views can suggest a 'God's-eye-view') or 'Good-bye, good-bye', depending on which emotions are floating about in the spectator's mind as a result of the rest of the film. Hence style is essentially a matter of intuition. There is no possibility whatsoever of an 'objective', 'scientific' analysis of film style – or of 'film' content. It is worse than useless to attempt to watch a film with one's intellect alone, trying to explain its effect in terms of one or two points of style. Few films yield any worthwhile meaning unless watched with a genuine interest in the range of feelings and meanings it suggests.[26]

Now let's continue by considering what Arthur does when he stands up.

The arc of flight

Having told Doreen how he and Bert, his cousin, used to play here when they were kids, Arthur turns to face the estate and throws a stone into the distance. Following existing logic, Arthur's action could be seen as the final act of defiance from a man who realises that it is time for him to start behaving more responsibly. This is certainly possible when we consider the way in which the following exchange between Doreen and Arthur is constructed:

[1]   Close shot of Doreen. She asks Arthur why he threw the stone.

[2]   Close shot of Arthur. The camera is positioned as if from Doreen's point of view.

[3]   Same as [1]. Doreen looks off screen and suggests that one of those houses might be theirs.

[4]   Same as [2]. Arthur tells her that he is not sure why he threw the stone.

[5]   Same as [1]. Doreen tells him that he should not throw things.

[6]   Same as [2]. Arthur looks down and tells Doreen that it will not be the last one he throws.

[7]   Same as [1]. Doreen silent.

[8]   Same as [2]. Arthur silent as well.

The editing strategy here does seem to imply containment. As they discuss the possible trajectory of their future life together, the exchanges between the couple are tightly framed. Despite Arthur telling Doreen that it will not be the last stone he throws, this sequence, and the film, ends with him reaching down to take Doreen's hand and walking down the hill presumably towards their new life. Once again, however, this moment, like before, is weighted with more than one possibility. Consider, for example, the shared silence which concludes their conversation in shots 7 and 8.

If we consider this moment to signal nothing more than Arthur's defiance and Doreen's resignation that her life with him may contain other episodes of 'stone-throwing' then this at least starts to free our reading from the earlier linearity. This shared silence implies an acknowledgement of the future struggle for (a kind of) independence within the confines of a highly structured life. It also signals a shared uncertainty about the way their lives will unfold. One further idea is that both Arthur and Doreen, for similar or different reasons, are lost for words. This moment indicates an equal split between the contradictory desires of settling down and remaining independent and this is because there is an interesting connection between the shared silence and Arthur's throwing a stone. This action can be seen as a simple act of defiance. As Arthur tells Doreen, it will not be the last one he throws. This is certainly in keeping with the way Arthur's character is presented, especially through the monologue that opens the film, when he talks about not letting anyone grind him down. We might see it as something less advanced than making a stand. It could just be an act of mindless vandalism, exactly the sort of thing that someone frustrated might do when they lack the opportunity for adequate personal expression. (This would connect Arthur's action here with his earlier shooting of Mrs Bullock.) Both indicate a willingness to lash out at the world without properly considering the consequences. Doreen sees it this way when she tells him that he should not do things like that, especially as one of the houses he aims at might be theirs one day. This view is also reinforced by Arthur's inability to say why he did it. As before, this act can be read in more than one way. Arthur's stone-throwing has a further connection with ideas of self-expression, of wishing for something or hoping that something might happen, even if it is not clear what this something might be. For a better understanding of this idea we need to consider another example of the same act from a different film.

In *It's a Wonderful Life*, George Bailey finds himself in a similar position to Arthur. Caught between his girlfriend's desire to settle down and his own desire to remain independent, George stops outside a deserted house and throws a stone. This action, as he tells Mary (Donna Reed), also requires you to make a wish. We know by this point in the film that George is desperate not to follow the pre-ordained path that will see him inherit his father's business and remain in his home town. Thus, his throwing a stone is accompanied by the wish that he will leave home and see the world. In this example, and unlike Doreen, Mary also throws a stone and makes her own wish.

The significance of Mary's action is that she keeps her silence when George asks her what she wished for. Despite this, it is made quite clear that she wishes for George to stay where he is so that the two of them can settle down together. The connection between these two films cannot be pursued too strenuously but I am interested in the idea that the narrative of Capra's film, like Reisz's, appears to direct its central character through a series of events which culminate in his containment. Admittedly, the character of Arthur appears to have more control over events than George. Nevertheless, the limits of the life he leads, irrespective of brief acts of rebellion, ensure that, ultimately, Arthur's life has a similar feel to George Bailey's. Further, and though the point is made more explicitly in Capra's film, George, like Arthur, appears caught between two conflicting desires. Though Arthur has never suggested that he wants to leave Nottingham in order to better himself, he is caught between the desire for an independent life, to whatever degree, and the kind of domestic life that would accompany settling down with Doreen. Though he does not actively make a wish when he throws his stone I still want to emphasise the ambiguity of this action. Even Arthur is not sure why he acts this way but it is this lack of clarity that allows us to give his action more than one interpretation. This ambiguity is the same one that Aldgate highlighted in his discussion but, rather than just agree with Aldgate, it is important to understand the way in which this ambiguity is related to the film's manner and meaning.

On each occasion, the moment in question defies a singular reading by allowing a variety of interpretations to circulate in place simultaneously. Rather than following the kind of singular linear route that charts the passage from Arthur's rebelliousness to his finally accepting responsibility, this is only one of several co-existing possibilities. The alleged linearity of Arthur's trajectory across the narrative might be better described as having a more circular sense, and this is derived from the various possibilities that happen to orbit each moment. Interestingly, as Ralph Waldo Emerson famously wrote, the life of a man 'is a self-evolving circle, which, from a ring imperceptibly small, rushes on all sides outwards to new and larger circles'. Inherent in this idea is the possibility of different outcomes. As Emerson explains:

> The extent to which this generation of circles, wheel without wheel will go, depends on the force or truth of the individual soul. For, it is the inert effort of each thought having formed itself into a circular wave of circumstance – as, for instance, an empire, rules of an art, a local usage, a religious rite, – to heap itself upon that ridge, and to solidify, and to hem in the life.[27]

The question here is one of perspective but I am happy to propose that the words of a nineteenth-century American Transcendentalist can help to shed light on two days in the life of a Nottingham factory worker.[28] As Joel Porte explains:

> Emerson, as he himself frequently insisted, is fundamentally a poet whose meaning lies in his manipulation of language and figure. The best guide to change, or growth, or consistency in Emerson's thought, is his poetic imagination and not his philosophic arguments or discursive logic. The alert reader can discover, and take much pleasure in discovering, remarkable verbal strategies, metaphoric repetitions and developments of sound, sense, and image throughout Emerson's writing.[29]

And Porte's words here, with his talk of developments and repetitions, are perfectly in keeping with the type of style-based criticism that should be applied to films such as *Saturday Night and Sunday Morning*. This makes the act of stone-throwing a suggestion, whether conscious or not, that the straight edges of the frame need not be as rigid as they would appear. This reading stands in stark contrast to the tight framing of the character, and this contrast hints at a dramatic tension that sits at the heart of this film. This, in turn, following Robin Wood, suggests a broader tension that can be said to exist between matters of ideology, theories of genre and questions of authorship.

It is the interaction of these three things which, for Wood, determines a richness and density of meaning. Wood is concerned with what he calls 'the great Hollywood masterpieces' and the films he discusses are Alfred Hitchcock's *Shadow of a Doubt* (1943) and *It's a Wonderful Life*. Nevertheless, he is keen to juxtapose films of 'comparable stature but of very different authorial and generic determination' in order 'to raise other and wider issues'. Capra's film bears sufficient comparison with Reisz's to allow this idea of juxtaposition to be entertained. As Wood continues:

> I want to stress here the desirability for the critic – whose aim should always be to see the work, as wholly as possible, as it is – to be able to draw on the discoveries and particular perceptions of each theory, each position, without committing himself exclusively to any one. The ideal will not be easy to attain, and even the attempt raises all kinds of problems, the chief of which is the validity of evaluative criteria that are not supported by a particular system.[30]

Certainly, the arc of flight of Arthur's stone ensures that it lands beyond the frame and this becomes a metaphor for the ongoing project of rethinking British cinema. As a correlation, close attention to the film's detail becomes one way in which we might break free from the rigidity of existing trends in British film criticism. It is only by relating pertinent moments of individual detail to broader questions of interpretation, meaning and the process of criticism itself that we can begin to redefine the straight-lined frames and rigid templates of history, the cocoon of context and the limits of existing critical approaches to British films. This is essential if we are to narrow the gap between (British) film studies and (its) cinema history.

Notes

1 Robin Wood, *Hitchcock's Films Revisited*, London, Faber and Faber, 1989, p. 43.
2 William James quoted in Stephen C. Rowe, *The Vision of James*, Rockport, MA, Element, 1996, p. 51.
3 Maya Deren, 'Cinematography: The Creative Use of Reality', in Gerald Mast, Marshall Cohen and Leo Braudy (eds), *Film Theory and Criticism: Introductory Readings*, fourth edition, New York, Oxford University Press, 1992, pp. 59–70, p. 69.
4 John Hill, *Sex, Class and Realism: British Cinema 1956–1963*, London, BFI Publishing, 1986, pp. 54–57.
5 David Bordwell and Kristin Thompson, *Film Art: An Introduction*, fourth edition, New York, McGraw-Hill, Inc., 1993, p. 82.
6 David Bordwell, *Narration in the Fiction Film*, London, Routledge, 1985, p. 157.
7 Douglas Pye, 'Bordwell and Hollywood', *Movie*, 33 (Winter 1989), pp. 46–52, p. 46. Janet Staiger was the third person involved in the writing of *The Classical Hollywood Cinema: Film Style and Mode of Production to 1960*, London, Routledge, 1985.
8 Pye, 'Bordwell and Hollywood', p. 47.
9 *Ibid.*, p. 52.
10 Elizabeth Cowie, 'Storytelling: Classical Hollywood Cinema and Classical Narrative', in Steve Neale and Murray Smith (eds), *Contemporary Hollywood Cinema*, London and New York, Routledge, 1998, pp. 178–190, p. 178.
11 Hill, *Sex, Class and Realism*, p. 177.
12 Jeffrey Richards and Anthony Aldgate, *Best of British: Cinema and Society 1930–1970*, Oxford, Basil Blackwell Publisher Limited, 1983, p. 6.
13 *Ibid.*, p. 8.
14 *Ibid.*, p. 14.
15 *Ibid.*, p. 140.
16 *Ibid.*, p. 141.
17 As Aldgate explains: 'In fairness to Reisz it should be said that by [1985, when Alexander Walker's *National Heroes* was first published] he was no longer "too keen" on the stone-throwing ending to the film. But if it was a "feeling of frustration" he was looking for as he was directing the film's final scenes, then he had certainly created that and a lot more besides. He had invested them with ambiguity and confusion.' Aldgate also highlights a further ambiguity over the film's handling of Brenda's abortion. As he continues: 'As with the stone-throwing end of the film, the question of Brenda's pregnancy was left unresolved. Sillitoe's original intent was

changed, and considerable confusion was generated as a result. In production integrity gave way to expediency, and clarity of purpose was rendered obscure.' (Brenda, played by Rachel Roberts, is the wife of one of Arthur's colleagues, Jack (Bryan Pringle), and falls pregnant while having an affair with Arthur.) Notwithstanding this potential obscurity, Aldgate is led to conclude: 'Without doubt, *Saturday Night and Sunday Morning* presented a faithful and realistic picture of an industrial working-class environment in a way that had rarely been evident in the British cinema before. It fully acknowledged the presence of sexuality and violence in the world it depicted and carefully detailed some of the changes that new-found affluence had wrought among the working-class in this country . . . In many ways, then, the film was indeed a film of 1960, and it was imbued with much of the spirit and vision that permeated the cultural revolution of its day. The times had changed, and *Saturday Night and Sunday Morning* reflected a good many of the changes and developments. Yet its vision was by no means unbounded or untrammelled; it was appropriately compromised from the start – the traditional dictates of the film-making process saw to that. To place the film in its context is to appreciate that in some respects the revolution had only just begun' (*ibid.*, pp. 142–143). See also Alexander Walker, *National Heroes: British Cinema in the Seventies and Eighties*, London, Harrap, 1985.

18   Jeffrey Richards and Anthony Aldgate, *Best of British: Cinema and Society 1930–1970*, London, I.B. Tauris, 1999, p. 235.
19   Jeffrey Richards, 'Rethinking British Cinema', in Justine Ashby and Andrew Higson (eds), *British Cinema, Past and Present*, London and New York, Routledge, 2000, pp. 21–34, p. 21.
20   *Ibid.*, pp. 21–22.
21   *Ibid.*, p. 22.
22   *Ibid.*, p. 22.
23   *Ibid.*, p. 25.
24   Bordwell and Thompson, *Film Art*, p. 213.
25   *Ibid.*, pp. 213–214.
26   Raymond Durgnat, *Durgnat on Film*, London, Faber and Faber, 1976, p. 27. This process is also aided by the film's manner which as Alan Lovell explains, almost constitutes an 'anti-style'. For Lovell, 'the camera does only enough work to tell the story as simply and directly as possible. Because of this the audience is encouraged to make judgements for itself' (Alan Lovell, 'Film Chronicle', *New Left Review*, 7 (January–February 1961), pp. 52–53, p. 52).
27   *Emerson's Prose and Poetry*, selected and edited by Joel Porte and Saundra Morris, London, W.W. Norton & Company, 2001, p. 175.
28   As Emerson famously wrote elsewhere: 'We live amid surfaces, and the true art of life is to skate well on them. Under the oldest moldiest conventions, a man of native force prospers just as well as in the newest world, and that by skill of handling and treatment. He can take hold anywhere. Life itself is a mixture of power and form, and will not bear the least excess of either. To finish the moment, to find the journey's end in every step of the road, to live the greatest number of good hours, is wisdom. It is not the part of men,

but of fanatics, or of mathematicians, if you will, to say, that, the shortness of life considered, it is not worth caring whether for so short a duration we were sprawling in want, or sitting high. Since our office is with moments, let us husband them' (Ralph Waldo Emerson, 'Experience', in *Self-Reliance and Other Essays*, New York: Dover Publications Inc., 1993, p. 90).

29 Joel Porte, 'The Problem of Emerson', in Porte and Morris, *Emerson's Prose and Poetry*, pp. 679–697, p. 685.

30 Wood, pp. 288–289.

Bodies, critics and *This Sporting Life*

If you're shooting dramatic material the kind of privacy and manoeuvrability you get in a studio is a great advantage. I should not like to have had to film *This Sporting Life*, with its extended dramatic scenes, on location. The world is on top of you on location, and this can often make it very difficult for the actors. But there is one very great advantage in working on location, which is that you engage your own unit, and can handpick them yourself. (Lindsay Anderson)[1]

Knuckles are being rapped all over the place; exhibitionist harangue has to be disentangled from useful truth. But at least there is an awareness that criticism is a discipline, although one which resists attempts to pin it down to a formula. (Penelope Houston)[2]

One can imagine criticism so perceptive and illuminating that it can also illuminate for the artist, show him what he has been doing, and tell him truths about himself he did not see. But in practice one seems to know the faults and virtues of what one has done more clearly than the people who criticise it. Perhaps this is because critics judge too much, and interpret too little. (Lindsay Anderson)[3]

The rules of the game

The key to understanding Lindsay Anderson's *This Sporting Life* (1963) can be in examining the relationship between the film's organisation of space and its deployment of characters within this space.[4] However, as crucial as this idea is I can hardly claim it to be a revolutionary one. The same could be said for almost any film in the history of narrative cinema. Yet, there are two compelling reasons why I want to consider Anderson's film in this way. To begin with, *This Sporting Life* demonstrates a remarkable predilection for filling its frames with bodies. In addition, the stylistic choices that Anderson makes in order to pursue this policy have resulted in some of the most interesting critical debates concerning a New Wave film.

Thematically, there is an overwhelming desire for personal expression evident in Anderson's film. As the film unfolds, the demonstration of this desire is accompanied by the inevitable dissatisfaction that comes from a lack of personal fulfilment. Internally, both of these things inform our understanding, contributing with equal ferocity to the wide spaces of the rugby pitch that Frank Machin (Richard Harris), the film's protagonist, plays upon and the narrow rooms of the house he shares with Margaret Hammond (Rachel Roberts), his landlady. Externally, also, questions of personal expression and an accompanying dissatisfaction extend beyond the frames of the film and will help shape the structure of my reading.

Following a trial, Frank leaves his job as a coal miner and becomes a professional rugby player. Success playing rugby, like any other team-based sport, is wholly dependent upon an understanding of the relationship between the spaces of the pitch and the positions players adopt in relation to these spaces. As the game unfolds, spaces on the pitch are occupied, left vacant, opened up and closed down. Whether in relation to team-mates or opponents, an understanding of positioning is vital. Even within the rigid conventions of tactics and rules, the nature of these positions can be fluid and constantly changing. Nevertheless, the game just would not work if its participants underestimated the importance of positions. Viewing the game in this way allows me to establish a correlation between the boundaries of the pitch and the edges of the film's frame. This is best understood if we realise that the dynamic relationship between positions and movements here corresponds perfectly well with the basic premises of the film's mise-en-scène. This is evident when we see players jostling for position on the pitch. Or when they find themselves crowded out, trapped by other bodies and are unable to move. At other times, when breaking free from a tackle or a scrum, players move to separate themselves from the close proximity of others by seeking wider spaces in which to act. The reverse is also true, as well, when we see players moving towards each other in a concerted effort to reduce the space between them.

The analogy between a film and a game of rugby is a difficult one to sustain successfully for any reasonable length. Yet, the positions adopted by characters within the frame, as well as the movement between these positions, are governed by a logic that is compellingly similar to the one on the pitch. Towards the end of the film there is a brief sequence of four shots that draw my attention to the possibilities they contain for viewing the film in this way. This sequence occurs after Frank has finally realised that his ambitions of a love affair with his landlady Margaret have no future. This is despite the fact that he has told her he loves her. After a violent argument, Margaret asks Frank to leave her house. Frank moves into a rundown boarding-house and disturbed by the seediness of his new digs, goes for a drive in the countryside. The four shots follow this.

Body and landscape

The four shots show Frank standing alone on a hillside overlooking a town. I am particularly interested in the first of these four shots because of what it reveals about the relationship between the film's spaces and the characters that inhabit them. The most interesting thing here is the position that Frank adopts in relation to these spaces. Simply put, this is the relationship between a body and a landscape. However, considering the fact that the film is particularly concerned with the physical relationship between Frank and its other characters then the absence of other characters here suggests the need to also consider the positional relationship between characters. Viewed from a wider perspective this view of Frank standing alone on a hill also reminds us of the critical concerns that developed over the uses of locations and landscape in films such as *This Sporting Life*. The relationship between body and body within the film is echoed externally by the relationship between critic and critic. This last idea is crucial because Anderson's film occupies a unique position within critical discussions of the British New Wave.

The first shot in this series is a long shot. The slope of a hillside is angled downwards from left to right and fills two-thirds of the frame. The other third is filled by the sky. Frank stands on the side of the hill looking out of the frame. The distance between character and camera ensures that Frank appears dwarfed by his surroundings. If the film reveals a particular fascination with the possibilities that a crowded frame might contribute to an understanding of Frank's unfolding life then this shot of him alone in the frame is the perfect starting-point. It acts as a useful reminder of the progress that Frank has made in his professional career. After all, it was at a trial game that Frank first stood out from the crowd of other hopefuls and got noticed by the selectors. This image is useful, then, on a literal level but does a lot more than just allow us to make a fairly obvious pun about the way in which Frank became a full-time rugby player. This image also offers a useful insight into the nature of Frank's professional life and his motivations. The image of Frank standing alone also urges us to reconsider his relationship with the other characters in the film. This is most relevant when it comes to Frank's relationship with Margaret. It was her rejection of his declaration of love that led to Frank standing here alone in the first place. Before we consider this relationship in more detail, we need to examine the development of Frank's professional life.

It is during one of the film's many flashbacks that we first get a glimpse of Frank's former life as a miner. The cramped spaces of the mine-shaft say something useful about the limited opportunities that such a career had to offer Frank. Underground in the semi-darkness, Frank's struggle at the coal-face invites us to imagine the frustration and desperation that must accompany a life of this kind. Frank, it appears, is lucky to have the opportunity to escape such a fate. For Frank's co-workers, however, a life of this kind leaves very little room for personal manoeuvre.

This brief flashback offers a useful insight into Frank's motivation. But this is only one use we might make of this recollection. As the film unfolds it is clear that Frank never leaves these confined spaces behind. It is only the nature of these spaces that changes. For a better understanding of this let us compare Frank's old job with his new one. Frank is a very talented rugby player and we see evidence of this during a league match. Receiving a pass from the wing he breaks for the line and rides a tackle before touching the ball down for a try. This is where the correlation between the edges of the pitch and the frames of the film becomes interesting. Shots of the action on the pitch are combined with shots of the crowd watching the game. Every time we see the crowd we see that the frame is packed with expectant faces. We also see shots of the directors and senior members of the club and their faces have the same expectancy etched upon them. As the spectators watch Frank and the team in action the soundtrack swells with the sound of their demanding voices.

The cramped confines of the mine-shaft gave Frank's life very little room for manoeuvre and it was clear that he would have to escape these confines in order for his life to develop. As we see the crowds ringing the pitch here it is sensible to ask whether much has really changed. The rugby pitch presents Frank with the opportunity to express himself in a way that being a miner never could but there are still some very restricting limits on his life. Coal-mining is a very private and intimate occupation. Despite its particular demands it still takes place away from the public eye. Rugby League, on the other hand, is an occupation that takes places in front of huge crowds and this gives its particular demands a very different sense. If you play well and score a try, as Frank does here, then the crowd are behind you and will give you their support. But the demands of the crowd, and the directors, for success means that Frank will now be expected to play well every week. This is something that Frank cannot maintain.

Despite the fact that he has made a positive change in his life by escaping the coal mine, Frank's professional life still demonstrates a level of confinement. It is true to say that his life is no longer bordered by the stifling limits of a job that offered very little in terms of personal expression. The problem is, as we can see from the crowds around the pitch, Frank's new career is now enclosed by the boundaries of demand and expectation. This takes us back to the image of Frank alone on the hill. This shot of Frank on the hillside is not the only time in the film when we see him standing alone in the frame. Yet, working back from this particular image does allows us to connect it with other moments that rhyme with it in the film and develops a more detailed understanding of *This Sporting Life*. For example, having scored the try, Frank is briefly shown alone in the frame as he receives the applause of the crowd. It was his try, after all, and it is only right that he has the opportunity to savour his success. Yet, there is an interesting problem here. On the one hand, success on the pitch brings him closer to his team-mates. At the same time, this same success makes him stand apart from them. There is further evidence of this last idea when we see Frank on a night out in a local club.

It is talent night at the club and a loud and drunken Frank is cajoled into singing before the crowd. Frank takes to the stage, instructs the band as to what song he will sing, and turns to face his audience. Frank launches into a rendition of 'Here in My Heart' and manages to carry the tune quite convincingly. Once again, the spotlight falls upon Frank's ability and once again he does not disappoint. The raucous crowd fall silent and just like before, Frank's performance is intercut with shots of an appreciative crowd. During his performance, the camera begins to move slowly backwards. With the band behind him, the camera's movement leaves Frank standing alone on the stage. In a similar way to the triumphant position he adopted on the football pitch, there is a feeling of success that we should attach to Frank's position. He has reduced the drunken crowd to silence. Nevertheless, these two examples of Frank's ability making him to stand out from the crowd are visually echoed by the later view of him standing alone on the hill and my memories of the earlier images manage to complicate my response to this later one.

As I watch Frank singing 'Here in My Heart', my initial impression is of a drunken show-off unwilling to lose face in front of his team-mates. Later, as he stands on the hill, with no crowd and no audience, the song's concern with feeling alone in one's heart take on a more frighteningly literal tone. With no crowd to please and no stage to perform on, the significant consequences of Frank's final isolation here begin to loom large. Having moved from the confining frames of the mine-shaft, where self-expression was impossible, Frank found that the space of the rugby pitch was the ideal place for him to demonstrate his ability. Though his new career was framed by the expectations of supporters and directors, he still found room to express himself. As his relationship with the team deteriorates, the demands placed upon him become almost as limiting as those of the mine-shaft and this is what makes this image of Frank alone on the hill so compelling. Away from the crowds and free momentarily, at least, from the demands placed upon him, Frank still appears as trapped as he has always been. The only difference being that this time Frank's image is framed with a sense of solitude and failure that is as constricting and as confining as any mine-shaft. The changing circumstances of Frank's professional life contribute to the crucial role that this single image plays in our understanding of *This Sporting Life*. This is only half the story, however. To complete the connection between this single image and the film's style and meaning it is now necessary to consider Frank's relationship with Margaret.

7 Margaret (Rachel Roberts) and Frank (Richard Harris) jostle for position in *This Sporting Life*.

Old boots and small rooms

On the whole, the relationship between Frank and Margaret takes place in the tight confines of the terraced house that they share. With her dead husband's boots in the fireplace as a constant reminder of the sorrow she feels, Margaret, it appears, has closed down the spaces of her life. Too tightly bound to the past and unwilling (or unable) to let go, the cramped sequences that take place in the house are framed by the film as the tragedy of a relationship that will never have the space it needs to develop properly. A useful indication of this is when we see Frank and Margaret wake up in bed together.

Despite his best efforts to convince her otherwise, Margaret tells Frank that she cannot let go of her feelings again. 'Say you've got some feeling for me', pleads Frank as Margaret sits up. This movement causes her to be framed alone. Frank's voice can be heard offscreen. The camera moves away slightly to accommodate Frank in the same frame as he sits up behind Margaret.

They are close together now, as close as you would expect lovers to be, but the composition here lacks a reassuring balance. The frame is divided vertically into three sections. Frank is placed on the far right, facing Margaret. Margaret is in the centre. The left-hand side is empty and it is these three parts of the frame that tell us so much about these two people. From his position, Frank wants Margaret to turn around and face him. The desire for such a simple movement is increased in its importance because an action of this kind would imply Margaret turning her life around and facing the prospect of sharing it with Frank. But Margaret is unable to do this and she chooses to look the other way. This marks her initial position here as one of opposition and resistance. The empty space that Margaret looks into is an inviting one for it gives her a way out of the commitment that Frank is asking for. We can expand the importance of this empty space by considering that it is filled with the memories of Eric, her dead husband. The composition that Margaret would see at this moment, were she able to step far enough back from her life, would be her positioned in the middle, flanked on either side by the past, as represented by her husband, and Frank, the future, on her right. Her dilemma comes from being caught in the middle of these two men and what they represent.

Margaret gets up from the bed and, as expected, moves into the empty space beyond the left of the frame. The camera moves with her and she is framed alone. She does not look at Frank because this might mean her having to look to the future. Instead, Margaret chooses to look down, and the direction of her gaze suggests that she really has nothing to look forward to. 'I cannot let my feelings go', she tells Frank. Even when Frank moves into the frame Margaret still does not look at him. She asks him to give her time and Frank places his arm around her shoulder. The gesture is a tender one but Frank, like Margaret, is also caught between two positions, tenderness and forcefulness, and this opposition makes his action here feel like the kind of move he might make on the pitch in order to pin down an elusive opponent. 'You keep fighting me', he says and his words make his gesture appear like a tackle. 'I've nothing more to give you', she says before leaving the room. It is Frank's turn to be alone in the frame now. 'You're so big', Margaret tells him and the closeness of the camera here means that his shoulders almost fill the width of the frame. Here, despite the fact that Frank's new career has given him the opportunity for expansion that the mine-shaft never did, the spaces of Frank's life are as enclosed as they must have been before.

An examination of this sequence offers a range of illuminating insights. Frank's clumsy efforts at closeness are starkly contrasted with Margaret's avoidance and this contrast gives us clear guidance that this is the way that this relationship will naturally evolve. In other parts of the film we see Frank strike Margaret and the sight of this makes his efforts at tenderness appear even more uncomfortable. This, in turn, returns us to the shot of Frank standing alone on the hill and allows us to understand that this shot stands as the only possible outcome of his relationship with Margaret. The harder he tries to get close to her, the further they end up apart. Sharing the frame here, just like sharing the bed, is no guarantee that the two of them will share a life together. Once we understand the forlorn inevitability that hangs over the relationship between Frank and Margaret, the range of responses derived from seeing Frank alone on the hill have the potential to become more varied and more eloquent.

At the very least, this image evokes pity but it is not quite as simple as this. Our response to this shot of Frank becomes intensified by witnessing the failure of his efforts to connect with Margaret. Even living as close together as the small house they share dictates does not help them to become closer emotionally. In fact, the cramped corridors and gloomy rooms actually help to force them further apart. This is not to say that the unfolding of their relationship takes place only indoors. There is one interesting moment when a change in the relationship between this couple and the spaces they share represents an opportunity for their relationship to take a different turn. This is the moment when Frank returns home with the new sports car he has bought and offers to take Margaret and the children out for a drive.

White cars and black coats

Frank has bought a white sports car and parks it outside the house. The car stands conspicuously in the street and looks like the kind of grand (but vulgar) gesture that you might expect from someone not used to having so much money. This car is just a little too obvious for its surroundings. Be that as it may, the car does more than merely represent new-found wealth, it also symbolises an opportunity for Frank and Margaret to do something together. This is why he asks her to come for a drive. It would get them both out of the house and a change of scenery might be what they both need. Frank's hope is that this will bring them closer together. These possibilities seem as obvious as the car itself but at least it does allow us to make a contrast with the difficulties of togetherness Frank and Margaret experienced in the bedroom. Sadly, however, the car's conspicuousness is problematic. It is certainly enough to make the neighbours stare, and this troubles Margaret. She is terrified of being seen as a kept woman and her reaction here shows that she is disturbed by Frank's extravagant gesture. But the car disturbs me as well.

This is the kind of gesture that people make when they try too hard to impress. Its very presence in the film confirms this. It is just too big and too bright and, like the clumsiness of Frank's gestures when he tries to be gentle, is just too heavy-handed. This is an uncomfortable moment. Frank cannot be blamed for wanting to impress Margaret with his new-found status. After all, impressing her is exactly what he feels he needs to do in order to win her over. Yet the more Frank strokes the car and the louder he proclaims its beauty to anyone who will listen, the greater the feeling grows that his efforts are doomed to failure. Margaret is not totally against the purchase. We do see her smile when she sees the car but she is too aware of the neighbours looking and what they might think and finds herself caught between conflicting desires. Frank finally manages to convince Margaret that they should all go out for a drive. Despite Frank's declaration that it is like driving around 'in your own front room', we cannot help but notice how cramped the car is with four people sitting in the front and this makes it more like driving around in their front room than Frank could ever imagine.

The sequence in the country begins with a shot of Frank and the two children, Ian and Linda, playing on a trail of stepping-stones that traverse a wide stream. The camera is positioned at some distance away from the three figures and this places an emphasis on the tall trees and open expanses of grass that surround them. As Frank skims stones with the children the film cuts to reveal Margaret standing alone and separate. She is taking stock of her surroundings and as she moves around the camera moves with her. The ruins of an enormous abbey come in to view and Margaret stops to stare.

The film cuts again, leaving Margaret alone with the ruins, and returns us to Frank. He turns to look off-screen, standing as he does so. The camera moves up with him but also moves inwards towards him, placing an emphasis on his looking offscreen. This emphasis is an understandable one because Frank has seen Margaret staring at the ruined abbey and the thought of this causes him to react. He suggests to Linda that they all go and play soccer, and this decision is motivated by the desire to get closer to Margaret and somehow distract her. The reason behind Frank's plan was to get them all out of the house and away from all that it represents. The last thing he wants here is for Margaret to be reminded of her loss by the ruined building. The sound of Linda laughing causes Margaret to turn around. There is another cut here and the camera is now positioned behind Margaret. Margaret begins to walk towards Frank and the children and her movement here signals the moment at which Frank and Margaret might begin to become closer. She has seen Frank playing with the children and it is clear that he is good with them. He has money and there is every possibility that he could provide them all with a comfortable future, but this movement towards the rest of her 'family' is not completed because moving forwards here means moving on, and this is something that Margaret is unable to do. Before she gets close enough, Margaret stops and the film cuts once again. Frank turns and looks to see where she has got to. A cut reveals her standing and watching from a distance.

This shot is interesting for several reasons. The sequence as a whole has attempted to demonstrate the distance that will always exist between Frank and Margaret. This is despite his best efforts, as the drive in the countryside demonstrates. However the car has already indicated that he is trying too hard and being too conspicuous in his efforts to get closer to her. Even bonding with her children fails to bring her closer. As he skims stones with Ian and Linda, or plays soccer, or chases them, Margaret

8 Margaret (Rachel Roberts) is trapped between the past and the future in *This Sporting Life*.

can only stand and watch. She does catch the ball when Frank throws it to her but even this simple act fails to bring them closer together. There is just something too difficult about the whole situation and this is reflected in the way the characters are positioned in relation to the spaces here. Most notable is the way that Margaret stands in the middle of the frame, and once again the space is divided vertically into three sections. This composition is something we saw originally in the bedroom sequence. There, the spaces on either side of Margaret allowed us to deduce that she had been presented with a choice of directions that she might allow her life to take. Here, the consequences of this choice are explicitly revealed. Margaret is positioned in the middle of the frame and on her left we can see Frank's car. On her right stands the ruined abbey.

The bright white of the paintwork on Frank's car stands in stark relief to the black coat that she pulls tightly across her breast. Though the car might suggest an obviousness and heavy-handedness, it still represents a certain hope for the future. The abbey, on the other hand, stands for darkness and ruin and the memories of something that once was perfect but is no longer. Like the abbey, the passing of time has taken its toll on Margaret and has eroded any hope she had of escaping from her past. As the colour of her coat suggests, all she will ever be able to do is remain irretrievably merged with the deserted ruins of her history. The symbolism here can be considered to be fairly primitive, obvious even, but this should not prevent us from incorporating these two images into our discussion. The idea of obviousness, after all, is something that the sequence has brought to our attention. With this in mind, and despite the stark contrast between the colours here, we should understand that the position Margaret finds herself cannot be simply viewed in terms of black or white. As her position demonstrates, Margaret will always be caught between two conflicting desires and our response needs to be shaded by this. Penelope Gilliat hints at the same idea in her discussion of the couple. As she suggests:

> There is something about her put-upon Englishwoman's silences that make him behave like a pig, and he could boot her for the way she droops over the memory of her dead husband; but at the same time there is a kind of purity about her withdrawal that somehow consoles him, although he does everything to wreck it . . . they make demands upon each other that are cruel because they cannot be met, cannot be communicated, cannot even be defined to themselves.[5]

Inevitably, this idea of conflicting demands leads us back to the image of Frank alone on the hill. The trajectory of Frank's professional life has been accompanied by a sense of enclosure and the change in his profession does little to remove this sense. It is also inevitable that Margaret is framed in a similar way by the film. As she stands looking on, watching Frank and her children, she will never be able to break free from the memories that corral her life. Sadly, there is a connection between the couple but one that finds its only expression at the level of the film's mise-en-scène. Frank's isolation in the frame is poignantly echoed by Margaret being placed in a similar position. Though they could never know it, Frank and Margaret are doomed to be (framed) alone, enclosed by the impossible demands that surround them both. It could be that these demands stem from the difficulties that accompany professional circumstances. These demands might also stand as the ultimate expression of conflicting emotional impulses that are impossible to reconcile. Whatever the case, the most enduring connection between Frank and Margaret is the solitude they share. This idea of two characters who want to come together but are forced by circumstances to stand apart from each other is made all the more apparent by the film's desire to fill its frames with bodies. Frank's life with Margaret is not like life on the rugby pitch. Even though the original connection between the boundaries of the pitch and the frames of the film still makes sense from a critical perspective, the sadness felt when watching *This Sporting Life* comes from watching Frank finally understand that the rules he adheres to on the pitch make no sense when he tries to apply them to other areas of his life.

It is painful to think that Frank has to learn the hard way that his relationship with Margaret is not something he can tackle with his usual aggression. Despite his efforts, best or otherwise, Frank cannot achieve the connection with Margaret that he desires and is doomed to be (framed) alone. Margaret is destined for the same thing. This is not to say that this couple fail to achieve any connection at all. Sadly, it takes the tragedy of Margaret's death to make this explicit.[6] Our witnessing of the unfolding tragedy that is Frank and Margaret's life together turns upon two images of these characters, each one framed alone. My examination of *This Sporting Life* has drawn repeated attention to the image of Frank standing alone but our knowledge of the way in which Frank was unable to escape the confining frames of his life means that we need to do more than view this image as simply a man standing on a hill overlooking a town. Instead, this image needs to read as a complex reflection on the fear of isolation and a life alone that forces people to take desperate action to avoid being alone in their world. The film's persistent foregrounding of the relationship between a character and the spaces within the frame is intimately connected to questions of self-expression and its opposite, denial. This is the position I have adopted in relation to Anderson's film. Other critics, however, have adopted other positions in relation to the film's framing decisions, and this is where the discussion of the relationship between critic and critic begins.

A kind of difference?

Let us return to the series of shots highlighted earlier. The second shot in this series is another long shot. The camera's position has shifted by ninety degrees. The slope of the hill is still visible in the foreground of the frame. The middle of the frame is filled by the sprawl of an industrial town. We can see tall chimneys belching smoke. Frank's car is visible in the bottom right-hand corner of the foreground. We might begin by asking what purpose this shot of the town from the hillside serves. This is, after all, a New Wave film, and townscape shots in these films have always made critics nervous. Historically, a shot of this kind is allegedly indicative of a series of flawed films that are themselves characteristic, stylistically, at least, of a flawed national cinema. As Julia Hallam and Margaret Marshment write:

> Critical re-evaluation of the New Wave films has tended to emphasise the formal aspects of mise-en-scène and shooting style rather than other elements of realism such as acting style and characterisation, thus equating New Wave films with an excess of 'surface' realism and an over-abundance of descriptive detail of place which is somewhat at odds with plot development and characterisation.[7]

My re-evaluation of this image has been dependent upon stressing the equal relationship between descriptive detail and plot development. This is essential if we are to avoid the making the same laboured assertions over surfaces that are always made when talking about a film such as this. The importance of this second shot comes from its organic relationship with the other details specific to *This Sporting Life* and the way in which these details make it different from *A Kind of Loving*, say. By continuing to stress the uniqueness of each film I have aimed to move away from the kind of generalisation highlighted by Hallam and Marshment. There are certain similarities but this shot is fundamentally different in almost every aspect from the view of the town we see when Vic and Ingrid meet each other in *A Kind of Loving*.

This distinction is solely an interpretative one. Nevertheless, it is an important one to make, and in order to make this distinction more effective it is useful here to consider the question of directorial intention. Here Lindsay Anderson is discussing the use of location and descriptive detail. As he writes:

> The case of the new British school is rather different. These films have also loosened up in style in a very healthy way, but with a quite different emphasis to the French. Here the first achievement has been the opening up of new territories, both of subjects and of the social backgrounds in which they are set. This has been a great development – in fact an indispensable one. But it could also be restrictive if we make films for too long with an eye on what is representative – films about 'working class people', looked at objectively, almost with a documentarist's vision. (Or a sociologist's, which is worse.) . . . Throughout *This Sporting Life* we were very aware that we were not making a film about anything representative: we were making a film about something unique. We were not making a film about a 'worker', but about an extraordinary (and therefore more deeply significant) man, and about an extraordinary relationship. We were not, in a word, making sociology.[8]

It was exactly this perceived sociological tendency that so disturbed critics in the first place, especially those writing for *Movie*. Yet not everyone at *Movie* felt the same way about Anderson's film, and it is here that the idea of the relationship between the spaces on a rugby pitch and the critical positions adopted in relation to the British New Wave comes to the fore.

Gavin Millar, for example, felt that the achievements of *Life* prevented it from being seen as just another new wave film delighting in what he called 'the Poetry of Squalor'. As he continues: 'Social concerns should find some more honest response to industrial wildernesses than graphic fascination.'[9] And *This Sporting Life*, for Millar, was able to do this. As he explains:

> *This Sporting Life* is in no sense a landscape picture. There are no establishing shots in it. We see no more of the surroundings than Frank does, and that is precious little. This would be perversity if it weren't clear that there is no room for 'environment'. Frank Machin, his body and his mind are the bursting centre of the film. His body drives on the action, his mind controls its

order and flow. Only at the moment when he is nearest defeat, spirit crushed
and body shrunk into itself, does the landscape dominate him: when he
stands on a remote ridge overlooking the city. Even then he is uppermost in
the frame.[10]

As Millar concludes:

> The film, obviously enough, is a personal one before it is a social one – if it is
> ever a social one. There is none of the usual manipulation of class caricature.
> There are no jokes at the expense of the working class, a la Richardson,
> Schlesinger, Clayton, though there are jokes about them. Anderson's [and
> Storey's] respect for the people shows itself in the lack of fuss made about
> their habits, beyond the attention to them which is relevant.[11]

What is important here is the difference in opinion generated by *This
Sporting Life*. As with the other New Wave films, these differences centred on concerns over the film's use of landscape, and this is the point
at which the film's local detail and those more global concerns that
surround it meet. If the first shot of Frank standing alone causes us to
consider his relationship with the film's other characters then this also
becomes the point at which we might consider Millar's argument in
relation to other critics writing about the film.

The last hope?

The third shot in this series echoes the first one. Once again, the hillside
slopes downwards from left to right. Frank is still small in relation to
the hill and the sky. This time, however, the camera has moved closer.
The film cuts and the fourth shot is now an extreme close shot. The
camera faces Frank straight-on and his head and shoulders fill the frame.
His arms are folded and the collar of his coat is drawn together.[12] Frank
looks towards the camera as if looking out at the town we saw in the
second shot. This final shot ends this brief series. Thematically, the
image of Frank standing alone is clearly meant to signal the end of
something. Critically, this same idea of an ending has been attached
to Anderson's film. This is the conclusion Robin Cross reaches in his
discussion. As he writes:

> Mistakenly hailed as a breakthrough when it was made, *This Sporting Life*
> marked the end of the process which had begun with *Room at the Top*. Films
> like Bryan Forbes' *The L-Shaped Room* (1962) and Peter Glenville's *Term of
> Trial* (1962) seemed more like identikit assemblages of the genre's clichés
> than films with a life of their own. When Rank entered the lists with their own
> laundered brand of realism in Ralph Thomas's *The Wild and the Willing*
> (1962) the writing was clearly on the wall. *This Sporting Life* was caught by
> the turn of the tide and left stranded like a beached whale on the sandbanks of
> fantasy which were to mark the changing mood in British society and cinema.[13]

Consider, also, what Gilbert Adair has to say:

> At their best, they recharged the British cinema's batteries with the dark energy of working-class themes and a greater candour in the handling of sexuality (aided by a concurrent relaxation of censorship). At the less persuasive end, they had a tendency to serve up thickly buttered slabs of pre-sliced life . . .
>
> In any event, our cinema's egalitarian spasm was short-lived; by the mid-sixties Salford had ceased to be a fashionable address. Reisz, Richardson, Clayton and Schlesinger all packed their bags for internationally impersonal projects, where and when they could set them up – in Britain, if convenient.[14]

As we saw in Millar's examination of the film, all this is despite the fact that *This Sporting Life* was seen as a more successfully realised film than its New Wave contemporaries. *Sight and Sound*, for example, irrespective of its growing pessimism over the developments made in the industry, viewed Anderson's film as representing the best (or, perhaps, the last) hope for defining an unmistakably British cinematic style. As Penelope Houston optimistically announced, in a tone partly reminiscent of *Movie*'s more antagonistic stance:

> We have asked our film-makers often enough why they cannot be Antonioni or Olini, Resnais or Truffaut. The question is still valid and no doubt we will ask it again. But let us also realise that we have in this country, at this moment, a cinema which commands quite a degree of public support; a cinema which could afford to take a few risks, and might surprise itself by getting away with them; and a cinema which has got to work out its own salvation, in its own way. This looks like the moment for the real breakthrough.[15]

Tom Milne was another contributor to *Sight and Sound* who felt that the time was now ripe for a British cinema of 'highly personal, creative scrutiny and formal experiment'. Admittedly, he, like Houston, felt it necessary to declare that 'we want more; of course we are impatient for a home-grown Antonioni, Demy or Resnais; but they are unlikely to emerge until a platform has been erected for them to work on'. He also believed that this would be possible only if British films were prepared to cast off 'the apron-strings of novel and play, so as to be free to invent a bit of film instead of filming a bit of script. It may not mean better films, but it will almost certainly mean bolder, more exciting, more potential ones.'[16]

Turning to *This Sporting Life*, Milne finds it impossible not to note its 'distinct family resemblance' to the same northern novels that inspired *Room at the Top*. Nevertheless, Anderson's film is distinguished 'by the fact that it concentrates primarily on neither local colour, frustration, social climbing, anger nor unrest'. Instead, as Milne continues, 'it focuses, with considerable power, on the tragedy of a man who achieves his ambition for fame . . . then helplessly steers himself, and the woman he genuinely loves to disaster'. This is also the conclusion that Millar reached. As Milne suggests, the result is the attempt to make 'a stylish film, neither rough-hewn or thrown together to convey the impression of raw life, nor self-consciously exploiting the new-found glories of location shooting'.[17] Milne felt that Anderson's film might be the first of its kind to stand apart from the films that had preceded it. Were this to happen then *Life* would be seen as a film in its own right and not simply labelled as another example, following in the footsteps of *The Loneliness of the Long Distance Runner*, of a disappointing series that had failed to realise fully both its potential and the expectations placed upon it. Finally then, for Milne, and by extension, for *Sight and Sound* as well as Millar, here was the one British film that might make the breakthrough.[18]

As the image of Frank standing on the hill indicates, standing out from the crowd can be interpreted in more than one way. It was this idea of a breakthrough that caused Ian Cameron to enter the field and outline his objections. Writing in *Movie*, Cameron was motivated by the fear that *This Sporting Life* would become 'one of the holy films of the resurrected British cinema' without proper attention being paid to its stylistic 'achievements'.[19] In a bid to tackle *Sight and Sound*'s claims, as well as those of Millar, Cameron began by objecting to its 'fragmentary technique' on the grounds that the director had not properly considered the effect that this technique would have upon the film's audience. Notwithstanding the film's obvious passion, Cameron was also concerned by *Life*'s predominant use of close-ups, fearing that this forced the feelings of the film upon the viewer. As he writes:

> Having chosen to make a passionate film, Anderson has attained his aim by the easy – one could say cheap – way of shooting his film predominately in close shots. Of course, the audience emerges battered. Of course the film has impact. But what use is it? The style expresses the intensity of feelings contained within the story, an intensity which should come naturally from the actors without needing to be forced on the audience by slugging it with close-ups.[20]

As he continues:

> I'm sure this line of investigation could be pursued further, but for my purposes, it is not relevant except in so far as it relates to my main point: the close-up style does not help us to see Frank Machin, but obscures our view of him. I have no objection to the close-up technique in itself, or to any other obvious 'style', except where it is damaging or simply not useful to a particular film.[21]

Far from obscuring our view of Frank, the 'style' of Anderson's film effectively conveys its thematic concerns. The relationship between the film's presentation of Frank and its interest in matters of personal expression is perfectly realised as the film unfolds. That the ultimate outcome of this relationship is a tragic one is something that only serves to bring us closer to the character and his motivation. Cameron, however, saw things in a different way.

For him, the continued use of close shots did allow Anderson to give Frank a tragic stature but also forced the spectator to identify with him at the expense of everyone else in the film. As Cameron argues:

> By presenting Frank Machin as he does, Anderson forces the camera into such a consistently close embrace with him that throughout the film there is an implicit invitation to admire Frank. The fact of having him rammed at us for the length of the film seems to indicate that Anderson sets a higher value on him than on the others. In other words, because we are invited to admire Frank at the expense of all the other characters, their inability to cope with him makes them seem in some way defective.[22]

And this, according to Cameron, has a serious effect upon the film's balance. As he is keen to suggest:

> By keeping his camera up against Frank for the whole film, Anderson does more than impose an emotional proximity: he removes the distance that is necessary if one is to 'see' him as a person. The balance between this sort of detachment and identification is a delicate one, but the two qualities are not mutually exclusive. There are dozens of films in which one identifies with a hero while remaining aware that he is not wholly admirable but has considerable moral defects.[23]

Finally, fearing the worst, Cameron felt the film to be flawed stylistically, constructed in such a way as to force identification with its central character by blurring the lines between objective and subjective. As Cameron concludes:

> But flaws in the subjectivity can only be taken as a criticism if the film is intended to be subjective, as it appears to be for most of its length. The film constantly raises problems of this sort. Its style makes us ask ourselves questions of directorial intention that its confused realisation prevents us from answering.[24]

Cameron's objections to the film are extremely interesting. Cameron outlines a series of stylistic objections which, he believes, damage the film and limit its achievements. This is perfectly reasonable and contributes to our understanding of the variety of positions critics adopted in relation to this film. However, bearing in mind Cameron's motivation for his criticisms, as well considering the antagonistic relationship between *Movie* and *Sight and Sound*, these objections have the same air of peevishness which characterises 'The British Cinema'. Like we first saw with Perkins and later with Gibbs, the style of Cameron's words (unintentionally) now become the point at which we might start to ask ourselves questions of critical intention. This is evident, for example, when Cameron decides that 'a rough definition of a subjective film is that the audience has a viewpoint thrust upon it, like it or not. Whose viewpoint? There are only two possibilities – Anderson's or Machin's.'[25]

As my reading has shown, the tragedy of Frank's situation is carefully balanced by the tragedy of Margaret's. The overriding image we have of each of these characters is of them being framed alone, Frank on the hill and Margaret in front of the ruined abbey. Though Frank is the film's principal subject, an understanding of how his life unfolded to this point would be impossible to sustain unless we account for it relation to the unfolding of Margaret's. From this perspective, Cameron's objections appear to do only half the work. Once again, this question of subjectivity returns us to the idea of the positions that critics take in relation to other critics.

Substance and significance

Anderson felt that the film's subjectivity was to be expected in relation to a novel written in the first person. Of course, and perhaps explaining part of the problem that Cameron had with the film, Anderson found this to be somewhat problematic. Partly this was because he was unwilling to use any of 'the traditional devices of voice-over narration or subjective camera tricks'. Also, as he explains:

> For me there was the additional difficulty of entering into a temperament very different from my own: for Frank Machin [the central character] and I had very little in common, and as a result I found the leap into his heart and mind a hard one. This made me continually liable to slip into an objective view of scenes that needed to be presented through Machin's own temperament.[26]

In addition, and helping to explain the film's potentially contradictory handling of ideas of identification and attachment, Anderson unrepentantly explains: 'It is a film about a man. A man of extraordinary power and aggressiveness, both temperamental and physical, but at the same time with a great innate sensitiveness and a need for love of which he is at first hardly aware.' As he continues:

> People are apt to say that tragedy is impossible today: that the age of Freudian psychology and atomic science has robbed the individual of the dignity and the significance which alone make tragedy possible. Well, flying in the face of fashion, we have tried to make a tragedy.[27]

Aside from the curmudgeonly criticism of Cameron's review, with its emphasis on the disjointed nature of Anderson's film, we should not forget that the antipathy shown by some of the *Movie* critics, exemplified not only by Perkins but also now by Cameron, towards this new spate of

British films was based on a broader concern that developments in British cinema compared unfavourably with those from elsewhere. Anderson's discussion of his film is a useful counterpoint to this argument.

Anderson, like Perkins, Houston and Cameron, was happy to look abroad for films and film movements to admire. However, he was also prepared to consider the possibility that the new French films, a movement much admired by critics, for example, were far from perfect. As he writes:

> Much as I admire many of the experiments made by the young French directors – and particularly their adventurous breaking away from the outmoded conventions of cinematic 'style' – I think that even in their best work there is apt to be a terrible lack of weight, of substance and human significance. Their very brilliance seems to trap them in facility and vogueishness.[28]

Critical debates about film 'style', both for and against, hang heavy not only over *This Sporting Life* but also over the others to which it bore a resemblance. This is not to suggest that this is a simple case of one critic being right and one being wrong. Film criticism does not tend to work that way. The debates that circulate around this film reveal a variety of critical positions and this returns us, yet again, to the film's mise-en-scène. The movement of characters through spaces articulated within the film is easily mirrored by the movement of critics through the critical spaces that frame *This Sporting Life*. For a final example of this idea consider what Peter Baker had to say on the subject. Writing in *Films and Filming*, Baker is keen to suggest that *This Sporting Life*

> has no excesses: its very balance of style and content is as disarming in its conventionality as Burton beer and Cheddar cheese. Yet the one provides as substantial a meal for the mind as the other does for the belly. In a period in world cinema when one can only be square like Hitchcock or Hawks provided the hep youngsters like Truffaut or Godard applaud you, when almost any experiment is praised by almost every critic just because it is an experiment, when even the Italian renaissance is in danger of losing communication with its audiences through sheer intellectualism, it is good to find a new director who believes that art of its very nature owes some allegiance to tradition.[29]

Returning to this idea of critic in relation to critic, I want to propose a final correlation between the boundaries of the pitch, the edges of the film's frame and the act of film criticism itself. Just like the game that Frank excels at, spaces within the boundaries of film criticism are occupied and left vacant, opened up and closed down. Also, negotiation of these spaces is entirely dependent upon a clear understanding of the positions occupied by others, whether sympathetic or not. Even within the rigid conventions of tactics and rules, of disciplines and formats, these positions can be fluid and constantly changing. Thus informed, the decision of where we place ourselves in relation to the other participants in this process is for each one of us to decide individually.

Notes

1 Ivan Butler, *The Making of Feature Films: A Guide*, Harmondsworth, Penguin Books Ltd, 1971, p. 64.
2 Penelope Houston, 'Critic's Notebook', *Sight and Sound*, Vol. 30, No. 2 (Spring 1961), pp. 62–66, p. 62.
3 Lindsay Anderson, 'Sport, Life and Art', *Films and Filming* (February 1963), pp. 15–18, p. 18.
4 Erik Hedling, for example, accounts for the film's use of cinematic space in a different way by suggesting that Anderson's use of 'closed' space is 'predominately theatrical'. This, he argues, marks the film's difference from 'the spatial strategies of other "kitchen-sink" films'. Further, citing André Bazin's discussion of the ontological differences between theatre and film, Hedling has this to say: 'Theatre, Bazin maintained, is characterised by a limited spatial microcosm, whereas film could expand space without limits. In theatre, actors and dialogue were focussed; in film, meanings were created through the integration of the actors and unlimited space. These distinctions pertain to *This Sporting Life*, which to a certain extent represents a symbiosis of the theatrical and the cinematic, since the film balances between theatrical and cinematic spaces as well as theatrical and cinematic acting conventions.' This symbiosis, Hedling continues, is 'supplemented by a complex narrative structure and an elaborate flashback pattern which dominates the entire plot'. Hedling's conception of the film's use of space differs from my own but his discussion provides a useful counterpoint to my own (Erik Hedling, *Lindsay Anderson: Maverick Film-Maker*, London and Washington, Cassell, 1998, pp. 53–54; p. 54).
5 'British Cinema, Attitudes and Illusions', *Film*, No. 36 (Summer 1963), pp. 16–24, p. 17.
6 I'm thinking here of the trickle of blood that comes from each of their mouths; Frank's after dental surgery and Margaret's when she dies in hospital. It is ironic, after all, that they have spent the whole film not being able to find the right things to say to each other but are still linked graphically by the mouth.
7 Julia Hallam with Margaret Marshment, *Realism and Popular Cinema*, Manchester and New York, Manchester University Press, 2000, pp. 46–47.
8 Anderson, 'Sport, Life and Art', pp. 16–17.
9 Gavin Millar, '*This Sporting Life*', *Movie*, No. 7 (February 1963), p. 33.
10 *Ibid.*, p. 33.
11 *Ibid.*, p. 33.
12 This gesture is mirrored by the gesture Margaret makes as she stands between the abbey and Frank's car.
13 Robin Cross, *The Big Book of British Films*, Bideford, Charles Herridge Ltd, 1984, p. 152.

14 Gilbert Adair and Nick Roddick, *A Night at the Pictures: Ten Decades of British Film*, Bromley: Columbus Books, 1985, p. 66.

15 'The Front Page', *Sight and Sound*, Vol. 32, No. 2 (Spring 1963), p. 55.

16 Tom Milne, '*This Sporting Life*', *Sight and Sound*, Vol. 31, No. 3 (Summer 1962), pp. 113–115, pp. 113–114.

17 *Ibid.*, pp. 114–115.

18 *Ibid.*, p. 115.

19 Ian Cameron, 'Against *This Sporting Life*', *Movie*, No. 10 (June 1963), pp. 21–22, p. 21.

20 *Ibid.*, p. 21.

21 *Ibid.*, p. 21.

22 *Ibid.*, p. 22.

23 Another consequence is the 'awkward and ugly' impact that this decision has upon the film's editing and soundtrack. As *Movie* continues: 'At its worst, the search for impact in the use of soundtrack, camera angles and shock cutting between sequences recalls the enormities perpetrated by Messrs. Dearden and Relph [supposed proponents of British 'quality' films]. The 'expressionist' devices that punctuate the film invariably result in disaster' (*Movie*, No. 10, p. 21).

24 Of course, as we would come to expect by now, of all the films cited by Cameron where this balance might be found, none is British. Instead, he cites Randolph Scott in *Decision at Sundown* (Budd Boetticher, 1957); Robert Ryan in *Day of the Outlaw* (André de Toth, 1959); Debra Paget in *The River's Edge* (Alan Dwan, 1957); Robert Mitchum in Richard Fleischer's *Bandido* (1956); James Stewart in Anthony Mann's *The Far Country* (1954); Marlon Brando in *On the Waterfront* (Elia Kazan, 1954); and James Stewart in Alfred Hitchcock's *Vertigo* (1958) (*Movie*, No. 10, p. 22).

25 *Ibid.*, p. 22.

26 Anderson, 'Sport, Life and Art', p. 17.

27 *Ibid.*, p. 16.

28 *Ibid.*, p. 16.

29 Peter Baker, '*This Sporting Life*', *Films and Filming* (February 1963), p. 32.

8 Single vessels and twisting ropes

> The business of film-going can be compared to a dialogue with people we care about. The discussion may often be affectionate, occasionally heated; but – no question – it should never be impersonal or indifferent. (Eric Rhode)[1]

> The question of what becomes of objects when they are filmed and screened – like the question what becomes of particular people, and specific locales, and subjects and motifs when they are filmed by individual makers of film – has only one source of data for its answer, namely the appearance and significance of those objects and people that are in fact to be found in the succession of films, or passages of films, that matter to us. To express their appearances, and define those significances, and articulate the nature of this mattering, are acts that help to constitute what we might call film criticism. (Stanley Cavell)[2]

> Pantheons, auteurs and the ranking of films and directors can be inhibiting, but – as with the *politique des auteurs* – can be liberating in shedding light on hitherto neglected areas. It is impossible to dispense entirely with a canon of approved films, but one can strive to make it broader and more fluid. (Robert Murphy)[3]

Back to the future?

This is the case I have made for reconsidering the style and meaning of the British New Wave. My examination of *Saturday Night and Sunday Morning*, *A Taste of Honey* or *Billy Liar* has been based upon the pressing desire to re-evaluate the mise-en-scène of these films. This has been achieved by applying the kind of British critical methodology that first suggested that such an approach was unnecessary. Whether sustained readings of whole films, examinations of significant moments, or the discussion of specific examples from the films that are accompanied by existing critical opinions, the preceding chapters have demonstrated the need for treating each film as an individual object of critical scrutiny. Ultimately, the kind of style-based film criticism originally advocated by *Movie* is a useful tool for reconsidering the nature and the status of this series of films. Reconsidering the nature of each of these films is made possible by concentrating upon the details of each one and allowing a discussion of these details to develop a deeper understanding of each *individual* film. The implications of this are twofold. Firstly, I am able to demonstrate clearly that it is not the methodology that is at fault, it is just the way in which the methodology has (not) been applied. The strand of British film criticism pioneered by Perkins and *Movie* is an impressive tool by which discussions of the British New Wave can be moved forward. The impressive nature of the methodology is further enhanced by the implications that such an approach has for other aspects of British cinema.

Secondly, it is important to understand that examining the style and meaning of *any* individual film allows that film's position within any kind of broader framework – whether historical, ideological or in any other reasonable context – also to be reconsidered. In the particular case of the British New Wave, this is vital if each of these films is to be sensibly discussed individually without continually having to resort to finding common features. This allows discussion to move forward and prevents it from just standing still. (Or, worse still, moving in endless and non-productive circles.) Once again, the implications for future discussions of British films are extremely exciting. Here, the results of my discussions concur with the observations made by Peter Hutchings that I used to initiate this investigation.[4]

Hutchings began by suggesting that, despite the fact that these films are normally viewed as a series, they are actually noticeably different from each other. As I have demonstrated, this is most certainly the case. For example, *Billy Liar* is a film about one man's desire to place a distance between himself and the world that he lives in. Ostensibly, Joe Lampton's ambitions in *Room at the Top* are similar. Yet this film is more concerned with arriving somewhere new and the possibility for self-expression that this entails than it is with the forlorn hope that leaving home will offer Billy Fisher the opportunity to express himself more effectively. The sense of frustration that governs the actions of Arthur Seaton in *Saturday Night and Sunday Morning* may appear to be of a similar kind to those expressed by Billy Fisher (especially those aspects of violence, real or fantastic, that they share) but the film's articulation of this frustration is achieved in a very different way. Violence is also one of the thematic concerns of *This Sporting Life* but here the film mediates this violence through a sustained consideration of what it really means to be truly alone in the world. *A Taste of Honey* is another of these films that is interested in the position a person occupies within their world, but its articulation of the threat of isolation varies significantly. With its images of Archie Rice alone on the stage, the same can be said for *The Entertainer*. Finally, as the title suggests, *The Loneliness of the Long Distance Runner* shares this concern but once again expresses it in a different way. Though there might be a sense of something similar the actual execution varies significantly from film to film.

Hutchings continues by noting the films' ability to neutralise what he calls a 'critical distance'. This distance can be best understood in the relationship between *Movie* and *Sight and Sound*. When it came to the British New Wave these two journals adopted very clear positions. Hopeful of a breakthrough in the development of British film style, *Sight and Sound* championed the early films of Tony Richardson and Jack Clayton. Though mindful of their fallibility, the journal hoped that films such as *The Entertainer* and *Room at the Top* were at the forefront of a movement in British cinema that would achieve a critical parity with films from other countries. *Movie*, on the other hand, saw things very differently.

Movie's position in relation to these films is a troubling one. Though keen to point out that its contributors were all capable of thinking independently, the journal's position in relation to the British New Wave smacked of consensus. This was evident from its opening salvo, Perkins's 'The British Cinema'. Placed on the opening pages of the journal's first issue, this article stated quite clearly why it was that the British New Wave was not worthy of the journal's positive critical attention. Admittedly, *Movie*'s project can be linked to the re-evaluation of other national cinemas, most notably, following the lead of Andrew Sarris and *Cahiers du Cinéma*, Hollywood. Nevertheless, it is evident from the critical literature of the period that *Movie*'s disavowal of these new British films was based less upon its preoccupation with the films of Nicholas Ray and more upon its hostility towards *Sight and Sound* and what it stood for.

In itself, this is hardly surprising. Movements of any kind are invariably reactions to the status quo, and the key to a successful development of critical ideas is the constant establishment of new positions in relation to those already in place. This last idea is evident in relation to *This Sporting Life*, one of the films that caused *Movie* the most problems. Yet the antagonism *Movie* displayed towards the style and meaning of these films, an antagonism that has lasted to this day, is not without its problems. Of course, as John Caughie has suggested, *Movie*'s 'new' approach to film criticism represented a radical shift in the way that people thought about films. Sadly, however, this radicalism now appears peculiarly conservative.[5] This is particularly interesting when we realise that the conclusions both journals reached regarding these films were essentially the same. In this way, the distance between *Movie* and *Sight and Sound* and, by extension, the distance between *Movie* and the British New Wave, is not as wide as the two protagonists originally imagined. The position I have adopted to both the films and the debates that surround them is an effort to reduce this distance once and for all. Once again, it is necessary to stress that my problem is not with the methodology promulgated by Perkins *et al.*, it is just their application in relation to this series of films. To understand this position better it is necessary to consider the questions of interpretation and meaning.

Noël Carroll has recently suggested that there are many ways to examine a film and that there is no reason to argue for the primacy of any of them. This means that there is still a case to be made for interpreting a film. When it comes to the British New Wave the case is more one of necessity than choice and this is because film interpretation, irrespective of its position within the broader concerns of film studies, still has a justifiable function. As Carroll continues:

> Interpreting a feature of a film is to offer an account of why that feature is present in the film. To interpret a film is a matter of explaining the presence of its features and the interrelationships thereof (or, at least, of explaining a substantial number of the pertinent features and interrelationships of the film in question). These features may be formal, expressive, and/or representational, and their interrelationships may be explained thematically in terms of what might be broadly called 'meaning', or in terms of their putative effects.[6]

This returns us to the account of film criticism that David Bordwell outlined previously. The suggestion is that film criticism is beset by the problems of appropriateness and novelty. Appropriateness requires a sufficiently compelling argument for the chosen film(s) to be considered worthy of critical interpretation. Though the British New Wave was not originally considered to be worthy of such an approach it is the question of novelty that is more pertinent here. This is because novelty consists of initiating a new critical method, revising an existing one, applying an existing method to a fresh instance or, if the film is familiar, pointing out significant aspects which have been previously ignored.[7] The preceding chapters have aimed to fulfil all of these criteria. In this way, my personal position might be better understood. In addition, returning to Stanley Cavell, the discussion of each film has been based upon the persistent exercise of my own taste in order to form what he calls an 'artistic conscience' through my encounter with specific films.[8]

The problem with the idea of a personal response is that it requires careful handling. It was a response of this kind that caused *Movie* to reject these films in the first place. Nevertheless, the exercising of my own taste not only allows me to reconsider the films for myself but also offers an opportunity for the continued critical emphasis upon the realist aspect of the New Wave to be reduced. Robin Wood previously suggested that the relationship between film criticism and theory is an inherently contradictory one. This is because theorists construct systems and critics explore works. This means that a personal response to a given work will be considered to be an irrelevance to a theorist. For a critic, however, mindful of the need to be constantly challenged, a personal response is essential. Of course, this is only an ideal and the problem with a personal response is often its subjectivity. Admittedly, as we saw from Richards's discussion of the relationship between film studies and cinema history, this is an area of considerable conflict.[9] Nevertheless, following Wood, provided we maintain a critical integrity and understand that the essential relationship between theory and criticism is one of checks and balances, there is little need for us to remove the subjective element from the criticism that we write.[10] This idea of balance is something we saw discussed by Perkins previously.

Continuing the idea of a personal response, Perkins suggested that there is little choice in the matter because the only viable alternative is restricting criticism to mere description. At the very least a descriptive analysis will have to make claims about the distribution of the film's emphasis and 'emphasis is as subjectively perceived, relies as much on a personal response, as judgement'.[11] If claims about the distribution of a film's emphasis are reliant upon a personal response then this explains Perkins's original stance concerning these films. However, there is still the need to move discussions of these films beyond simple description.

Other approaches have chosen to emphasise or re-emphasise the distribution of landscapes and locations. Adhering to the logic of Perkins's argument, it is essential to reconsider and thus redistribute the emphasis of each film. In this way, fears over the repeated emphasis upon the films' deployment of landscape and the damage that this emphasis has done to the films can be allayed. Ironically, a reassessment of this kind returns us to Perkins's earlier observations about the value of a positive claim being given more weight than a denial of critical worth. As he continues: 'If we fail to perceive functions and qualities it may well be because we are looking for them in inappropriate ways.'[12] Historically, this idea of inappropriateness can be linked to *Movie*'s antagonism towards the support *Sight and Sound* offered to the British New Wave. This antagonism, however, is not sufficient to damn such an important chapter in the history of cinema. Indeed, as Perkins interestingly concluded elsewhere, 'a failure to discern quality is not a demonstration of its absence'.[13] Clearly, then, the time is right for *Movie*'s original position to be reconsidered.

Admittedly, Perkins avoids the term 'social realism' in 'The British Cinema'. Nevertheless, his concerns over the mismatch between locations and characters amount to a dissatisfaction with the same thing. John Hill made this connection in his discussion of these films, linking the films' presentation of action and events with the ideas of redundancy and 'noticeability' leading to a critical vulnerability.[14] We can see the enduring quality of these criticisms when we consider that they were also made by Thomas Elsaesser ten years after Perkins.[15] There truly is a certain tendency to view the British New Wave in such a critically negative way.

A continued emphasis upon the collective failings of the films is incompatible with the desire to make an evaluative assessment of the style and meaning of each individual film. This is especially true when we relate this desire to Perkins's involvement in the promulgation of style-based evaluative film criticism in Britain. Forty-odd years on from the introduction of such an approach into British criticism it seems nonsensical that Perkins's claims have never been properly reconsidered. One of the alleged problems with the conventions of realism is their susceptibility to corruption through overuse. From a current critical perspective, this idea of corruption through repetition moves away from the films themselves and becomes more applicable to existing discussions of them. In order to avoid this we need to try to find new ways to talk about the films. This is important if we are to free the British New Wave films from the critical constraints that 'The British Cinema' and its subsequent legacy imposed on them. With this in mind, echoing Bordwell's earlier claims for 'novelty', the act of interpretation is not designed to tell people something they already know. Instead, 'we read interpretations in order to gain *new* insights concerning the way films work'.[16]

This interpretative hunt for new insights is inextricably linked with 'the problem of meaning'. Meaning is not a passive attribute of books, films and other objects. Instead, it is the result of people making sense of something that they confronted by. As Geoffrey Nowell-Smith continues:

> This making sense goes on in the presence of real-life situations as well as artefacts. If I find myself face-to-face with a scene in which there is a car smashed up against a lamp post, a body on the ground being given resuscitation, and a policewoman directing traffic, my response will be composed in more or less equal measure of emotional shock and an intellectual (or intellectualising) desire to reconstruct what has happened. Is the body that of a pedestrian? Did the car perhaps swerve to avoid him, strike him a glancing blow, and then end up crosswise against the lamp post?

Admittedly, as Nowell-Smith continues, 'Nobody compels me to perform this sense-making activity but nevertheless I do it.' The reason why we are compelled to try and make sense of a film we see is because, whether actively or passively, 'there is no possibility of the film meaning anything without the creative intervention of the spectator in determining what to pay attention to and what sense to give it'.[17]

Nowell-Smith outlines a simple model about how we respond to the films that we watch. Yet we need to be more expansive here. Allowing for the accident described to represent a film is one thing; making sense of what have we seen is something else. In either case, neither traffic accidents *nor* films occur in isolation. Both are dependent upon a chain of events for their existence. Nowell-Smith partly acknowledges this when he suggests that 'the meanings on offer [in a film] have been channelled in a particular direction as a result of actions undertaken by the film-makers'.[18] Yet, there is a further complication here, one which justifies my extending the original analogy.

Bad driving or biased accounts?

Imagine that I came across the same accident as Nowell-Smith. Like him, I would try to make sense of what I was seeing but it is very likely that I might have a different interpretation of events. Obviously, this is a problem that occurs from not having been present at the time the accident occurred and I, like Nowell-Smith, would be left to retroactive speculation. Was the driver distracted by using his mobile phone and therefore didn't see the pedestrian step into the road? Did the driver try and stop but could not because his brakes were faulty? Was he driving too fast to stop in time? There is a certain allure to speculations of this kind yet, ultimately, they are next to useless. They do very little to help us make sense of what has happened. Unless the driver gives a written statement to the policewoman, provided he was not killed, how can we possibly know what his intentions were? Maybe we will never know. This is the point at which complications can arise.

Whether faced with a car-crash or a film, we feel compelled to try to make sense of what we have seen. We have to decide what to pay attention to and what sense to give it. We would need to avoid speculating about intention because without written evidence to guide us this does little to aid our understanding. Instead, we need to deal in certainty, allowing the details to be our principal guide and using them to create a version of events that concurs with the reality of the situation. In this way, our understanding arises organically from the facts of the matter rather than descending upon them from an already established position elsewhere. Imagine I arrive at the scene of the accident after it happened and I meet two people who saw what happened. I talk to both of them in turn and they tell me what they saw. Potentially, both accounts will be useful to help me make sense of the accident. They were present at the time and this gives both of their stories a significance. Yet, I still need to be careful here. What happens if the first witness had a close affinity with the driver? This witness acknowledges that the driver might have made mistakes in the past but is prepared to overlook this by believing that the driver has learnt from his erroneous past. The second witness, however, sees things very differently. He has heard the first witness's version of events and becomes alarmed. He, too, knows the driver and has had first-hand experience of his driving. Unlike the first witness, however, he cannot forgive him for his earlier mistakes. To make matters worse, the second witness is also concerned that the first witness's account will artificially enhance the driver's standing and give him a reputation that he does not really deserve. As the second witness tells me, 'There are far better drivers elsewhere! They are the ones we should be interested in.' (I soon discover that there is a history of animosity between the two witnesses. They have clashed before over similar situations.) Ultimately, however, irrespective of their positions, both witnesses express a disappointment with the driver that is more similar than either would care to admit. The end result is that I am left with two conflicting accounts of the same event. Admittedly, the situation I have outlined is a simple one and there will always be a wider range of accounts than I have suggested. Yet, as this model demonstrates, the question becomes one of where to place oneself in relation to the (critical) perspectives on offer. This question of personal positions moves us neatly on to Hutchings's final point.

Hutchings felt that the central position that cinematic realism holds in relation to British cinema cannot be denied. Nevertheless, the ongoing desire to deconstruct it has had severe impact upon these films.[19] 'The British Cinema', for example, took great exception to what Perkins saw as the flawed relationship between character and background. This was further compounded by what he saw as the constant need to establish 'place' through 'inserted shots'.[20] Thomas Elsaesser was also concerned with this idea. For him, the use of landscape shots in these films was indicative of a misplaced visual emphasis and tantamount to the exploitation of their social milieu. To make matters worse the shots of industrial landscapes found in these films quickly became clichéd and formulaic.[21]

To criticise these films in this way is to pour scorn on their efforts towards establishing a new mode of representation. It is now common practice to consider a film like *A Taste of Honey* to be gritty and offering a slice of life hitherto unseen on the British screen. Words of this kind, when accompanied by the ideas of clumsy repetition and an over-reliance upon certain shots said to be characteristic of a specific time and place, create the impression of vulnerability. The style of the British New Wave has always been susceptible to adverse criticism and this series of films has always been considered guilty of what John Hill calls 'stylistic "manipulation"' and an iconographic obtrusiveness.[22] Once again, however, this is all just a question of emphasis. Approaches of this kind place their greatest emphasis on viewing the New Wave collectively, stressing the (social realist) similarities they share and using the fact of these similarities to include the films in broader debates about class, gender and/or ideology. Dissatisfied with this tendency, my intention has been to take an alternative approach and consider each of the films individually. This is not to deny that the similarities between these films do not exist. Nevertheless, for the sake of revivifying the study of British cinema, I see little methodological sense in being content to merely reproduce existing critical discussions. This, as Andrew Tudor suggested elsewhere, is little more than adding yet another interpretation on to 'the already creaking cart'.[23] Instead, I have aimed to circumvent this process by defining my own critical position and demonstrating that we might fruitfully consider the detail of an individual film without having to continually re-emphasise the similarities it might share with other related films.

Crucially, as Robin Wood concluded previously, a film defines its own reality through its 'method, presentation, style, structure' and, therefore, '"Realism" is relative, not absolute, and can only be judged by reference to the work's internal relationships'. This means, for Wood, that a better notion of realism might be 'a particular artistic method or strategy'. Logically, then, the relativity of realism becomes clear through the question of the emphasis placed upon it. In this way, by questioning the emphasis and refusing to accept an absolute standard of judgement, one that can then be applied to define a series of films collectively, the precise nature of our involvement will 'differ appreciably' from film to film, with 'each writer or director determining our relationship to his characters through method and style'.[24]

There is something extremely attractive about avoiding the repetition of existing critical views about British films, and part of this attraction comes from how the implications of this approach might be extended into other perceptions of British cinema. For example, Andrew Higson demonstrates a concern for what he calls 'the instability of the national'. Primarily, Higson concentrates upon the opposition between viewing British cinema as depicting what he calls 'a stable centred nation' and as a 'a plural, complex, heterogeneous and hybrid nation'.[25] I have not been interested in addressing specific questions about the position these films occupy in relation to their national cinema. Primarily, this has been because my re-evaluative stance has caused me to place greater value on the specific mise-en-scène of each film than on the position each film occupies within broader debates about nation and ideology. Instead, I have constructed a series of sustained readings that account for the details of each film and thus allow an understanding of that film to develop organically from within it. This has allowed me to avoid viewing the British New Wave as a series of identical vessels into which the usual external concerns can be poured without an apparent concern for each vessel's relative capacity.

Interestingly enough, however, my approach is not as far removed from Higson's concerns as it might appear. As he continues:

> British national cinema appears increasingly heterogeneous, eccentric, even unhomely. On the one hand, unfamiliar films are given a new significance. On the other, the films that were once seen as constructing a familiar consensus, imagining the nation as a solid, stable, centred space and people, now seem to express the contingency and fragility of the national, and the fractured and shifting nature of identity.[26]

Underlying Higson's concern here is the fear of critical fashion, and this prompts him to ask whether this is 'no more than a question of interpretation, one reading of a film replaced by another?' As he continues:

The question of interpretation, the question of where meaning resides, or how it is created, has of course become a central issue in Cinema Studies. An increasing number of scholars now question the legitimacy of textual analysis divorced from historical context. Interpretation is increasingly grounded in the historical study of reception. We should be wary then of cultural analysis that lacks such grounding.[27]

Nevertheless, the process of one reading replacing another is not something that we are forced to view suspiciously. Clearly, it is all a question of projects. Higson is right to suggest that textual analysis divorced from historical context might arouse suspicion. Yet my project is very firmly placed within a historical context. The only difference is that my readings need to be located within the ongoing history of British film criticism and not specifically in the identification of the distinguishing features of a national cinema.

Admittedly, in a similar way to the peevishness that Perkins suggested underlined 'The British Cinema', an element of belligerence can be attached to my approach. This is evident in my desire to re-evaluate existing critical positions and question their relevance or continued importance. Following the logic of Nowell-Smith's car-crash analogy, I have been extremely unwilling to accept other people's accounts of events. Instead, I have chosen to establish my own critical position in relation to both the films and the debates that surround them. To this end, I am reminded of Robin Wood's introduction to his account of Satyajit Ray's Apu trilogy. As he begins:

> One likes to begin a book with a bit of controversy, punching a few critical noses and offering one's own for the return poke or smash that all too seldom comes. The reader always enjoys finding a few insults bandied around: aside from the dubious pleasure of sharing in a probably quite unjustified feeling of superiority, it gives him the sense that there must be some issue at stake for him to make up his own mind about.[28]

There *is* an issue at stake here, one that requires our immediate attention. Despite reports to the contrary, the British New Wave films are vibrant, fascinating films that have always been critically undervalued. This is something that needs to stop now. It is essential that the existing critical emphasis is redistributed more evenly. Only in this way can we overcome defensiveness, hostility and empty posturing. Only in this way can we reclaim the interpretative project that is normally reserved for more 'deserving' films. Stagnant debates needs to be stirred up. Established positions need to be questioned. Existing methodologies need to be appropriated for new purposes. British films need to be considered in ways that will allow fresh debate to be generated. Ultimately, the process of British film criticism needs a new direction, and here I am guided by Stanley Cavell's thoughts on the subject of developing a critical opinion of one's own. As he suggests with a particular pertinence:

> Cynics about philosophy, and perhaps about humanity, will find that questions without answers are empty; dogmatists will claim to have arrived at answers; philosophers after my heart will rather wish to convey the thought that while there may be no satisfying answers to such questions *in certain forms*, there are, so to speak, directions to answers, *ways to think*, that are worth the time of your life to discover.[29]

Notes

1 Eric Rhode, *Tower of Babel: Speculations on the Cinema*, London, Weidenfeld & Nicolson, 1966, p. 9.
2 Stanley Cavell, 'What Becomes of Things on Film?', in *Themes Out of School: Effects and Causes*, Chicago, University of Chicago Press, 1984, p. 183.
3 Robert Murphy, 'Popular British Cinema', *Journal of Popular British Cinema*, No. 1 (1998), pp. 6–12, p. 11.
4 Peter Hutchings, 'Beyond the New Wave: Realism in British Cinema, 1959–63', in Robert Murphy (ed.), *The British Cinema Book*, second edition, London, BFI Publishing, 2002, pp. 146–152.
5 John Caughie (ed.), *Theories of Authorship*, London and New York, Routledge, 1981, p. 49.
6 Noël Carroll, *Interpreting the Moving Image*, Cambridge, Cambridge University Press, 1998, pp. 5–6.
7 David Bordwell, *Making Meaning: Inference and Rhetoric in the Interpretation of Cinema*, London, Harvard University Press, 1989, pp. 29–31.
8 Stanley Cavell, 'The Thought of Movies', in *Themes Out of School*, pp. 10–11.
9 Jeffrey Richards, 'Rethinking British Cinema', Justine Ashby and Andrew Higson (eds), *British Cinema, Past and Present*, London and New York, Routledge, 2000, pp. 21–34.
10 Robin Wood, *Personal Views: Explorations in Film*, London; Gordon Fraser, 1976, pp. 10–12.
11 V.F. Perkins, *Film As Film*, Harmondsworth, Penguin Books, 1972, p. 191.
12 *Ibid.*, pp. 190–191.
13 *Ibid.*, pp. 190–191. Though Perkins is writing some ten years from his 1962 article, the relevance of these later quotations can be found in the fact that there has been no real attempt on his behalf to modify his views on the British New Wave. Therefore, the time that has elapsed should have very little bearing on the use of these quotations.
14 John Hill, *Sex, Class and Realism: British Cinema 1956–1963*, London, BFI Publishing, 1986, p. 64.
15 Thomas Elsaesser, 'Between Style and Ideology', *Monogram*, No. 3 (1972), pp. 2–10.
16 As Carroll explains: 'At points, I may speculate about how a device moves viewers. But my account of why the device is designed that way and about how it achieves its postulated purpose should rarely be taken as a claim

about the way in which the audience actually conceptualised the relevant feature or features of the film in question. The interpretations are my own hypotheses. They are not meant to stand in as reports of the surmises of the average audience member (whoever that might be)' (Carroll, p. 9).

17 Geoffrey Nowell-Smith, 'How Films Mean, or, From Aesthetics to Semiotics and Half-way Back Again', in Christine Gledhill and Linda Williams (eds), *Reinventing Film Studies*, London, Arnold, 2000, pp. 8–17, pp. 10–11.

18 *Ibid.*, p. 10.

19 Hutchings, 'Beyond the New Wave', pp. 146–147.

20 Perkins, *Film As Film*, p. 5.

21 Elsaesser, 'Between Style and Ideology', p. 7.

22 Hill, *Sex, Class and Realism*, pp. 127–132.

23 Andrew Tudor, 'The Many Mythologies of Realism', *Screen*, Vol. 13, No. 1 (Spring 1972), pp. 6–36, p. 27.

24 Wood, *Personal Views*, p. 81.

25 Andrew Higson, 'The Instability of the National', in Justine Ashby and Andrew Higson (eds), *British Cinema Past and Present*, London and New York, Routledge, 2000, pp. 35–48, p. 44.

26 *Ibid.*, p. 45.

27 *Ibid.*, pp. 45–46.

28 Robin Wood, *The Apu Trilogy*, London, Movie Paperbacks, 1972, p. 6.

29 Stanley Cavell, 'The Thought of Movies', p. 9.

Bibliography

Adair, Gilbert and Nick Roddick, *A Night at the Pictures: Ten Decades of British Film*, Bromley, Columbus Books, 1985.

Affron, Charles, *Cinema and Sentiment*, Chicago, University of Chicago Press, 1982.

Allen, Robert and Douglas Gomery, *Film History: Theory and Practice*, New York, Alfred A. Knopf, 1985.

Anderson, Lindsay, 'Sport, Life and Art', *Films and Filming* (February 1963), pp. 15–18.

Armes, Roy, *Film and Reality: An Historical Survey*, Harmondsworth, Penguin Books Ltd, 1974.

——, *A Critical History of the British Cinema*, London, Secker & Warburg, 1978.

Ashby, Justine and Andrew Higson (eds), *British Cinema: Past and Present*, London, Routledge, 2000.

Aumont, Jacques, Alain Bergala, Michel Marie and Marc Vernet, *Aesthetics of Film*, trans. Richard Neupert, Austin, University of Texas Press, 1992.

Babington, Bruce, *Launder and Gilliat*, Manchester, Manchester University Press, 2002.

Baker, Peter, '*This Sporting Life*', *Films and Filming* (February 1963), p. 32.

Barr, Charles, 'CinemaScope, Before and After', in Gerald Mast and Marshall Cohen (eds), *Film Theory and Criticism*, third edition, New York, Oxford University Press, 1985, pp. 139–193.

Barr, Charles (ed.), *All Our Yesterdays: 90 Years of British Cinema*, London, BFI Publishing, 1986.

——, *Ealing Studios*, London, Studio Vista, 1993.

Bazin, André, *What Is Cinema?* Vol. 1, Berkeley, University of California Press, 1967.

Bellone, Julius (ed.), *Renaissance of the Film*, London, Collier-Macmillan Ltd, 1970.

Belton, John, *Widescreen Cinema*, London, Harvard University Press, 1992.

Bennett, Tony, Susan Boyd-Bowman, Colin Mercer and Jane Woolacott (eds), *Popular Television and Film*, London, BFI Publishing, 1981.

Bloom, Harold, *The Western Canon*, London, Papermac, 1995.

Bogdanor, Vernon and Robert Skidelsky (eds), *The Age of Affluence 1951–1964*, London, Macmillan and Co Ltd, 1970.

Booker, Christopher, *The Neophiliacs*, London, Collins Clear-Type Press, 1969.

Bordwell, David, *Narration in the Fiction Film*, London, Routledge, 1985.

Bordwell, David, *Making Meaning: Inference and Rhetoric in the Interpretation of Cinema*, London, Harvard University Press, 1989.

Bordwell, David and Kristin Thompson, *Film Art: An Introduction*, fourth edition, New York, McGraw-Hill, Inc., 1993.

Bordwell, David, Kristin Thompson and Janet Staiger, *The Classical Hollywood Cinema: Film Style and Mode of Production to 1960*, London, Routledge, 1985.

'British Cinema, Attitudes and Illusions', *Film* No. 36 (Summer 1963), pp. 16–24.

Britton, Andrew, 'In Defence of Criticism', *CineACTION*, Nos 3/4 (Winter 1986), pp. 3–5.

———, 'Philosophy of the Pigeonhole: Wisconsin Formalism and "The Classical Style"', *CineACTION*, No. 15 (Winter 1988/89), pp. 47–63.

Brown, Geoff, 'Paradise Found and Lost: The Course of British Realism', in Robert Murphy (ed.), *The British Cinema Book*, London, British Film Institute, 1997, pp. 187–197.

Burton, Alan, Tim O'Sullivan and Paul Wells (eds), *Liberal Directions, Basil Dearden and Postwar British Film Culture*, Trowbridge, Flicks Books, 1997.

Butler, Ivan, *The Making of Feature Films: A Guide,* Harmondsworth, Penguin Books Ltd, 1971.

Cameron, Ian, 'Attack', *Film* No. 25 (September–October 1960), pp. 12–14.

———, 'Against *This Sporting Life*', *Movie* No. 10 (June 1963), pp. 21–22.

Cameron, Ian (ed.), *Movie Reader*, London, November Books, 1972.

———, 'Introduction', in Ian Cameron (ed.), *Movie Reader*, London, November Books, 1972, p. 6.

Carroll, Noël, *Interpreting the Moving Image*, Cambridge, Cambridge University Press, 1998.

Caughie, John (ed.), *Theories of Authorship*, London and New York, Routledge, 1981.

Cavell, Stanley, *The World Viewed*, enlarged edition, Cambridge, MA, Harvard University Press, 1971, 1974, 1979.

———, *Themes Out of School: Effects and Causes*, Chicago, University of Chicago Press, 1984.

———, *Contesting Tears: The Hollywood Melodrama of the Unknown Woman*, Chicago, University of Chicago Press, 1996.

Chibnall, Steve and Robert Murphy (eds), *British Crime Cinema*, London, Routledge, 1999.

Chion, Michel, *Audio-Vision*, New York, Columbia University Press, 1994.

———, *The Voice in Cinema,* trans. Claudia Gorbman, New York, Columbia University Press, 1999.

Cook, David A., *A History of Narrative Film*, New York, Norton, 1981.

Cook, Pam and Mieke Bernink (eds), *The Cinema Book*, second edition, London, The British Film Institute, 1999.

'Correspondence', *Sight and Sound*, Vol. 32 No. 1 (Winter 1962–63), pp. 49–50.

Cowie, Elizabeth, 'Storytelling, Classical Hollywood Cinema and Classical Narrative', in Steve Neale and Murray Smith (eds), *Contemporary Hollywood Cinema*, London, Routledge, 1998, pp. 178–190.

Cross, Robin, *The Big Book of British Films*, Bideford, Charles Herridge Ltd, 1984.

Deleuze, Gilles, *Cinema 1: The Movement-Image*, trans. Hugh Tomlinson and Barbara Habberjam, London, Athlone Press, 1992.

Deren, Maya, 'Cinematography: The Creative Use of Reality', in Gerald Mast, Marshall Cohen and Leo Braudy (eds), *Film Theory and Criticism: Introductory Readings*, fourth edition, New York, Oxford University Press, 1992, pp. 59–70.

Durgnat, Raymond, *A Mirror for England: British Movies from Austerity to Affluence*, London, Faber and Faber, 1970.

——, *Durgnat on Film*, London, Faber and Faber, 1976.

Dyer, Peter John, 'Counter Attack', *Film* No. 26 (November–December 1960), pp. 8–9.

——, '*Saturday Night and Sunday Morning*', *Sight and Sound*, Vol. 30 No. 1 (Winter 1960/61), p. 33.

Dyer, Richard and Ginette Vincendeau (eds), *Popular European Cinema*, London, Routledge, 1992.

Elsaesser, Thomas, 'Between Style and Ideology', *Monogram*, No. 3 (1972), pp. 2–10.

Emerson, Ralph Waldo, *Self-Reliance and Other Essays*, New York, Dover Publications, Inc., 1993.

Emerson's Prose and Poetry, selected and edited by Joel Porte and Saundra Morris, London, W.W. Norton & Company, 2001.

Fell, John L., *Film: An Introduction*, London, Thomas Nelson and Sons Ltd, 1975.

Freeland, Cynthia A. and Thomas E. Wartenburg (eds), *Philosophy and Film*, New York, Routledge, 1995.

Friedman, Lester (ed.), *British Cinema and Thatcherism: Fires Were Started*, London, UCL Press, 1993.

Geduld, Harry M. (ed.), *Film Makers on Film Making*, Harmondsworth, Penguin Books Ltd, 1967.

Geraghty, Christine, *British Cinema in the Fifties: Gender, Genre and the 'New Look'*, London, Routledge, 2000.

Gibbs, John, *It Was Never All in the Script: Mise-en-Scène and the Interpretation of Visual Style in British Film Journals, 1946–1978* (University of Reading, 1999, PhD Thesis).

——, *Mise-en-scène: Film Style and Interpretation*, London and New York, Wallflower Press, 2002.

Gillet, Philip, *The British Working Class in Post-war Film*, Manchester, Manchester University Press, 2003.

Gledhill, Christine and Linda Williams (eds), *Reinventing Film Studies*, London, Arnold, 2000.

Godard on Godard, translated and edited by Tom Milne, New York, Da Capo Press, 1968.

Graham, Peter, *The New Wave*, London, Secker and Warburg, 1968.

Hallam, Julia and Margaret Marshment, *Realism and Popular Cinema*, Manchester and New York, Manchester University Press, 2000.

Harcourt, Peter, 'I'd Rather Be Like I Am', *Sight and Sound*, Vol. 32 No. 1 (Winter 1962/63), pp. 16–19.

Harrington, John, *The Rhetoric of Film*, New York, Holt, Rinehart and Winston Inc., 1973.

Hedling, Erik, *Lindsay Anderson: Maverick Film-Maker*, London and Washington, Cassell, 1998.

Higson, Andrew (ed.), *Dissolving Views: Key Writings in British Cinema*, London, Cassell, 1986.

——, 'Space, Place, Spectacle: Landscape and Townscape in the "Kitchen Sink" Film', in *Dissolving Views: Key Writings on British Cinema*, London, Cassell, 1996, pp. 133–156.

——, *Waving the Flag: Constructing a National Cinema in Britain*, Oxford, Clarendon Press, 1995.

——, 'The Instability of the National', in Justine Ashby and Andrew Higson (eds), *British Cinema: Past and Present*, London, Routledge, 2000, pp. 35–48.

Hill, Derek, 'A Writer's Wave', *Sight and Sound*, Vol. 29 No. 2 (Spring 1960), pp. 56–60.

Hill, John, *Sex, Class and Realism: British Cinema 1956–1963*, London, BFI Publishing, 1986.

——, *British Cinema in the 1980s*, Oxford, Clarendon Press, 1999.

Hjort, Mette and Sue Laver (eds), *Emotion and the Arts*, Oxford, Oxford University Press, 1997.

Hodsdon, Barrett, 'The Mystique of Mise-en-scène Revisited', *Continuum: The Australian Journal of Media and Culture*, Vol. 5 No. 2 (1990), pp. 1–12.

Hoggart, Richard, *The Uses of Literacy*, Harmondsworth, Penguin, 1958.

Holt, Seth, 'A Free Hand', *Sight and Sound*, Vol. 28 No. 2 (Spring 1959), pp. 60–64.

Houston, Penelope, '*Nowhere To Go*', *Sight and Sound*, Vol. 28 No. 1 (Winter 1958/59), p. 38.

——, '*Look Back in Anger*', *Sight and Sound*, Vol. 28 No. 1 (Winter 1958/59), pp. 31–33, p. 32.

——, '*Room at the Top*', *Sight and Sound*, Vol. 28 No. 2 (Spring 1959), pp. 56–59.

——, 'Into the Sixties', *Sight and Sound*, Vol. 29 No. 1 (Winter 1959/60), pp. 4–7.

——, 'The Critical Question', *Sight and Sound*, Vol. 29 No. 4 (Autumn 1960), pp. 160–165.

——, '*The Entertainer*', *Sight and Sound*, Vol. 29 No. 4 (Autumn 1960), pp. 194–195.

——, 'Critic's Notebook', *Sight and Sound*, Vol. 30 No. 2 (Spring 1961), pp. 62–66.

——, *The Contemporary Cinema*, Harmondsworth, Penguin Books Ltd, 1963.

Hutchings, Peter, 'The Histogram and the List: The Director in British Film criticism', *Journal of Popular British Cinema*, No. 4 (2001), pp. 30–36.

——, 'Beyond the New Wave: Realism in British Cinema, 1959–63', in Robert Murphy (ed.), *The British Cinema Book*, second edition, London, BFI Publishing, 2002, pp. 146–152.

——, *Dracula*, London, I.B. Taurus, 2003.

Jacobs, Lewis, *The Emergence of Film Art*, New York, Hopkinson and Blake, 1974.

Kael, Pauline, 'Is There a Cure for Film Criticism?', *Sight and Sound*, Vol. 31 No. 2 (Spring 1962), pp. 56–66.

Kirkham, Pat and Janet Thumin (eds), *Me Jane: Masculinity, Movies and Women*, London, Lawrence and Wishart, 1995.

Klevan, Andrew, *Disclosure of the Everyday: Undramatic Achievement in Narrative Film*, Trowbridge, Flicks Books, 2000.

Kuhn, Annette and Jackie Stacy (eds), *Screen Histories: A Screen Reader*, Oxford, Clarendon Press, 1998.

Landy, Marcia, *British Genres: Cinema and Society, 1930–1960*, Oxford, Princeton University Press, 1991.

Lassally, Walter, 'The Dead Hand', *Sight and Sound*, Vol. 29 No. 3 (Summer 1960), pp. 113–115.

Lay, Samantha, *British Social Realism: From Documentary to Brit Grit*, London and New York, Wallflower, 2002.

Lellis, George, 'Recent Richardson – Cashing the Blank Cheque', *Sight and Sound*, Vol. 28 No. 3 (Summer 1969), pp. 130–138.

Lindgren, Ernest, *The Art of the Film*, London, George Allen & Unwin Ltd, 1963.

Lovell, Alan, 'Film Chronicle', *New Left Review* No. 7 (January–February 1961), pp. 52–53.

——, 'Robin Wood – A Dissenting View', *Screen*, Vol. 10 No. 2 (March/April 1969), pp. 42–55.

——, 'Notes on British Film Culture', *Screen*, Vol. 13 No. 2 (Summer 1972), pp. 5–15.

Lovell, Alan and Jim Hillier, *Studies in Documentary*, London, BFI/Secker & Warburg, 1972.

Lovell, Terry, 'Landscape and Stories in 1960s British Realism', in Andrew Higson (ed.), *Dissolving Views: Key Writings on British Cinema*, London, Cassell, 1996, pp. 157–177.

Lowe, Victor, *Understanding Whitehead*, Baltimore, Johns Hopkins Press, 1966.

Lowenstein, Adam, '"Under-the-Skin Horrors": Social Realism and Classlessness in *Peeping Tom* and the British New Wave', in Justine Ashby and Andrew Higson (eds), *British Cinema: Past and Present*, London and New York, Routledge, 2000, pp. 221–232.

Luckett, Moya, 'Travel and Mobility: Femininity and national identity in Swinging London Films', in Justine Ashby and Andrew Higson (eds), *British Cinema: Past and Present*, London, Routledge, 2000, pp. 233–245.

McFarlane, Brian, 'A Literary Cinema? British Films and British Novels', in Charles Barr (ed.), *All Our Yesterdays: 90 Years of British Cinema*, London, BFI Publishing, 1986, pp. 120–142.

Mackillop, Ian and Neil Sinyard (eds), *British Cinema of the 1950s: A Celebration*, Manchester, Manchester University Press, 2003.

Manvell, Roger, *Film*, Harmondsworth, Penguin Books, 1944.

——, *New Cinema in Britain*, London, Studio Vista, 1969.

Marcorelles, Louis, 'Conversation with Jean Renoir', *Sight and Sound*, Vol. 31 No. 2 (Spring 1962), pp. 78–83.

Martin, Wallace, *Recent Theories of Narrative*, Ithaca, Cornell University Press, 1986.

Marwick, Arthur, *The Nature of History*, London, Macmillan, 1970.

——, *The Sixties*, Oxford, Oxford University Press, 1998.

Mathews, Tom Dewe, *Censored: What They Didn't Allow You to See, and Why: The Story of Film Censorship in Britain*, London, Chatto and Windus, 1994.

Medhurst, Andy, 'This Septic Isle', *Sight and Sound*, Vol. 8 No. 2 (February 1998), pp. 28–29.

Merleau-Ponty, Maurice, *Sense and Non-Sense*, trans. Hubert L. Dreyfus and Patricia Allen Dreyfus, Eranston, Northwestern University Press, 1964.

Millar, Gavin, '*This Sporting Life*', *Movie* No. 7 (February 1963), p. 33.

Milne, Tom, '*This Sporting Life*', *Sight and Sound*, Vol. 31 No. 3 (Summer 1962), pp. 113–115.

'*Movie* Differences: A Discussion', *Movie* No. 8 (April 1963), pp. 28–33.

Murphy, Robert, *Sixties British Cinema*, London, BFI Publishing, 1992.

——, (ed.), *The British Cinema Book*, London, British Film Institute, 1997.

——, 'Popular British Cinema', *Journal of Popular British Cinema* No. 1 (1998), pp. 6–12.

Naremore, James, *Acting in the Cinema*, Berkeley, University of California Press, 1988.

Neale, Steve, *Genre and Hollywood*, London, Routledge, 2000.

Neale, Steve and Andrew Higson, 'Introduction, Components of the National Film Culture', *Screen*, Vol. 26 No. 1 (1985), pp. 3–8.

Nichols, Bill (ed.), *Movies and Methods: An Anthology*, Berkeley, University of California Press, 1976.

Nowell-Smith, Geoffrey, 'Movie and Myth', *Sight and Sound*, Vol. 32 No. 2 (Spring 1963), pp. 60–64.

——, 'How Films Mean, or, From Aesthetics to Semiotics and Half-way Back Again', in Christine Gledhill and Linda Williams (eds), *Reinventing Film Studies*, London, Arnold, 2000, pp. 8–17.

Palmer, R. Barton, 'What Was New in the British New Wave? – Reviewing *Room at the Top*', *Journal of Popular Film and Television*, Vol. 14 No. 3 (Fall 1986), pp. 125–135.

Perkins, V.F., 'The British Cinema', *Movie* No. 1 (June 1962), pp. 2–7.

——, *Film As Film*, Harmondsworth, Penguin Books, 1972.

——, 'A Reply to Sam Rohdie', *Screen*, Vol. 13 No. 4 (Winter 1972/73), pp. 146–151.

——, 'Moments of Choice', in A. Lloyd (ed.), *Movies of the Fifties*, London, Orbis, 1982, pp. 209–213.

——, 'Must We Say What They Mean? Film Criticism and Interpretation', *Movie* 34/35 (Winter 1990), pp. 1–6.

Perry, George, *The Great British Picture Show*, London, Pavilion Books, 1985.

Petley, Julian, 'The Lost Continent', Charles Barr (ed.), *All Our Yesterdays: 90 Years of British Cinema*, London, BFI Publishing, 1986, pp. 98–119.

Phillips, Adam, *On Kissing, Tickling and Being Bored*, London, Faber and Faber, 1993.

Phillips, William H., *Film: An Introduction*, Boston and Bedford, St Martins, 1999.

Pirie, David, *A Heritage of Horror: The English Gothic Cinema 1946–1972*, London, Gordon Fraser, 1973.

Porte, Joel, 'The Problem of Emerson', in *Emerson's Prose and Poetry*, selected and edited by Joel Porte and Saundra Morris, London, W.W. Norton & Company, 2001, pp. 679–697.

Putnam, Hilary, *Realism with a Human Face*, edited and introduced by James Conant, Cambridge, MA, Harvard University Press, 1990.

Pye, Douglas, 'Bordwell and Hollywood', *Movie* No. 33 (Winter 1989), pp. 46–52.

——, 'Movies and Point of View', *Movie* No. 36 (Spring 2000), pp. 2–34.

Reisz, Karel, *The Technique of Film Editing*, London, Focal Press, 1968.

Rhode, Eric, '*A Kind of Loving*', *Sight and Sound*, Vol. 31 No. 3 (Summer 1962), pp. 143–144.

———, *Tower of Babel: Speculations on the Cinema*, London, Weidenfeld and Nicolson, 1966.

Richards, Jeffrey, *Films and British National Identity: From Dickens to Dad's Army*, Manchester, Manchester University Press, 1997.

———, 'Rethinking British Cinema', in Justine Ashby and Andrew Higson (eds), *British Cinema: Past and Present*, London and New York, Routledge, 2000, pp. 21–34.

Richards, Jeffrey and Anthony Aldgate, *Best of British: Cinema and Society 1930–1970*, Oxford, Basil Blackwell Publisher Limited, 1983.

———, *Best of British: Cinema and Society from 1930 to the Present*, London, I.B. Tauris, 1999.

Richardson, Tony, 'A Free Hand', *Sight and Sound*, Vol. 28 No. 2 (Spring 1959), pp. 60–64.

Robinson, David, '*Look Back in Anger*', *Sight and Sound*, Vol. 28 Nos 3/4 (Summer/Autumn 1959), pp. 122–125.

———, 'Case Histories of the Next Renascence' *Sight and Sound*, Vol. 38 No. 1 (Winter 1968/69), pp. 36–40.

Rohdie, Sam, *Screen*, Vol. 13 No. 4 (Winter 1972/73), pp. 137–143.

Rosen, Philip (ed.), *Narrative, Apparatus, Ideology*, New York, Columbia University Press, 1986.

Rothman, William, *The 'I' of the Camera: Essays in Film Criticism, History, and Aesthetics*, Cambridge, Cambridge University Press, 1988.

———, 'Cavell's Philosophy and What Film Studies Calls "Theory": Must the Field of Film Studies Speak in One Voice?', *Film and Philosophy*, Vol. 2 (1994).

Rothman, William and Marian Keane, *Reading Cavell's The World Viewed: A Philosophical Perspective on Film*, Detroit, Wayne State University Press, 2000.

Roud, Richard 'The French Line', *Sight and Sound*, Vol. 29 No. 4 (Autumn 1960), pp. 166–171.

Rowe, Stephen C., *The Vision of James*, Rockport, MA, Element, 1996.

Salt, Barry, *Film Style & Technology: History and Analysis*, 2nd expanded edition, London, Starword, 1992.

Sarris, Andrew, *The American Cinema: Directors and Directions 1929–1968*, New York, E.P. Dutton & Co., Inc., 1968.

———, 'Film Criticism in the Seventies', *Film Comment*, Vol. 14 (January/February 1978), pp. 9–11.

———, '*You Ain't Heard Nothin' Yet*': The American Talking Film, History and Memory, 1927–1949*, Oxford, Oxford University Press, 1998.

Scruton, Roger, *England: An Elegy*, London, Pimlico, 2001.

Shivas, Mark, 'Letter from London', *Film Culture* No. 27 (Winter 1962/63), pp. 21–22.

Sight and Sound, Vol. 30 No. 2 (Spring 1961).

Sight and Sound, Vol. 32 No. 1 (Winter 1962/63).

Sinyard, Neil, *Jack Clayton*, Manchester, Manchester University Press, 2000.

Staiger, Janet, 'The Politics of Film Canons', *Cinema Journal* No. 3 (Spring 1985), pp. 4–23.

Stead, Peter, *Film and the Working Class: The Feature Film in British and American Society*, London, Routledge, 1989.

Stephenson, Ralph and Guy Phelps, *The Cinema as Art*, revised edition, Harmondsworth, Penguin Books, 1989.

Stonier, George, 'A Taste of Honey', Sight and Sound, Vol. 30 No. 4 (Autumn 1961), p. 196.

Street, Sarah, British National Cinema, London, Routledge, 1997.

——, 'Ealing Comedy to the British New Wave', in Elizabeth Ezra (ed.), European Cinema, Oxford, Oxford University Press, 2004, pp. 176–193.

'The Critical Issue', Sight and Sound, Vol. 27 No. 6 (Autumn 1958), pp. 270–279.

'The Front Page', Sight and Sound, Vol. 31 No. 2 (Spring 1962), p. 5.

'The Front Page', Sight and Sound, Vol. 32 No. 2 (Spring 1963), p. 55.

Thomas, Deborah, Reading Hollywood: Spaces and Meaning in American Film, London and New York, Wallflower Press, 2001.

Tudor, Andrew, 'The Many Mythologies of Realism', Screen, Vol. 13 No. 1 (Spring 1972), pp. 6–36.

——, Theories of Film, London, Secker and Warburg, 1974.

Turim, Maureen, Flashbacks in Film: Memory and History, London, Routledge, 1989.

Turner, Graeme, Film as Social Practice, London, Routledge, 1988.

Vas, Robert, 'Arrival and Departure', Sight and Sound, Vol. 32 No. 2 (Spring 1963), pp. 56–59.

Walker, Alexander, Hollywood, England: The British Film Industry in the Sixties, London, Michael Joseph Ltd, 1974.

——, National Heroes: British Cinema in the Seventies and Eighties, London, Harrap, 1985.

Walker, John A., Cultural Offensive: America's Impact on British Art since 1945, London, Pluto Press, 1998.

Warnock, Mary, Existentialism, Oxford, Oxford University Press, 1970.

Wilson, George M., Narration in Light: Studies in Cinematic Point of View, Baltimore, Johns Hopkins University Press, 1986.

——, 'On Film Narrative and Narrative Meaning', in Richard Allen and Murray Smith (eds), Film Theory and Philosophy, Oxford, Oxford University Press, 1997, pp. 221–238.

Wittgenstein, Ludwig, Philosophical Remarks, Oxford, Basil Blackwell, 1975.

——, The Blue and Brown Books, Oxford, Basil Blackwell, 1975.

Wollen, Peter, Signs and Meaning in the Cinema, London, Secker and Warburg, 1969.

——, 'The Last New Wave, Modernism in the British Films of the Thatcher Era', in Lester Friedman (ed.), British Cinema and Thatcherism: Fires Were Started, London, UCL Press, 1993, pp. 35–51.

Wood, Robin, 'Ghostly Paradigms and H.C.F: An Answer to Alan Lovell', Screen, Vol. 10 No. 3 (May/June 1969), pp. 35–48.

——, The Apu Trilogy, London, Movie Paperbacks, 1972.

——, Personal Views: Explorations in Film, London, Gordon Fraser, 1976.

——, 'Editorial', CineACTION, Nos 3/4 (Winter 1986), pp. 1–2.

——, Hitchcock's Films Revisited, London, Faber and Faber, 1989.

Wright, Basil, The Long View: An International History of Cinema, London, Secker and Warburg Ltd, 1974.

Index

Page numbers in italics indicate an illustration.